The World of Burmese Women

Mi Mi Khaing

To
Sao Saimong Mangrai

Zed Books Ltd., 57 Caledonian Road, London N1 9BU

The World of Burmese Women was first published by Zed
Books Ltd., 57 Caledonian Road, London N1 9BU, in 1984.

Typeset by Sapphire Set
Proofread by Ros Howe
Cover photo courtesy of Maung Maung
Cover design by Lee Robinson
Photos courtesy of the author
Printed by The Pitman Press, Bath

British Library Cataloguing in Publication Data
Khaing, Mi Mi
    The world of Burmese women
    1. Women—Burma—Social conditions
    I. Title
    305.4'2'09591   MQ1735.7
    ISBN 0-86232-179-4
    ISBN 0-86232-180-8 Pbk

US Distributor
Biblio Distribution Center, 81 Adams Drive, Totowa,
New Jersey 07512

Erratum
*Due to a printing error the author's name on the cover has
been misspelt.*

Contents

Introduction

The aim of this book is to bring within its two covers all aspects of women's participation in the society of one small country. That country is Burma. Its population is just over 30 million.

Two reasons make Burma a good subject for a case study. First, less has been written about Burmese women in post-Independence years than about women in other parts of the world. Second, when all over the world, this century has seen changes in the status of women, particularly with regard to social life, the control and disposal of property, marriage etc., no such change has been visible in the lives of Burmese women. Yet, despite the fact that Burmese women have not lacked the power to protest or demonstrate either in the past or now, there has been no feminist movement of note in the country. And indeed, there are certainly areas in our lives which can be said to need change, and which have been pointed at by Western women. Perhaps then, this book, in describing the life and world of Burmese women and in tracing their history, may provide material for discussions on sex roles and how women achieve their place in the sun elsewhere in the world.

The aim of this book is no doubt ambitius even for a writer who is native to and seasoned for many decades in the environment to be investigated. It would be useful to clear the ground first to see what material does, in fact, exist on the subject of Burmese women.

It is well known that no foreign sociologist has been able to carry out field work in Burma since 1962. Of the studies done before that date, the most noteworthy is Manning Nash's *Golden Road to Modernity* based on his research (during residence) in two villages near Mandalay in Upper Burma. He says, quite rightly, that other books on Burma have given a picture at the national level, ignoring the villages and huts of the country in which the majority of Burmese live. However, while he looks at rural Burma, hitherto ignored, he is not able to throw much light (a fact that he recognizes) on the question of women, although where he does make brief descriptions of the domestic load he is surprisingly accurate and perceptive.

Manning Nash has also worked, together with his wife June, on a study called *Population Growth in Upper Burma*. This is a useful and informative work and far better than the two chapters written by me in two compilations *Women in the New*

Asia (B.E. Ward) and *Women in the Modern World* (R. Patai). It is partly to offset my own unfavourable recollections of these two articles that I so keenly wanted to do the present work. In addition, the fact of being on an American university campus where I would be able to make the time to write, such as I would not in Burma, was also encouraging. Apart from the time thus available, it was stimulating to be in Ann Arbor. If foreign sociologists had been cut off from Burma during the last 15 years, we readers of books in English had been equally cut off from the world of such books. Now, in the Graduate Library, I could see that works on women in Javanese, Malay, Indonesian and Thai societies abounded. Their contents pointed clearly to a gap where Burmese women and society were concerned. By assiduously attending conferences where papers were read, I became familiar with the well-reiterated concepts to be sought out and stated. It became clear to me that while the place to write was here in Ann Arbor, the only place for sufficient field work was in Burma. I could not hope to go back for field work and return to write as American scholars are funded to do. Even if I had the funds to return home, the procedure necessary to get out again would cut seriously into my working time. Due to recently discovered aberrations in my physique, I did not feel sure of being able to count on more than another two years of reading sight.

I had, before coming, made some notes on certain areas of the study, but these were far from being adequate for my new purpose. I did, however, have at home in Burma a good number of young people linked to me by blood or other strong ties. This enabled me to ask their active help in searching out data, conducting interviews, and sending summaries of the scenes I had already located. I therefore spent the first six weeks of my work planning the chapters in detail and drafting the scores of questions. There is a lack, even in a well-equipped place like Ann Arbor, of statistical material on Burma. In Boserup's book *Women's Role in Economic Development*, which is rich in tables, there was, in many of them, a note opposite Burma saying 'figures not available', 'for urban areas only' whereas other Southeast Asian countries had full figures. In my letters to my band of helpers I implored them to beg, cajole and press, to obtain information. I tried friends at the U.N. from where, too, no statistical data was available. I tried a week in Washington, where at the Library of Congress, Helen Po came to me, loaded down with volumes and a magnifying glass. I took down the little I could find and decided I would have to think out a way to write which would use all the personal experience at my command against the background of the poor amount of statistical data available at the national level. The chapters on the household were easy, as my young helpers were able to interview some 150 households in village, country-town and capital-town with questions, the answers to which I could use as a check on my own experiences and observations. Though the questions asked by such sensitive Burmese of their own country folk could not be so many as can be put by unembarrassed foreign questioners, we could try to direct the few at the areas most vital to the housewife's view of her household management.

The chapters on the economic input of women would suffer most from the lack of statistical data, especially the one on modern industrial labour. In certain matters I decided to exploit to the full the fact of my being Burmese. This was the case with the chapter on kinship. Professor Robbins Burling has written an analytical paper on the Burmese kinship system debating the pros and cons of two approaches to classifying or enumerating a comprehensive list of relationships. Manning Nash has given summaries of relations within the family. I would be able to add to these works data which a foreign observer could not be expected to perceive in kinship terms and associations.

For the chapters on Family Law and Practices, I was fortunate enough to find sufficient books in the Law Library of the University of Michigan. For other chapters (such as the one on the Education and Training of Women) I was able to get data from friends in London and Rangoon. The chapter on Women in Religion was enjoyable to write as it came mostly from sources so far published only in Burmese and from personal accounts by people who had known the women in that line. Chapter I, in which I give an account of women's activities during past centuries of Burmese history, might appear to some as an attempt at a potted history of Burma in a linear trail of notes on women. I have depended, as most writers on Burma must depend, on the work of scholars headed by the great professors, Tin and Luce, writing in journals of The Burma Research Society. I have, however, selected material which, after so many centuries, is reflected in the activities of women today, as found in my own field studies. This chapter, showing as it does, women and girls in economic, social and religious positions so familiar to us today, I regard as the keynote of this book in that it reflects the continuity of tradition in Burma. I have therefore attempted, in the closing chapter of the book, to look more closely for trends and signs of change which might correct my reading of this theme.

*   *   *   *

This book should have been completed by October 1977. When it was half done, around January 1977, family matters in Burma took a turn which necessitated our presence there; we knew, however, that we would need to return to the U.S.A. to honour our commitments.

At the same time my eyesight began to worsen and I required brain surgery to try saving whatever vision remained. Finishing my duties at the end of April 1977, I went into hospital for that surgery. I had had a brain operation in 1974 and had left hospital only 9 days after it, and was riding tubes and buses in London a month later. I therefore reckoned that I could be operated on in early May, recuperate in U.S.A. right till the end of June, then fly the long journey to Burma in early July when the fatigues of the journey would be amply offset by the care I would receive from relatives, especially two loving daughters, three sisters and doctors at every turn to consult. I could fill all the gaps in my material, do visits and interviews during the two month summer vacation and return to Ann Arbor to write better.

Alas for human conceit when it believes it can plan according to need. My system did not respond as I had always known it to do. I never seemed to get well – so that no fieldwork could be done in Burma and, due either to the rigours of the operation, or the passage of time and inevitable deterioration of my original pathology, I lost even the power to read which I had had up to the time of the operation. I thought it would come back gradually if I trained my eyes on print long enough, but it never did. I thus learned that one feature of the operation had failed and my general vision also was deteriorating alarmingly so that I might, before long, be blind.

I could do nothing and was idle. Fortunately, one of my daughters had come to Michigan with me, in case I needed help, and help was certainly needed now. She could read to me and was alert enough to enjoy recapitulating the chief points in the material for me to jot on stark white paper with a thick felt pen. I 'read' but I didn't write. I had to believe that my reading vision would return and then I would chain myself down to write and rewrite. My chief pleasure in writing, as with other writers I think, lies in the scoring out of most of the dreary first draft, to an acceptable degree of readability. For this I thought I depended, not on hearing but, on reading slight only.

Realizing the hopelessness of writing plans based on the ability to read and amend what I had written, I became very depressed. Fortunately, a friend with a personality that can influence his associates deeply, visited me soon after. He was, besides being a dear friend, the Director of the Center for South and Southeast Asian Studies, which was our host department and to which I felt accountable for making my stay here fruitful. The way, he, L.A. Peter Gosling, spoke to me convinced me that he could quite clearly see through to the shambles of my wrecked willpower. In a determined effort to retain his good opinion, I sat down to all the notes and drafted chapters I could not read. Contrary to the writing procedure I adopt normally, I worked on each sentences as read out by my daughter. It is my earnest hope that readers will view leniently the shortcomings of this book due to my handicap in not being able to remedy them by reading over what has been written.

My acknowledgements of deep gratitude must be long. First those Burmese friends and relatives, who have supplied me with information. Headed by my scholar cousin U Lu Pe Win, they are: Sao Hso Hom, Sao Soe Tint, U Aye Maung and Daw Hla Kywe, Sao Hseng Sandar. Thi Thi Ta, U Toe Aung Kyaw, Patricia Kingham, San Thida, U Kham Leng, Daw Khin Thein, Daw Toke Gale, U Ba Aye and Daw Yin Yin Mya the professional women whose careers are outlined in Chapter X, that superb reader of Burmese material, Ma Tu Mar, and Hpyu Hpyu Soe for her proficient secretarial help at the most needed time. For figures of the British period and other material in London I am grateful to my lifelong benefactor, FS.V. Donnison, who has also exerted himself in seeking out a publisher. For proofreading I thank another lifelong friend, Peter Murray.

I owe more than I can say to my daughter Ta Ta for secretarial and reading help before our return to Burma in July 1978, and to my niece San Thida and my nephew Leng Boonwaat for the same help after July 1978. My friends Betty Musgrave and Karen Payne, I deeply thank for their generous gift of reading and typing help.

There are also my Ann Arbor friends and colleagues: Professor A.L. Becker who was responsible for my being able to reside in the University of Michigan campus, who would like this book to be written better than it can be by me, and who must help even more than he has already done in the final reading of the manuscript. There is also L.A. Peter Gosling whose influence I have already acknowledged in this introduction. There are Professors Tom Trautman, Gayl Ness, Rhoads Murphey, Robbins Burling and others based on Lane Hall, South State Street, Ann Arbor, who with their wives not only showed me so much warmth of welcome but have also encouraged and helped me in my work. In the great blessing of Ann Arbor's system of being able to call colleagues on the phone and get information on that colleague's field of specialization, perhaps the best is John Musgrave, always ready to tell or to track down whatever one needs, with so much kindness and knowledge. I do thank him deeply.

There are the distinguished friends and relatives whom I have asked to read over the draft of the manuscript: the eminent writer and jurist Dr Maung Maung who made time from his national responsibilities at the highest level, and U Lu Pe Win who read so quickly as not to delay.

Finally, I must thank the Ford Foundation who helped me to work at this book without the need to seek wage support. I thank also John D. Rockefeller III Associates for help in getting me home to Burma where secretarial services have been within my means so as to enable me to complete this book. In this, it is Leng Boonwaat who has been with me in the last weary pushes to the finish.

However, when I felt that I had completed my work on this book I found that the end result still needed revision and some cleaning up. In this it was only the supervision and help of my husband Sao Saimong which provided me with the finished product and enabled me to produce a bibliography and source notes.

*　　*　　*　　*

In attempting to show what I have called 'the world of Burmese women', I have felt it desirable to give a fully-rounded account of the society in which they function. Such a full description of the Burmese social background may sometimes appear tedious and may even draw the reader's attention from the main focus of the book. However, I have no doubt that the thoughtful reader will soon be able to focus on the central point again and indeed, she may find that she has added something to her perception of her Burmese sisters from the background material. I have supplied. I have several reasons for having chosen this method: I have a certain amount of national pride in the conditions of women in my country. Then, several times at meetings and conferences I have read speakers get up and declare the high position enjoyed by women in their countries. I do not wish to prove any such thing by statement alone. Instead, I prefer to give here as full a picture as I can and let the reader make her own conclusion.

Thus, when dealing with the kinship system for example, I have given a fairly detailed account of all its terminology in order to show it as a truly bilateral system. In dealing with family law I have gone back as far as the original sources of Burmese Buddhist law in order to show what a strong place it has in people's lives today. I have also tried to show how, in spite of new legislation having been passed, people still prefer to go by the old laws.

The spirit of any women will be derived from the spirit of the society in which they exercise their personalities. Though the Burmese embrace the austere doctrines of *Theravada* Buddhism, they are not an austere people. I would rather say they are a fun-loving and happy people. This aspect of their character is most easily evident in certain community festivities which, unfortunately, I shall not be able to describe in this work. Suffice it to say that, as in various other aspects of life, certain community and religious festivities allow an equal role for men and women.

In giving the account of the housewife's work load I have, once again, given a fuller account than is perhaps strictly necessary. Partly I have done this for the reasons outlined above. But partly I have also emphasized certain aspects of her role in order to show how different Burmese society is from that of its more industriaized neighbours.

Finally, I would like to place one other point about my work in front of the reader. This book is not written on the basis of national-level statistics. Much of what is contained in it comes from the experience of one who has strong roots in her native community. Some of the profiles of women, especially those who work in the so-called 'non-professional' jobs, are given in great detail in order to make them alive. In doing this I hope also to be able to retain the flavour of Southeast Asia in the context of which this book on Burmese women should be read.

1. The Historical Background

The Historical Background — Women in the Making of Burma

Our first historical glimpse of women in Burma is in the Pyu Kingdom of Sriksetra or Old Prome near Burma's southern coast. Today Prome is 180 miles north of the sea; then it was much nearer.

Chinese sources refer to Buddhism as having already arrived in Burma in the first half of the third to fifth centuries and note an orderly kinship and societal system among the Pyu (Luce (i) pp 308-9). But it is in the ninth century descriptions of the Old Tang History (ibid, p. 318) that women spring to life:

'When they come to the age of seven, both boys and girls drop their hair and stop in a monastery where they take refuge in the Sangha. On reaching the age of twenty, if they have not awaked to the principles of the Buddha, they let their hair grow again and become ordinary townsfolk' (ibid, p. 319).

This is arresting information, for to go to a monastery and take refuge in the Sangha (Order of Monks) is one of the greatest privileges given to human beings in the Buddhist world. It is exciting to find girls of that time given it with boys. (Did they go to monasteries of ordained nuns, or was it to monks they went for teaching? The records do not say.)

The fact that girls were admitted to the Sangha becomes all the more interesting when we note that the basis of monastic life is to keep distractions of sex away from the monks. And the women of the Pyu period, it would seem, would certainly have been considered in that light. 'Married women wear their hair piled in coils on top of the head, and ornaments with silver and strings of pearls. They wear blue skirts of silk cotton and throw about them pieces of gauze silk. When out for a walk they carry a fan' (ibid pp. 319-20).

The Pyu Kingdom came to an end in 832 A.D. Soon after this, in the southeast, another people of Burma, the Mons, gained prominence. Though few traces have been found, as yet, of their kingdom, a woman's voice still reaches us from it. It says, in an inscription on an image of the Buddha found in Kawgun cave near Pa-an: 'This image of Buddha, it was I, queen of Martaban dwelling in the town of Duwop who carved it and made this holy Buddha. The votive tablets of earth in Duwop and elsewhere in this kingdom, it was I and my followers alone who carved them' (Nai Pan Hla, p. 70).

1

The highest devotional act in Buddhism is to set up and dedicate an image before which others can gain merit by their own devotions. A duplicate of this inscription was found in Thaton, the capital of the Mon kingdom of Ramaññadesa which was in the north of present-day Tenasserim, a coastal region streaming southward from the main body of Burma. Among stories of important Thervadha Buddhist monks (such as Sona and Uttara who are said to have brought the doctrine in Asoka's time in the third century B.C., and of the scholar Buddhagosa who brought the Pali scriptures from Ceylon in the fifth century A.D.) we come across one of a young Mon girl, Talahtaw (Harvey, p.6), who is said to have converted the heretic king of Pegu (which lay northwest of Thaton). The story says she gained her knowledge by her frequent outings with her parents when she listened to doctrinal discourses.

Maung Maung

Pagan panorama: 11th Century foundations of Burmese civilization

The Classic Period — 11th to 14th Centuries

The dry air of this inland region preserved its wealth of monuments, and from their inscriptions we can now see that Burmese women were active in many fields besides the religious. The inscriptions are not accounts, as such, of daily or secular life. They are religious dedications which only incidentally make references to other activity, and so make their revelations about women all the more rewarding.

It is not surprising to find women in agriculture, in paddy and cotton fields, or in spinning and weaving, but they were also engaged in trade (Luce (ii) p. 352), thus confirming a role which has come down the centuries till today. Their economic role included large-scale purveying and contracting of supplies such as betel, selling of curries and rice, and appointments such as 'keeper of all-important granaries' (Pe Maung Tin, p. 413).

Betel was a highly relished, symbolically cherished, stimulating chew. Its trade, monopolized by women, was an extensive business. Female purveyors, sellers, and servers of betel provided quids not only to court, monks and public, but also laid them before images and scriptures, by the thousand daily in some cases (Luce (ii) p. 352). It was an elaborate culture, with buildings donated specially for chewing betel, with jewelled silver or lacquered betel containers, with gourd or gold phials for lime paste to go with it. Quids required a variety of products, which presumably the women had to procure and assemble: areca nut for astringence, grown mostly in wet regions south; green betel-leaf also from wet regions for fresh tang and aroma; burnt and slaked lime to smear on the leaf and blend the taste of the two; cutch, boiled from heart-wood of *Acacia catechu* grown in their own dry region, to cool down the lime; and tiny bits of spices to heighten fragrance.

The fields in which these women worked had a developed agriculture, with an irrigation system based on tributaries of the Irrawaddy. Crops included rice and millet, sesame for oil, cotton, fruits like banana, mango, jack and bael, vegetables such as beans, cucumber and pumpkin, spices, sugarcane, tamarind and toddy (ibid, pp. 328, 333, 353). This important toddy or palmyra palm was planted all over the dry landscape to give drink as well as sugar, and women must have been involved in its use, as one of the best-known proverbs to stress fair division of labour roles between male and female says: *lin ka htan tet, maya ka htan chet* – husband climbs the toddy tree, wife cooks it into jagaree (palm-sugar).

The glory of Pagan was in its temple building and dedication. Thousands of structures were built over several centuries, of which the remains standing within call of each other, make of these sixteen square miles beside the great river, one of the world's devotional wonders. Though kings caused the great temples to be built, the inscriptions abound with names of donors who gave other temples, monasteries, lands and labourers, and these include women as well as men.

The inscriptions are meant to show piety but their relevance here is their indication of the status of women at the time. They obviously had rights not only to own property but also to dispose of it as they wished. (This latter right is still being fought for in equally Buddhist Thailand next door where women now own large properties, but cannot dispose of them as they wish.) Inscriptions of dedication also showed the rights of women in law cases. They could sue and could defend themselves if sued. One noteworthy case is the Phiyon lawsuit from the Kyaukse area west of Pagan.[1]

Commenting on the decision of the judges to uphold a woman's rights in this case as well as in other cases in this area, Professor G.H. Luce says, 'Women ... could earn, own and inherit property in their own right apart from their husbands' (Luce (iii) p. 95).

Most of the law-suits recorded are about the ownership of 'slaves' and involve women suing each other. The word 'slave' is a misleading translation. Though there were domestic 'slaves', the majority were labourers attached to the pagodas and monasteries. Their duties were agricultural labour on lands donated, or upkeep and offerings at temple, image or monastery, decorating them or providing song and dance at festivals in their grounds.

Women donors, like men, often showed concern for the welfare of such pagoda subjects. Some reserved land for their use (Than Tun, p. 42), another (woman) gave detailed instructions to ensure their food (ibid, p. 44), another stipulated that when her pagoda subjects got old or ill the monks must give them proper treatment (ibid, p. 45).

'Slaves' could rise above their station by becoming monks or nuns. Equally, women could become nuns if they wished.

The decision made by the Buddha in about 500 B.C. to allow women into an Order was a revolutionary step in the social history of the world. It gave to a woman the right, unknown in other religious systems of Asia even today, to choose to leave the duties of home and hearth in order to attend to her spiritual growth as an individual, just as a man is entitled to do. Though she will be behind a man in this spiritual path, she is still entitled to pursue it with respect from society. The Order of *Bikkhunis* has died out since. It is not known whether the Nuns of Pagan were of that tradition with ordination, continued from the Buddha's time, or whether they were like the nuns of today as described in Chapter VI. Professor Luce thinks they were ordained nuns (Luce (iii) pp. 95-6).

Nuns in Pagan could rise high. A solemn dedication in a cave (temple) records eight Lords of religion (Pe Maung Tin, p. 413), chanting the *Pareit*, one name among them is a women's, an Abbess it is thought.

Religion and letters were synonymous, and part of the reverence accorded to monks comes from their task of educating boys. Although girls in this period could not benefit from this monastic medium, there was no denial of learning to them, and, as women were much to the fore in the society's life, literacy among them is to be expected.

This period in Burmese history saw the birth of the Burmese script from the Mon, the Mon script still in use, the Pyu not yet lost, and Pali in all maturity as the language of religion. So learning was in the order of the day, and women were said to chant *pyissi pahtan* (extracts from the *Abhidhamma*) over their spinning, weaving and cradle-rocking Kyi Mah, p. 20). When monks came for almsfood offering (and women then, as now, obviously took their place in the assembled laity) a twelve-year old girl distinguished herself in a discussion of Pali grammar with the monks (Pe Maung Tin, p. 413).

Pagan was the bastion of Buddhism. G.E. Harvey in his *History of Burma*, writes of the Pagan kings,

> To them the world owes one of the purest faiths mankind has known. Brahminism had strangled it in the land of its birth. In Ceylon its existence was threatened again and again. East of Burma it was not yet free from priestly corruptions. But the kings of Burma never wavered, and at Pagan the stricken faith found a city of refuge.

Monks came from other countries to imbibe the doctrine. One such novice monk from abroad·was stopped by a girl tending a cotton field as he crossed it, and engaged by her in a cathechism duel in Pali. At court, Princess Thanbyin, daughter of King Kyaswa, who debated with monks, left a treatise on Pali cases called *Vibhattyattha*. A woman court secretary is mentioned. A woman, Uiw Cau San, records that she wrote her own inscription (Kyi Mah, p. 20). And even female 'slaves' are listed as literate. In a batch of nine literate 'slaves' in 1227, four are girls; in another batch four girls and thirteen boys are listed as literate (Than Tun, p. 47).

Women are also shown in administrative positions. Women 'headpersons' (*sukhri*) of villages, women elders (*sankri*) and assistant elders (*sanlyan*) in charge of community projects are mentioned. These same titles were also held by men, and in the case of *sankri* the title was used even for monks in charge of some other project. At court, women officials are mentioned, women were given titles carrying the royal order, offices such as Keeper of Royal Fans and Charge of the Maids of Honour existed for women, and also an Inner Service of Palace Women, just as for men of the palace (Pe Maung Tin, p. 414).

A note on names then is relevant to the system prevailing today. Women's names had female prefixes (i, ui, in, im, uwi, etc.) though it is not known if these, like *Ma* and *Daw* of today denoted marital status. Like today, there seems to have been no rigid rule as to whether a woman would name herself as an individual or, suppressing her name, describe herself as wife or daughter. They appear to have followed wish and circumstance, and where (as in the great majority of cases of donation) being a wife or daughter was something to boast about, they stressed it, sometimes with the female parent being named. Thus inscriptions show women referred to in different ways.

Given below are a few more instances of activities women were involved in seven or eight centuries ago; records of later periods do not give us such details about women. For example, there is the story of two daughters coaxing their father to purchase 20 maids. The two girls themselves weighed out the 'copper' and 'live silver' needed for the purchase (ibid, p. 418). Other vignettes included women players of the xylophone-like *pattala*, a woman singer who weighed out money for a paddy-field purchase; dancers; slave women dealers in meats; and most successful among this humble company, a wet nurse. To his wet nurse Prince Yan gave a golden palanquin, a ceremonial umbrella, a painted awning with bells attached, land, slaves, cows. When he died, King Cansu – (*Sithu*) who came after him said 'I too was suckled at the breast of Mother Ui Pon San. I give her as the price of the milk I drank . . .' and confirmed the gifts (ibid, p. 414).

The noble prayer of this King Cansu has been quoted to show the measure of moral greatness of the Pagan. Equally, there are records of prayers by women. Here is an ideal of attainment as expressed by one woman, a minister's wife who dedicated a cave at his grave-side.

After calling blessings on king and realm for their share in her merit, she says:

> May the queens also and all the ladies in waiting share it. May they look at one another with eyes of love, without one speck of anger or cloying . . . May those who desire worldly prosperity get it. May those who prefer to do good deeds do them. For myself I pray that I may never be covetous, insatiate, wrathful, bullying, ignorant, dull, stingy, mean, unfaithful, frivolous, forgetful nor inconsiderate. But I would cross samsara full of the good graces – modest in my wants, easily satisfied, mild of temper, pitiful, wise, conscious of causes, generous, large-handed, faithful, earnest, unforgetful and affectionate . . . (ibid, p. 419).

All women could not be so worthy. Here is quite another woman's prayer and a more materialistic approach:

> Before I attain Nirvana by virtue of the work of merit I have done on such a big scale, if I'm born as a man, I wish to have prosperity and happiness above all men. If I am born a spirit, I wish to be endowed above all spirits with noble and thralling beauty of complexion and especially, I wish to be long-lived, free from sickness, beautiful, sweet-voiced, well-proportioned in limb, abundant of gold, silver, rubies, pearls, corals and other inanimate things, and elephants, horses and other such living things. I wish to be great, through my power, influence, retinue and fame (ibid, p. 419).

Women in Regal and Administrative Roles

In the 13th century the Kingdom of Pagan broke up for reasons which need not be discussed in this work. Burma was split into warring kingdoms in the two centuries following. As these centuries contained the reign of the great Mon Queen, Shin Saw Bu, I will refer here to Burmese traditions of Queenship and of the rule of women when found at other levels, including the village level.

Before considering Shin Saw Bu, it is relevant to look at Burma's traditions regarding women in the regal aspect, as ruling queen or consort.

From the Pyu period, there was a tradition of queenship. The *Taungdwingyi* chronicle tells of the Panhtwa Princess who ruled in Peikthano. The *Yazawingyi, Yazawinlat,* and *The Glass Palace Chronicle* tell of Queen Nam Hkam, or Malasandi who ruled in Thagya-in on the site of the later Sriksetra. After the fall of the Pyus, also, when Kyakhatwaya town was built on the site of Toungoo, a woman was installed to rule it. In Arakan, the coastal region across the western ranges, an inscription records the rule of Queen Kywaypi at Wethali from 334 to 341 A.D. (Kyi Mah, pp. 11-12). And an Arab traveller of the tenth century notes: 'In India there is a realm called Rahma (Burma). Its ruler is a woman' (Harvey, p. 10).

As a consort, the *Mibaya Khaung* or Chief Queen, had strong status. A king's coronation was not complete if he did not have such a consort. At ceremonies, she had a separate set of offerings placed before her (Kyi Mah, p. 24). She was regarded as the king's adviser, and was praised or blamed for the state of the kingdom. She was consulted, as were the other queens in her absence, about the succession (ibid, p. 24). A successor always tried to win strength from an alliance with the Chief or other queens of his predecessor. In the chaotic Burma we have now arrived at, one such queen, in her frightened moments of fleeing during a take-over, was assured by a follower: 'Many men have seized the throne, but none has ever harmed the crowned Queen of his predecessor.' The assurance proved right. Shin Bo Me, a cruel woman herself, went on till she had been queen to five crowned heads (Harvey, pp. 96, 324).

Queen Shin Saw Bu of the Mons was somewhat different. Of her reign from 1453 to 1472 the historian Harvey writes: 'She ruled well, leaving behind so gracious a memory on earth that four hundred years later, the Talaings (Mons) could think of no fairer thing to say of Queen Victoria than to call her Shin Saw Bu reincarnate' (ibid, p. 117).

Daughter of the hero king Razadarit, she had been taken to Ava as a prized Queen. There she asked for two Mon monks to come to the palace to teach her. With them she later fled down the river to the Mon capital of Pegu. After the death of her father and her brother who succeeded, she became Queen.

The duties of a good Buddhist ruler are to keep enemies at bay and to promote religion. Both of these she achieved. Except for a few incidents, there was peace, and subsequent rulers continued her tradition of humaneness.

Shin Saw Bu suffered from taunting not different in spirit from that suffered by latter-day feminist aspirants to high office. Once, when out in state with crown and sword, an old man was hustled out of the palanquin's way. He shouted: 'Old fool am I? Not so old that I can't get a child which is more than your old Queen could do!' She accepted the rebuke as meekly as any Buddhist woman and often referred to herself thereafter as 'the old Queen' (ibid).

She retired before old age set in. She invited the two monks who had helped her escape to take alms. In one of the two alms bowls she had put the symbols of kinship and lay life. The monk who got these left the Order, married her daughter, and reigned as Dhammazedi, among the best of kings.

Shin Saw Bu retired to Dagon, the site of present Rangoon. The Shwedagon Pagoda there had always been sacred from the eight hairs of the Buddha which it enshrines, but its aspect was not then as it is now. Shin Saw Bu built a terrace fifty feet high and three hundred feet wide; she also built an immense balustrade with stone lamps; beyond this she built other encircling walls, and between them she planted palm trees. With successive raising of the spire by subsequent kings, the Shwedagon stands today, the premier shrine in the Buddhist world, a golden wonder dominating Rangoon from its wooded Theinguttra Hill, and it was a woman who set it thus.

Away from the court the villages continued under the control of local *Thugyis* or 'Headmen' which really means 'Head person'. Such an office was most often hereditary, and where a woman became at one time the head person of a village, the position was carried on by her female descendants. In the revenue inquest compiled in 1767 for example, the deposition made by headwoman Mi Ain, age 36, of Myethindwin village in Pagan township takes us back to earlier decades thus:

> This village my great-grandmother Ma Nyein administered. When she was no more my grandmother Mi San administered. When she was no more, my mother Mi Way administered. When she was no more, I, from 1119 (1757) till now have administered (Furnival, p. 50).

Exact boundaries, detail of monastery and pagoda, lands attached to them, crops and taxes, were part of such depositions. A head person had not only to be familiar with lands, crops, and taxes, she was also responsible for lists of people. This might be complicated because of a system of hereditary 'classes' or groups that gave specified service and remained under the authority of a group leader who, by migrations possible to all, might now be distant from a member. Distance entailed written communication. An Italian traveller, Manucci, writing of conditions in about 1700 remarked: 'It is a kingdom governed by the pen, for not a single person can go from one village to another without a paper or writing.' Harvey's comment is that such 'obstructive' Government control was facilitated by the unusually high standard of literacy. In this I include the literacy of women.

The persistence of such hereditary headwomen in Burmese history led J.S. Furnivall to explore the possibility of a matriarchal tradition in Burma. Perhaps it is closer to the truth to say that there was a principle of not denying to women the rights and responsibilities which circumstances may offer them, though as a rule, such circumstances did not occur often, and it was the men who held office by consensual tradition.

I have mentioned that these were times of war and desolation in many parts of Burma. It is at such times that the small falicities of life are cherished, and the notes I have made on women's contributions during this period show female participation in much the same roles as it takes today. In the flowering of literature which occurred at this time, wives of ministers at court, led by queens and followed by handmaidens wrote verse and prose, keeping as they do today, to such 'womanly' topics as the treatise by maid-of-honour Yeway Shinhtwe on fifty-six hairstyles of women, while village women like those of Nyaungyan and Byetayaw kept alive traditions of folk poetry (Kyi Mah, p. 20-1). Consider also the women of Toungoo who, according to an inscription, cooked rice twice a day to feed hundreds, much as women of today do. Consider again the Princess wife of Pyanchi of Toungoo who stood before an altar in Pagan, and having cut off her hair and lit it into a torch, prayed to be born again as her husband's wife and not as a man (Bennet).

However, this is only one side of the picture. There were other aspects of Burmese women's activity.

The strong dynasty set up by Alaungpaya in 1752 and continued by the more illustrious among his sons had not only unified Burma but expanded its boundaries. The Burmese went into Siam and destroyed forever the capital of Ayuthia; they repulsed Chinese invasions for four successive years; they incorporated the coastal kingdom of Arakan more fully into the empire than before; they settled succession disputes in Assam and Manipur which they overran from time to time. These westward expansions brought them into contact with British power in India, border incidents multiplied, and war broke out in 1824.

This war, fought bravely by a people hitherto victorious in mobile, stockaded fighting, depending on formidable musketry, was lost to seaborne invasion and heavy artillery. It is in the battle of Wettigan that its chronicler Major J.J. Snodgrass records seeing 'three young and handsome women of high rank, dressed in warlike costume, who rode constantly among the troops inspiring them with courage, and ardent wishes for an early meeting with the foe'. One fell from a wound in the breast, another while riding near a thicket to urge the troops, one was hit in the head by an exploding shell and tumbled into the water (Snodgrass, pp. 231-2). These were Shan women.

A Foreigner's First Observations of Burmese Women

As a result of this war, the coastal strips of Tenasserim and Arakan had to be ceded. For the first time in Burma's history she was conclusively defeated on her own soil, and the modern world, in the person of Britain, had got its foot in her door.

The nature of Burmese records had so far precluded any descriptions of women in personal and family life. Once foreign observers, more interested in recording this kind of detail, came into the country, we began to get observations of this aspect of women in Burma.

Howard Malcolm, an American, President of the University of Lewisburg, Pa., visited Burma shortly after this annexation. He was deeply committed to Baptist evangelical efforts, which had begun in monarchic Burma without much success. Now, the efforts, concentrated in British-ruled territory showed rosier prospects, and after seeing these in the south in Tenasserim, Malcolm went up the river into Burmese territory where society was still untouched by British influence. This is what he saw:

> Women usually wear a *te-mine* or petticoat of cotton or silk-lined muslin. It is but little wider than is sufficient to go round the body and is fastened by merely tucking in the corners. It extends from the armpit to the ankles . . . being merely lapped over in front and not sewed, it exposes one leg above the knee, at every step . . . in addition, an ingee or jacket open in front with close long sleeves . . . It is always made of thin materials and frequently of gauze or lace (Malcolm).

He sketches this, adding 'a cigar, as is common, in her hand'.

Despite the showing of thigh, the Burmese woman retained her 'modesty'. 'The female dress certainly shocks a foreigner by revealing too much of the person; but no woman could behave more decorously in regard to dress. I have seen hundreds bathe without witnessing an immodest or even careless act' (ibid).

A traveller of the early nineteenth century found much distasteful. The Buddhist religion appeared 'spiritual death', the people 'a nation of liars', hygiene and government abominable. But where women were concerned, a different scene unfolded:

> Their (women's) intercourse is unrestricted, not only with their own countrymen but with foreigners. The universal custom is to give them the custody of their husband's cash; and by them is done the chief part of all buying and selling, both in shops and bazaar. They clean rice, bring water, weave, and cook; occasionally assisting in the management of a boat or the labours of the field . . . But hard work of all kinds, the universal custom assigns to men. They (women) are by no means denied education, nor is any impediment placed in the way of attaining it; but the monastic character of the schools prevents admission there. Private schools for girls are common in large places (ibid).

He goes on to describe harmony in work roles and gives this glimpse of a poor family at home:

> Children are treated with great kindness, not only by the mother, but the father who, when unemployed, takes the young child in his arms, and seems pleased to attend to it, while the mother cleans her rice, or perhaps sits unemployed by his side. In this regard of the father, girls are not made secondary to boys (Lu Gale, pp. 157-67).

Yet, to this man of God, divorce seemed 'shockingly common', because it was simply a matter of both parties agreeing to one. If one party did not agree, it was more trouble and involved a trial. Then, 'women may put away their husbands in the same manner, and with the same facilities, as husbands put away their wives' (Foucar, p. 157).

Much of our understanding of early Burmese women through the centuries is thus confirmed in this early account by a foreigner.

He also noted that: 'females of the higher classes do not condemn industry and affect the languid listlessness of some Orientals' (Kyi Mah, p. 24) and that they were not secluded. When he was granted an audience with the Mekhara Prince, uncle to the king, the wife was present. At the audience with Surawa Prince who later became king, 'his lady was introduced, with a lovely infant two or three years old' (White, p. 14).

Around 1853 the British, having fought another war, took this time the belly of the country, the delta plains south of Prome where we first saw the Pyu. Burma was particularly rich in teak, prized for ships, and she would soon be turned by the British into a great asset for rice, with Indian labour to hand nextdoor, the Suez canal open for quick export to Europe, the monsoons and rich delta lands, and the Burmese tradition of rice growing.

On the eve of this transformation of the lower country into the world's foremost rice exporter, we take a look at women in rice-work, the basis of life for most women in Burma.

Here is a description of paddy transplanting by scholar U Lu Gale in the village headman's field at Myaunggyi village during King Mindon's reign, in the year 'after repairs to the reservoir at Sinkut' (ibid, pp. 68-9).

Early in the morning the girls gathered together and went down to the fields in small groups. They dispersed into adjoining plots, each with a leader, and started quick transplanting – a batch of plants in one hand. As they planted, and as mood took them, they sang well-known or improvised poems, singly or in chorus as the tempo moved, poems of man-woman work-nature relations, love and scorn, fun and tenderness. Each line called for an answering line matching in rhythm, its chief element, with rhymes. In challenge and answer one field matched another at intervals throughout the long working day.

Hlaing Hteik Khaung Tin, the leading woman of letters at this time also wrote love lyrics. They were philosophical and sad. She was married to the King's brother, an unfaithful husband whom she continued to love. She was a noble woman, and she lived in the Mandalay palace of teak, with multiple roofs ascending, with vermilion and gold walls, glass mosaic pillars, and carvings that enlivened every panel and roof hang. The last mistress of this palace, Queen Supayalat, was the opposite of Hlaing Hteik Khaung Tin. Young and ambitious, she has been depicted by foreign historians as unscrupulous and cruel as well. A Burmese view of her which will be found in the profile of author Dagon Khin Khin Lay in Chapter X should be read to offset the foreigner's depiction of her. She is often blamed for the tragedy of the last reign. In fact, imperial policies made this final annexation inevitable.

On 29 November, 1885, British forces led away the King and his immediate family in a plain cart which drove down to the river. There a boat waited to take them to island exile on the far west coast of India. The feeling of the young king, descendant of the dynasty whose armies had marched victoriously up hill and down dale from Siam to India, and heir to even more glorious dynasties before it, can only be imagined. No words were spoken by the people watching that cart rumble on.

Suddenly, a slender hand is thrust out. It holds a cheroot, it is Queen Supayalat in need of a light. The British soldiers hasten to give it, the arm is withdrawn. The last movement in the ringing down of the final curtain on monarchic Burma is a woman's gesture, which still today is the most familiar one among Burmese women – the lighting of a green cheroot (Nisbet, p. 450).

Interlude of Resistance – the 19th Century

Pin Khin Khin was a woman guerilla who wielded a country sword in company with her uncle, U Min Bo, a rebel leader in central Burma. She introduces this interlude when, faced with the actual fact of direct foreign rule, the countryside rose in resistance. 'Throughout the whole of the villages and hamlets on the plains ... there was probably hardly a household where some male member had not issued to join one or other of the rebel gangs,' said a British official of the time. Khin Khin was not the only girl fighter. In hills where Kachins and Chins fought fiercely for many years to preserve their independent way of life, we hear of the expedition led in 1889 by Major Shepherd being met, at Tar Tan village of the Siyin Chins, by a unit of women and men combined. In this battle, eight Chin women were killed (Cochrane).

Women's Adjustment to the 20th Century and Colonialism

It took from four to ten years to put down this resistance. Meanwhile, others took the view that life must go on. Women, being more pragmatic, accommodated themselves early. Thirkell White in *A Civil Servant in Burma*, relates that immediately after the annexation when Chief Commissioner Bernard went up to Mandalay, he was, at Pakokku, received by the wife of the local authority,

> A lady of large bulk, of high spirit, and of cheerful humor, she was administering the town and district in the name of her son . . . Her position was quite in accordance with the practice in Burma as already stated, women take a prominent part in public affairs.

He adds later:

> If one has business with a police sergeant or Thugyi and finds him absent, one does not seek a subordinate, but discusses and settles the matter with the *Sazingadaw* or *Thugyigadaw* (sergeant's wife or headman's wife). It is on record that prisoners being brought to a police station in the absence of any of the force, the sergeant's wife puts them in the cage, and herself shouldering a dah, did 'sentry-go' till relieved.

Victorian Englishmen often expressed delight with a society which included women in spheres not invaded by their own women at home. Sir George Scott:

> The Burmese are probably the most engaging race in the East. The Japanese are the nearest to them . . . but the Burmese woman is far ahead of her lord in the matter of business capacity, and the Japanese woman is equally far behind. The Japanese wife is not only supposed to obey her husband, but actually does so. The Burmese wife shows her capacity by the way in which she rules the household without outwardly seeming to exercise any authority. The Japanese wife treats her husband as an idol, the Burmese as a comrade.

Big business had arrived in Burma. In it the Burmese would have little or no share as, in the wake of British companies, keen Indians and others fully conversant with the new commerce swarmed in. One cannot wonder that Burmese men, especially, felt out of place with things lost and changed. The gallant 'business-as-usual' aspect of Burmese women at this time is all the more to be appreciated.

'At all the large centres of trade' says Nisbet in *Burma Under British Rule and Before*,

> Burmese women have now to undergo a very keen competition from Parsis and other natives of Upper India from Bengal to Bombay. Burmese men would have no chance against . . . the subtle, watchful, greedy and alert Bengali – the Graeculus esurius of the East . . . but the Burmese girl holds her own, and will still hold it for some time yet – in the 'bazaar arts of persuasion and bargaining'.

A different observer, H.P. Cochrane, a missionary who found life in Burma as devoid of virtue as of comfort and ease, on rare occasions did see something which merited grudging approval:

> The Bazaar is almost wholly run by the women, each having her own stall and keeping her accounts in her head. Vastly better than her indolent husband or brother, she knows how to make money and keep what she makes. While Mohammedan and Hindu women are shut up in harems and zenanas, the Burmese women walk the streets with head erect, puffing their huge cheroots without the slightest thought of being the 'weaker vessel'. The energy of the Burmese women saves the race from going to the wall.

Maung Maung

Thuigyan, new year water festival

2. Kinship and Society

Kinship and Society

This chapter discusses terms and relationships between kin, the concept of kinship, and the most important mores underlying interpersonal relations in Burmese society.

The Nuclear Family

In Burmese, certain terms, in the basic meaning of their monosyllabic components, are indicative of relationship concepts. Thus the term for the family is *mi-tha-su*, meaning 'mother-offspring-group' or *tha-mi-tha-hpa*, meaning 'offspring-mother-offspring-father', and for the parents *'mi-hpa*, meaning 'mother-father'. In these terms the mother is placed first, or is the only parent mentioned, thus making the family unit basically one that comprises the mother and her children. The debt of life to the mother is repeatedly acknowledged: in merit-sharing the prayer leader calls out: *mway-the-mikhin mway-the-hpakhin*, 'the mother who gave (me) birth, father who gave (me) birth', again placing the mother first. While the mother is seen as the family's base and strength, the term used for the father, *ain-oo-nat*, describes him as the 'spirit head of the house' or its crown.

The prefix *a* before a kinship term denotes respect and authority and is found in terms used for all older relations, whether male or female. Thus the mother is called *amay* or, more formally, *mikhin*, and the father *aphay* or, more formally, *hpakhin*. The more familiar and intimate versions of the terms are *hpay-hpay* for the father and *may-may* for the mother. The term used for offspring is *tha-thami*, son: *tha*, daughter: *thami*. The older use of *tha* extended to both male and female offspring, sometimes with and sometimes without a suffix to qualify it. It means 'of the flesh'.

Married couples are known as *lin-maya* meaning 'husband-wife' or *zani-maunghnan* meaning 'wife-husband'. Interestingly, the wife refers to her husband as *khinpun* (friend). Other terms used are *aintha* (man of the house) or, least used, *yaukya* (man). The wife is referred to by the husband as *zani*, *amyothami* or *meinma* to correspond with the above terms for the husband. In addressing each other the husband and wife may use more indirect references such as 'the children's mother' or they may be more direct and use a sibling term or a modification of the name. In address a wife often uses sibling terms to her husband, for example *Ko Ko* (elder brother) or *Maung* (younger brother), to denote affection.

Relationships within the Nuclear Family
(a) *Husband and wife*: The husband and wife relationship is said to be based on the perceived differences between the spiritual, physiological and psychological natures of the two sexes. The term *ain-oo-nat* or spirit head of the house, indicates the higher spiritual plane on which the man is placed. In practice what this means is that while women are denied no practical powers and the male is given no especial domestic or social advantage, the concept of male dominance is still accepted and often even eagerly embraced by women.

This concept rationalised the importance of the position of the male in Buddhist terms. Buddhism, which has formed the way of life in Burma for more than nine hundred years now, was given by the Buddha who, as a man, gained enlightenment and showed the path for all to follow. As a man he attained the highest spiritual level and only as a man can another human being hope to do likewise. All living beings have a cycle of life after life, with the action of one shaping the next. It is possible for a woman to be born again as man (if she acts accordingly in doing good in this life). Meanwhile, every woman has a brother, husband, father or son, and she takes pride in this male quality called *hpon*, which is enshrined in him, in his attaining the peak of being born as a human and male. This *hpon* will be cherished and guarded by her no less than by the man himself.

The attitude of a wife to her husband is set by this concept. Even in private it is the ingrained habit of the wife to respect her husband's *hpon*. She does not stand or sit higher than him, or with her feet thrust in his direction, and instinctively treats his clothes with the same regard as she pays his person. She sleeps on his left as the *hpon* resides in his right, she keeps her clothes at the foot of the room, and as her *longyi* (skirt) is the symbol of her sex, it does not overlie anything connected with him. In public she defers to him, not advertising her decision-making in their affairs. All this, because it is so deeply ingrained, comes easily, and to do the opposite would, for many women, entail a wrench.

The degree of a woman's belief in the concept of *hpon* can be gauged when, in conflict, a wife 'desecrates' her husband's *hpon* by reversing the usual manners respecting it. To her, this is a more irrevocable act than smashing his property.

Here, it should be stressed again that the reason why this concept is still largely unquestioned today is because, as the previous chapter shows, it has through the centuries run parallel with a full life for women. A Burmese proverb says of every man: 'three steps down and he is a bachelor'. Three steps refer to his descent from the slightly raised front verandah of his marital home. Traditionally, the universal 'male' quality allows a man much sexual freedom, whether he be married or not. However, the constraints of religion and society make monogamy and marital stability the prevailing norms. By contrast to the man, the woman is seen as having stronger physiological links with the family. She is the earth and the man the seed; or if he is likened to the rain she is likened again to the earth. Being the bearer of children she is said to find her pleasures in being able to keep as close to the home as she wishes, while a man can go afield to work. Adultery on her part would have to mean an involvement of her emotions towards a new base, whereas for the potential 'bachelor' adultery does not necessarily mean a desire to change. These concepts also underlie the distinctions made between the sexes by customary law in conditions permitting divorce. (See Chapter III). They underlie the choice of roles in joint ventures, or in women's activity outside the home as Chapters VIII, IX and X will show. show.

Face of three generations

The Burmese do not hold the Hindu view of women as the irrational sex, easily swayed by emotions. Man, who has the energy, is the volatile spirit. He is also the sensitive one, easily hurt and humiliated. He is less able to bear the injustices of life, is trusting, and easily deluded by others. Woman is the conserver and guide. She is pragmatic and can bear reverses and injustices without injury to her spirit. Not easily hoodwinked, she is the negotiator and trader, speaker of smooth placatory and equivocal words. She therefore looks after difficult situations, often pleads for her husband's job promotion, advises him at all turns, sets the price for trade purchases or handles the labour in their joint ventures. *See-te-yay, hse-te-gazin* means 'the water which flows, the ridge which conserves it', defines the sex roles with an analogy from rice-planting. Water is heaven-sent and because of it, rice, the life-giver is obtained, yet without the little ridges built to keep it in, its great potentiality would be lost. Man is flowing water and woman the restraining influence which husbands his energies towards fruition.

In public, a husband shows no physical affection or attention to his wife: the bond of marital love is considered the stronger for being private. In the streets the man walks in front of his wife. This is partly because of his 'senior' status, and partly because it is embarrassing to be seen walking thus in public. The bond between man and wife however, must be extremely close – a complete identity of interests: *lin-nhin-maya, sha-nhin-thwa* 'as the tongue and teeth, so the husband and wife' so close as to clash often, yet never apart.

The love which grows from the union must be entire in its commitment. In terms which men use to refer to their wives, 'life' is the recurring theme: *thet-htar, thet-hsut, thet-nhin, thet-pan, thet-le*; 'life entrusted, life plucked (and given), life conferred, life a flower worn on hair, life exchanged'. In return for such complete entrusting, wives are reminded by elders to follow the *taw-lay-wa*, the four exemplary wives from the *Jatakas*, Amara, Sanda-Kainnari, Madi and Thambula, wives respectively of Mahawthahta, Sanda-Kainnara, Wesandra and Sothisena. They served their husband's interests entirely. Yet subservience is not demanded: 'she of a Lord who stands in fear is not a true wife' said the Buddha, and again, when asked, 'What here below is the comrade supreme?' He replied 'The wife here below is the Comrade Supreme.'

Apart from conjugal love and fidelity, the entirety of the mutual commitment between husband and wife makes for an identity of interests and the need for complementing each other in mutually supportive roles rather than emotional dependence. However, it must be said that emotional dependence in the East is not the same as in the West: i.e. limited to a romantic ideal of the relationship for the ties which bind parents and siblings continue strongly, and kinship and societal demands make it difficult for the partners to have a singular emotional involvement in each other.

(b) *Parents and children:* Children have several positive value-roles for parents, as will appear in later chapters. They are a domestic and economic help in the great majority of families, as from a young age they work alongside parents and take on duties at home, in the field or in business. At the same time, great love and indulgence is given them, as they are considered to be 'precious'. Even the *sonma saga* 'admonitory epistles' which are a part of classical literature for common quotation are filled with golden associations for the offspring: 'gold hill, gold egg, gold nugget, gold reed'. The Buddha, Dhama and Sangha are the Three Jewels, but the same term of *yadana* in 'daughter-jewel' or 'son-jewel' is used as a common expression. The poet Shin Maharahtathara says in his *Kogan Pyo*: 'The faces of children, like cool clear water; it needs but one drop to fall, and parents' hearts rise in happiness.'

Burmese parents also value their children as vehicles for the discharge of their (the parents') duties as human beings. The novitiation of all boys into a monastery for a symbolic stay is the noblest merit-making deed for the lay person. For a woman, such a deed sanctifies her role in life. If she has a son, this ensures that she will perform this ritual. If, however, she has no son but still wishes to perform the ritual she can do so for another boy. There is no such ceremony for girls. The traditional equivalent is that of having their ears pierced, but this does not carry the same importance. A mother's duty towards her daughter includes arranging her (the daughter's) marriage. Interestingly, marriages are the concern of the bride's family and they most often link the couple closer to the family than to the bridegroom's.

Children are also valued for the support they are expected to give to their parents in old age, although this expectation is not made explicit. Indeed, all through life the old give to the young and parents, for as long as they can, continue to give a great proportion of their assets to their children.

In studies of Southeast Asian societies, the close familial link between the mother and the daughter has often been pointed out. In Burmese society, while this tie is close, it is not the only one, nor is it always the strongest. The tie between two sisters may equal it and often outlast it. Although mothers and daughters are often seen together because they share domestic tasks and leisure activities, the ties between fathers and daughters and mothers and sons are also very strong. In their own places the mother and daughter exercise a particular power over their men: the mother will often 'use' the daughter to persuade the father to do certain things; equally, she will use her influence over her son to do the same.

The ideal set-up for the relationship of children to parents is *chit-kyauk-yothay* a 'love-fear-respect' compound that underlies the easy relationship of daily life and emerges to take effect in a crisis. In poorer families the help given by children in a variety of tasks, as will be seen in Chapter IV, is in response to the instructions of the parents. In better-off families requiring less help, the children still respond to the beck and call of their parents. The manners they acquire suggest respect in one form or another: they take second place in voicing opinions, often sit companionably silent (and without complaint) through long periods of adult gathering. These manners, like other junior-to-senior manners, are more or less ingrained because they are accorded to all elders and are not behaviour personally demanded by a parent.

When offspring deviate much from this pattern it is regarded as trouble. Girls' trouble invariably takes the form of keeping 'sweethearts' at an early age or falling in love with and meeting the 'wrong' boy. Daughter-rebellion of any other sort is rarely seen for, while daughters are not handled more strictly than sons (other than being chaperoned), a girl is associated with family responsibilities from a young age and identifies with parents easily.

(c) *Inter-sibling relationship:* Between siblings the elder brother or sister are the same to both male and female younger siblings who are expected to give them some respect. The *a* in *ako, ama* as mentioned earlier in this Chapter, shows the traditional regard due to them.

The eldest sister in a family takes on household responsibilities from an early age, as I have said, and may occupy a position very close to that of the mother's, both in what she does for the younger children and in the respect and dependence they feel towards her. The term for elder sister, *ma ma*, is, it should be noted, what maids in domestic service call their mistress employers. Its undoubted connotation is of respect. Today, in university hostels for female students, for example, the wardens who are invested with much authority, being senior faculty members, are addressed by the girls as *Ma Ma*. The age difference would normally call for the term 'aunt' but the elder sister term is used because it carries more authority, tempered with love.

Grandparents help the children off to school

Ko Ko, the term for elder brother, does not carry the same power outside the family.

A girl's younger sister and a boy's younger brother bear the same terms *nyi* and *nyima* denoting a helper, that is, in two siblings of the same sex, the younger is the helper of the elder in the domestic tasks they are expected to do together. When the siblings are of mixed sexes, the picture changes: a boy's younger sister is not a female helper to him, but a cherished girl, dear to the heart, *hnama*, in which the *hna* is the same as in the word *hnalone*, heart. A girl's younger brother is also someone special to her. The term *maung* comes from the word *mauk*, 'heaped high'. She will keep him high and at the same time tend to his creature comforts. In marriage, a wife who calls her husband *maung*, 'younger brother', wishes to show more tenderness than if she called him 'elder brother'.

Unfortunately, I do not have the space here to go into details of other consanguineous and affinal kin. I hope one day to be able to produce a full monograph on the Burmese kinship system. This will, hopefully, be of interest both to students of linguistics as well as anthropology.

Nature of the Kinship System

The Burmese kinship system is completely bilateral – in terminology (except where a section of the people distinguish paternal aunt and uncle), as well as in actual practice. The duties of both paternal and maternal kin are the same. The greater closeness of one side or the other is not openly recognized. In practice, however, as the mother is more involved with family management, a closer attachment grows between the children and her own kin. There are frequent visits, a married daughter goes to her mother to have her first child, a woman's own relatives often live with her and help in caring for the family. But this is not always the case, and often paternal kin can be closer.

Despite the absence of bonds created by ritual between kin, kinship ties are greatly valued, kept up by close and frequent association, and extended outside of the family. The word for kin, *hsway-myo*, 'the friendly kind', is often pronounced, *shwe-myo*, 'the golden kind'. The word 'gold' symbolises the most cherished possession.

The counting of kin extends both formally and informally and often friendship is clothed in kin terms and classed as a firm family tie. When my niece married, her husband became my nephew. A first cousin of his, as his 'brother' thus also became my nephew. His own younger brother's wife was a beloved and special sister to him; thence, her sisters also became most affectionate and helpful nieces to me.

Interpersonal Relations and Society

Between the fringe of kin and close friends the dividing line is an unclear one. Kin merge easily into a society of friends, and from there into a community.

I cannot hope here to explain more than the salient attitudes underlying inter-personal relations in this society; other attitudes must emerge as different spheres of activity are discussed in their place.

Sex distinction operating on the principle of regard for the male *hpon* is present in all relationships. The belief in 'suitable' feminine behaviour is very strong. Participation in every activity makes it all the more important to retain the ideal of modesty in deportment as depicted in the manners of a wife towards her husband. On public occasions and big feasts, people sit (on carpets or mats) according to sex in a roughly defined division, with the men generally in front, women behind or on the other side, and latecomers anywhere they can, regardless of sex. It is division, rather than segregation, and the arrangement is considered more thoughtful and comfortable than a mixed one. Women, for example, are more at ease, especially when such occasions stretch long, if it is another woman they must nudge against in a crowd.

In private houses, if a party is small, everyone sits together in the same circle, but again, if there is more than one circle, the sexes divide. However, an exceptional couple may, if they wish, join the other circle without censure.

Age, the other factor in interpersonal relations is ever-present, and young people are respectful of elders. As age advances, it takes precedence over sex, so that grown men for example, will give obeisance to an old aunt.

An important factor in interpersonal relationships is in the prefixes to names. A detailed note can be found on the name system in Chapter V. Here it must suffice to say that names, given individually, without patronymic or change on marriage, are never complete without the relevant prefixes – *Ma* for a girl, *Daw* when she is adult, *Maung* for a boy, *Ko* for a young man, *U* when he is adult. In address a prefix is indispensable to the full name. Names are used without it if they are used as diminutives, or if there is already a euphony such as a repeated first syllable, for example, of *Maung* (for a boy), and of *Khin* (for a girl).

In colonial times Englishmen, used to addressing each other as Taylor or Richardson, did not seem to realize how strange their Burmese colleagues found it to be called Chit Tun or Tun Byu. A friend of mine decided to forestall this by registering in an American Baptist School under the name of Ma Ma Khin, so that she made sure of being addressed with a *Ma* by her American teachers. Others less adroit must have tried the painful remedy of writing in a 'Mr' to stand before their Burmese name.

The Burmese are a friendly people and close relationships are immediately struck up over the simplest of things: a meeting, a social event, etc. Friends are often then made 'kin' and addressed in kinship terms. In the 'professional' forms of address, there are both 'office' and trade terms of address for the people concerned. In such cases the term of address for the wife is a respectful one. She is called the *kadaw* which implies a certain status. For the Burmese, such an address is an indication of the association of the wife, and the recognition of her contribution, in the prestige attained by her husband.

I would now like to turn to some concepts of social behaviour. One such that has been noted by foreign observers is the concept of *ahnade*. The literal meaning of this word is 'the strength hurts', i.e. that your feelings are constrained and uneasy when you think you have caused inconvenience or discomfort to anyone. Thus, you feel *ahnade* if you are unable to do someone a favour they have asked of you; equally when you have to ask someone to do something for you. Linked to this is the idea of 'face' – if you do anything that is not considered socially acceptable, you run the risk of 'losing face'. Thus, social acceptability in Burma can be said to be achieved by not asserting overmuch one's self or opinions and by developing a high degree of self-control. Often seen by the West as the much talked about Asian 'passiveness', and indeed it can often be such. But this kind of accommodation also makes it possible to live easily within a community network and therefore to prevent isolation and alienation. Of course, often this lack of open, direct speech can lead to problems.

Continuity of Tradition in Social Relations

Burma shares with other Buddhist countries a tradition of enumerating family and societal duties, some of which have already been referred to. The basis of these lies in the Buddha's teachings. I note, for interest, the origin of these duties as given by the Buddha in the Digha Sikaya Sutta No. 3, sometimes entitled 'Admonition to Singala'. As this dates from such a distant time and clime, it will reveal the continuity of traditions to quote the original and then see what the Burmese have made of it, and how much of it is still prevalent. Here is a vivid glimpse of an early morning in the 5th century B.C. in the great plain of India near the present Rajagaha.

> Lord Buddha went out from the Bamboo Grove towards Rajagaha with his alms-bowl. He saw a young householder, Siggala, with face and hands still wet from his early dawn ablutions. He was doing reverences towards all points of the compass as well as above and below. Lord Buddha asked him what he was doing and found the young man rather vague about the meaning of his actions which he thought were what his dead father had told him to do. At this, Lord Buddha told him the meanings he should put into his reverences. Identifying various seniors with the points of the compass as well as above and below, he defined the duties between people in kinship and society. Thus: A son to his parents: . . . 'should maintain them in their old age; he should perform the duties which formerly devolved on them; he should maintain the honour and traditions of his family and lineage; he should make himself worthy of his heritage; and he should make offerings to the spirits of the departed.' His parents 'should restrain him from evil; encourage him to do good; have him taught a profession; arrange for his marriage to a suitable wife; and transfer his inheritance to him in due time.'
>
> A husband should serve his wife: 'by honouring her; by respecting her; by remaining faithful to her; by giving her charge of the home; and by duly giving her ornaments.'
>
> A wife 'should be efficient in her household tasks; she should manage her servants well; she should be chaste; she should take care of the goods which he brings home; and she should be skillful and untiring in all her duties.'

From that, which was preached 2500 years ago, the Burmese have made felicitously pithy rhymes, with a few adaptations of these duties, especially of husband and wife, parents and son (which they apply to children of both sexes). They say: Husband to wife: Don't belittle her, entrust the property to her, don't commit adultery, give dress and ornaments, hold her in love and esteem.

Here, in the place of 'give her charge of home' the Burmese have put 'entrust the property to her'. They are specific about clothing and jewellery. They have retained the stress on the need for holding her in high regard.

Wife to husband: Do the house tasks, keep the treasure bag secure, don't commit adultery, distribute fairly, don't be lazy. Here, the old injunction to manage servants well has been dropped and a reminder to share fairly (with relatives of both sides) is substituted. The two separate injunctions stressing responsibility for the home are kept, as is care of the finances.

Parents to children: Prevent them from bad, guide to the good, let them learn knowledge, share out capital for earning, settle them in marriage.

3. Family Law and Practices

Sources of Law

In this chapter I will try to explain why Burmese women have, in general, not tried to bring about any alteration in their status and rights, even in areas where observers see them as being less privileged than men. In family law, perhaps more than in any other aspect of life, tradition is of more importance than actual legislation. Even in systems which appear from the outside to be oppressive to one sex, the keepers of the tradition, human beings who live within it, find values in it to cherish. The less advantageously placed make their smaller felicities within it; the more privileged see in it safety and protection for themselves and those whom they control.

When new and non-traditional laws have been passed in recent times in Burma, in order to change the low status of women, they have been slow to take effect. Indian legislations barring child-marriage, sanctioning remarriage of widows, and allowing for daughters to inherit property; or the law against polygamy in the China of the 1930's, were disregarded by families who felt safer with traditional ways. In Burma too, where the government (made up largely of Buddhist Burmese) persuaded the Muslim community to agree to a law, in 1952, allowing Muslim women to initiate divorce, the law has never been taken advantage of, as the Islamic tradition against it was too strong for women to feel bold enough to do so.

Legislation also takes time to become known to those whom it seeks to benefit. Indian village women cannot know that they are suddenly entitled to sue for divorce or inherit property on the same terms as their brothers. And even when directly informed they do not have the means to seek legal redress. Even to urban people conversant with the law, legal proceedings are often the last resort, especially in family matters.

Family relations, which set a premium on trust and amity, should not, it is generally felt, seek the help of legal safeguards. A Thai woman's pre-marriage property, if merged into the joint property on marriage, passes out of her hands and lies entirely at the husband's disposal, by traditional laws. New laws now allow her to register this property at the time of marriage as hers, in which case she retains rights over it. Many women find, however, that on attempting to do

25

this, the bridegroom reacts: 'Why! Don't you trust me?' Rather than spoil marital harmony at this juncture, the bride desists from registering (Dharmasakti, pp. 110-23).

In all such circumstances, leading spirits among women are stirred to push and fight, exhort and inform those among them who are timid and backward. Put on their mettle by the need for such efforts, they carry on with zeal and struggle to invade new fields of activity and challenge old ideas of male prestige and competence.

In Burma no such challenges to women have arisen, no legislation in modern times has been considered necessary, as customary laws ensure for women a position suitable to present-day concepts of equality. Except for the Burmese Women's Special Marriage Acts of 1939, 40 and 54 which safeguard the position of Burmese women who marry foreigners, family law is based entirely on traditional and customary codes. These laws are fully operative, and have been so for centuries. They ensure a certain degree of parity between the sexes, and it is perhaps this near-parity which leads to neglect in amending the small points of differentiation which still remain, such as ineligibility for marriage, causes for divorce and recognition of desertion.

But in the main it may be said that Burmese women have found customary law and their traditional roles reasonably comfortable and, hence, have not felt any great need to push for new legislation on their own behalf. This early advantage – i.e. their position in traditional law – has in a sense resulted in their having fallen behind in the present march of women. They have not got up the spirit to seek new fields to conquer nor acquired new attitudes to challenge the traditional concept of male *hpon* and prestige.

The customary law governing Burmese family matters is known as Burmese Buddhist Law. It must be understood that it is not in any sense a system of law laid down in Buddhism, but is the law which Buddhist Burmese have developed through the centuries, and have applied to themselves interpreting it in the light of changing social conditions, as customary law. It is worthwhile dwelling briefly on the origins of this law if only to disentangle the native spirit in it from the Hindu inspiration with which our early cultural contacts are usually associated.

Those who claim Hindu origins for Burmese law trace them to the influx of Hindus overland into northern Burma since the 9th century B.C. when the kingdom of Tagaung was set up. The assumption is that the Hindus married with the inhabitants there and developed a law combining their own with customs prevalent there. More definitely, later, maybe about the 5th century A.D. or earlier, Buddhist Indians came over by sea. Either they or the Pyu and Mons of Southern Burma who became Buddhists developed a system of law which later and extant books showed to be quite different from the Hindu. As noted by Sir John Jardine, Judicial Commissioner of Lower Burma, in his notes on the Burmese law books in 1882:

> Buddhism profoundly affects the position of women; and the changes of
> sentiment, manners and aspiration have left distinct marks on the written law of

marriage, divorce, inheritance and succession. The sacramental ideas of the Hindus have disappeared, being inconsistent with Buddhist theology. The Hindu religious obligation to beget a son is likewise left out. The succession to inheritance in accordance with the right and duty to perform *shraddh* or funeral for the same reason is, so far as decisions show, unknown to Buddhist law. The religious reasons given for the degradation of the widow and her burning with her deceased lord are entirely repugnant to Buddhist opinion and to Burman law. The widow on the contrary, at once becomes emancipated and may marry again at her own will.

This gives some idea of the laws which the Mons of southern Burma wrote and kept in monasteries. These were, in the following centuries adapted and added to in a series of law books called the *Dhammathats* (which followed Mon customary law and later that of the Burmans who succeeded them in dominating Burma). Till the mid-18th century the series of eleven such books were more in the manner of moral treatises. With the rise of Burma's last dynasty, the Konbaung, and the extension of effective rule to the sea-coasts, a new modified form of the *Dhammathats* was written. Though many *Dhammathats* followed till a total of 36 is recorded, two were most prominent – the *Manukye* and *Manu Wonana*.

The jurisprudence in these books was by now Burmese but a Hindu mouthpiece was still considered desirable for investing them with authority and learning. The *Manu* in the titles was the Hindu sage Manu, known as law-giver throughout Southeast Asia. He had become for the Burmese a mythical Burmese figure. The *Manukye* was used as the chief source of Burmese customary law when British Burma first came into being in 1826. From it, later, notes were made by Sir John Jardine for the guidance of judges. After the final annexation in 1885 however, U Kaung, the former minister Kinwunmingyi to the deposed King Thibaw, compiled a digest from all 36 *Dhammathats*, and the result, *Kinwun Mingyi's Digest*, replaced the *Manukye* as the chief reference.

In many respects, the *Dhammathats* referred to a society different from that of modern Burma, so decisions based on these traditional sources have usually been made by interpreting them in the light of prevailing customs. Accommodation is the spirit of Burmese Law. An observer of the courts before 1885 says 'In deciding civil suits the principal aim of the Judge is, if possible, to satisfy both parties, the result being, in almost all cases, a compromise' (ibid).

In traditional Burmese law consensus is the best way to settle a dispute and when agreement has been reached it can be taken that the law has been successfully administered. Thus, such law lists six types of 'judges'. These, in ascending order for recourse, were: 1) The parties themselves who might agree to a decision; 2) One or more arbitrators of their own choosing; 3) Unpaid but officially appointed and recognized arbiters whose court is called *khon*; 4) The town court; 5) The court of the capital city and 6) The King (ibid, p. 15).

It is to be noted that agreement between parties or by local elders of the parties' choosing is classed as having the same legal sanction as the law courts. In fact, as will be seen, marriage, divorce and other family matters are given legal recognition through the presence of local elders as witnesses. The guiding line for arbiters in civil cases was 'Let big words become small words and let small words disappear.' Payment made to arbiters would be after agreement was reached, and pickled tea-leaf eaten to mark it. In the sections that follow therefore, the laws are given as reference to the customary and prevalent practices. They are invoked only when disputes cannot be settled otherwise. In the majority of cases, marriage, divorce, partition and inheritance are settled, and given recognition without recourse to the courts.

Courtship

Although the norms governing the behaviour of young boys and girls in Burmese society are strict, certain rituals are looked upon with tolerance. Courting is one such, but even here a premium is placed on chastity. Pre-marital sex is also considered wrong both socially and according to religion. In addition, there are the constraints society imposes on demonstrativeness in public.

There is however a fairly open and tolerant attitude towards young people, particularly the *apyos* (young virgins) and *lupyos* (young boys/men).

As part of the ritual several *lupyo* will often visit the girls of their choice, sometimes together, sometimes with companions waiting outside while the accepted *lupyo* goes in alone. The girl waits by the light of an oil-lamp, dressed and expectant. Across the mat wall in the next room the parents ensure that only subdued talk and laughter goes on. This is considered respectable but meeting alone during the day is not. If a girl keeps a stall at a night-bazaar however, it is respectable to visit her there, a tribute to the importance of a Burmese woman's sales profession.

This old custom has, however, changed now. In the co-educational schools, universities, community life, bazaars and work places there is ample opportunity to make a choice and even meet clandestinely if need be. A favourite routine among young urban people is walking out, in the late afternoons before or after supper, in groups of four or five. *Lupyo* also walk up and down in groups. They will greet each other, perhaps talk briefly or simply exchange glances. The line of public behaviour is drawn finely. In high school girls always occupy the front rows in the classroom. Those who are so inclined talk freely with boys between lessons. At breaks, however, girls go with girls only. They may meet and sit with boys over a dish of noodles at the snack shop but they go there only with girls.

At the university the rise in status is recognized and a boy and girl occasionally seen walking to class together are acceptable, but anything regular is seen as a commitment towards marriage, which, if broken entails 'spoiling one's name'. This often acts as a brake, young people, even in their twenties, still worry about parental reactions. In villages and bazaars girls more easily slip away into meetings after their choice is made but among urban or middle-class girls, meetings in private are few and have to be contrived with the connivance of girlfriends to provide alibis.

It is to supplement these brief encounters that the well-worn institution of handing letters is resorted to. 'To give a letter' is synonymous with the sending of a love-letter. Such letters express love in stereotyped terms, and often speak of its core – the liver with its network of branching blood tendrils. But from this unromantic base rises some of the finest love poetry. For example, the troth plighted in the poet U Ponnya's words:

> Till oceans drain and a rabbit may in them stand
> Till earth's center stars and moon and sun appear
> Till in space the creeping earth grass grows I'll not stop loving you
> The Pole Star may drop away but my heart's pledge never
> True like the word of the quail born as Buddha to be
> If my troth swerves like the crookedness of King Sediya
> Let the earth break open and swallow me.

With such ardent letters the boy often uses an intermediary. Often the intermediary and girl fall in love over the handing of three or four such letters.

However free the choice, the parent's participation must now be sought before the matter can go further. They may be pleased, may need to be coaxed, or may refuse adamantly to agree, (of which more later). In other cases the parents and relations may actually choose or influence the choice of a partner by arranging meetings in conducive circumstances, and this is quite acceptable in the majority of cases where offspring have reached the mid-twenties or later without having found anyone on their own.

In all such cases it is the boy's parents who must take the initiative. Whereas the young people's choices follow no standards different from the universal phenomena of sexual attraction, parent's choices are rationalized into seeking a girl who is chaste and decorous, fair skinned and pretty if possible, rich, well-educated or skilled domestically. They choose a boy for sobriety, earning power and steadiness, not good looks. It is worth noting that scholarship in a girl is no deterrent to young men choosing her.

Betrothal

This is the setting against which the following laws regarding eligibility for marriage stand. These are invoked when there is cause for dispute about the legality of a marriage. The consent of both parties to the marriage, freely given, is necessary. The *Dhammathats* are silent on prohibited categories of kin in eligibility for marriage and the principle observed is not to contract a union unacceptable to society. Cousins through the maternal line, especially children of two sisters, do not marry. There is strong disapproval of any first cousin marriages but cross-cousin marriages are heard of now and again. Cognates, that is, kinsmen descended from a common ancestor are not actively disfavoured provided the woman is on the same generation line as the man or below it. Generally speaking however, non-kinsmen are favoured above kinsmen, though some closely knit families marry kinsmen without active disapproval from society. Marriage with the deceased brother's widow, or with the deceased wife's elder sister is not favoured, but that with a deceased wife's younger sister is very common.

A girl may be given in marriage by her relations in the following order: father, mother, brother, sister, nearest relations or guardian. There is no male dominance in this particular role. The woman must be free from marital ties, but a man does not need to be so free provided that the woman consents to his marriage situation. A widow or widower, and divorcees of both sexes are eligible to marry.

Once a couple are engaged, it is taken as an agreement to contract a marriage. The actual ceremony can be formal or fairly simple. I would like to emphasize here that the whole ceremony, like the courtship that precedes it, is taken quite seriously as a long-drawn out ritual. The couple, although central to this ritual, are not themselves the principal players. The play is, in a sense, played out around the couple by their immediate families, the elders, their parents, aunts, uncles, cousins, the community -- in a word, society. I give below two examples of engagement ceremonies I was present at. These illustrate the importance of ritual among different classes.

Soe Soe, a 15-year old girl, was brought to domestic service from 500 miles away by her paternal 'aunt'. This aunt, Daw Su, was a part-time trader, part-time housekeeper.

Soe Soe's father was Daw Su's cousin. He agreed to Soe Soe's employment on the promise that she would be treated as one of the family by the employer who was, after all, 'related'. The employer, in turn, needed a relative rather than a servant to look after her new baby while she went to work.

Soe Soe worked well. She shared a room with her aunt, from which she regularly emerged to hang the laundry on the back verandah. This overlooked a small house where a young couple had staying with them the husband's cousin (who had a job), and his younger brother (who was still a high-school student). The salaried brother fell in love with Soe Soe. He wrote her letters and sent them through his young brother. Soe Soe and the intermediary fell in love; unknown to others they met often.

One day the head of the small house called on the big house. He broke the news that his young cousin and Soe Soe wished to get married. He was told that there was no objection on the employer's part but her parents' permission was required, so 'let's take time to consider'. At this, the visitor broke out in embarrassment: 'Can't take time Sir, they've gone beyond the limit.' Soe Soe was pregnant.

A date was set for 'asking'. The aunt Daw Su, hearing the news ran up the stairs, slapped Soe Soe's face, gave her a kick or two and called her a shameless creature. This took care of the required 'formalities' and the employer could now write and inform the parents.

On the appointed day, the farm superintendent and his wife, having collected two couples who were their most senior relatives, arrived. The most senior kinsman formally asked for Soe Soe's hand to be given to his junior relative, promising to place him in a job within his giving. Soe Soe's employer accepted the proposal, the wedding was fixed for the week following, tea was served and Soe Soe became engaged for a week.

When Ta Ta and Maung Lin Myaing got engaged, their families decided to make it a fairly big affair. Verbal invitations were sent to about 50 couples. Each of the two families chose an eminent and respected couple to represent them.

On the appointed day the representative of Maung Lin Myaing's family stood up and 'asked' for the girl's hand. He spoke of having known the man as a boy, emphasized his good qualities, his present job and the prospects ahead. In reply, the man representing Ta Ta's parents spoke of her worth and accepted on behalf of the parents. Each made his own speech, following no set formula. (But I have attended ceremonies in the Shan State where old traditions persist longer. There, if Nang Onmar's hand is asked for by the boy's representative, the girl's family representative may counter 'which Nang Onmar?' There are three here. One is young and beautiful. Another is not so young. She is surrounded by children. She looks tired and worried. The third Nang Onmar is an old lady, wrinkled and grey. Which one will you take?' The answer of course is all three, after which proceedings continue.)

At Ta Ta's engagement her fiancé presented her with a ring. This is a modern custom as Burmese tradition does not recognize a ring as symbolic. According to tradition, gifts are given to the bride. Among the Shans, who remained under a traditional system of rule till 1959 and retain more of old traditions, the groom is expected to 'put up' something, usually jewellery and a set of clothing at the time of asking. The latter day practice among an affluent stratum during the colonial period when bachelors in British Government service were considered heaven born eligibles, of endowing the girl with jewellery, money or a house was perhaps a form of 'husband-catching' and not part of a traditional dowry system.

The real tradition is for both sides to give (the bride) whatever property they can, for the joint use of the couple. The *Wagaru*, oldest of the *Dhammathats*, says 'Fathers and mothers should provide their sons and daughters with a suitable amount of property when giving them in marriage.'

In modern law, this is suggested in the term 'kanwin' the legal term for the presents given to the bride by the groom and relatives of both sides for joint use in the marriage.

Expenses for a wedding were traditionally borne by the groom's family, but in practice there is no hard and fast rule. Among better-off families, the bride's side often takes pride in bearing the costs and having the marriage take place from their home. This custom seems to be replacing the older tradition. In many other cases the two families come to an agreement for both to contribute. Much depends on personal situation and financial resources.

Marriage

The *Manukye Dhammathat* announces three ways to effect a valid marriage. These are: 'First, a man and woman given in marriage by their parents who live and eat together; second, a man and woman brought together by the intervention of a go-between who live and eat together; third a man and woman who came together by mutual consent, who live and eat together' (Lahiri, p. 6).

The essential point is to 'live and eat together' and to show evidence of it. No sacrament attaches to this. What is required is to establish the intention to live as man and wife before a group of elders, pay them respects, and serve a few refreshments to all assembled to mark the occasion. On this essential base are built several different types of marriage ceremonies. But it must be explained that Burmese society has a homogenous culture and such differences that exist in the various ceremonies have to do much more with wealth and financial resources, and social pressure, rather than with the fact of people being rural or urban.

Ritual has an important place in the marriage ceremony – whether the couple are rich or poor – and the couple always pay their respects to the 'elders'. A wedding ceremony can be simple – at one I recently attended there were hardly any guests, the couple made offerings to the *nats* (spirits traditionally honoured by their parents), and to the mother of the bride as she was the only parent present, and the ceremony was complete. Soe Soe, whom we met earlier, had a rushed and modest wedding. She and her fiancé were exhorted to take marriage seriously, told to pay their respects to the assembled elders and then the actual marriage tie (when the groom puts his hand out, palm upwards, the bride lays hers on it, the hands are then tied together with a scarf and water, the indivisible element, poured over them) was made.

Ta Ta's wedding was somewhat more elaborate. Hundreds of guests were invited. An eminent couple were chosen, and their consent obtained, to perform the marriage tie. A Brahmin was engaged to be the 'ceremonial master'. The bride and groom both wore elaborate and traditional costumes of silk and brocade for the occasion. On the prenuptial night the couple made devotions together at the shrine and paid homage to the 'parental *nats*'.

At the actual ceremony the couple sat together in front of the *Saya* or master of ceremonies, with a bowl of eugenia sprigs in front of them. At each call of the *Saya*, the couple made obeisance to the Three Gems, Buddha, *Dhamma* and *Sangha*, to all spirits, to elders, parents and all the company. This they did by holding the sprigs between folded hands. The marriage tie was then performed by the officiating couple and as water was poured over their hands the couple were told: 'May your life together be free from the heat of strife as this cold water is. May your union be safely contained as this water lies in this bowl without spilling or leaking.' The master of ceremonies then read a poem, and this completed this part of the ceremony. Several other interesting rituals followed. These, although they add colour to the marriage, are not directly relevant here.

Just married: Maung Lin Mying and Thi Thi Ta in traditional wedding dress

Soon after marriage, the young couple is expected to visit close elder relatives in turn, paying respects together as man and wife. They will also visit the pagoda and pray to be reunited in the next life. They usually stay with the bride's parents for the short while (as the equivalent of the honeymoon) even if their own house is ready to move into. In the past, in a purely agricultural society, the groom was expected to live with and help his in-laws with farm work for three years (thus living matrilocally or nearby) before moving to a neo-local residence. The *Manu Wonana* said: 'If the girl who is loved is given, three years service must be done to the mother and father, in the father and mother's house.' This custom, however, has fallen into disuse in its entirety and, except for the initial short stay, the couple subsequently live where they wish to. It is true to say however that there is far less sanction for a virilocal residence. So that while: 'In absence of any justification the wife should live with her husband in the same house. The husband has the right to select the residence and the wife should comply,' there is also the provision that: 'but when the husband is able to live separately from his parents, the wife is not bound to live in the same house with her parents-in law' (ibid, p. 37).

It is not necessary, in Burma, to register marriages as registration does not make them any more legal. However, couples do register marriages nowadays.

A word now must be said about cases where parents refuse to agree to a marriage desired by their child. To marry then and continue with the normal terms of life would amount to unfilial defiance which to this day, few youths care to show. Instead they elope – another ritual, the sudden flight, the hiding into which they go, is all in accordance with the love-fear-respect they must show to their parents. Friends of the peer group always help with shelter either in the same town if it is a big one, or in another. A few couples are found and brought back on the same day by their parents, the girl's parents taking her back on the assumption that she is still a virgin. More often the couple hide successfully for a few days while a lot of running to and fro among the families takes place. When the couple are found, they are brought back, by now in fact man and wife. The boy's family then collect some elders mutually friendly with both families and take the couple to go and beg forgiveness from the girl's parents. If they do not agree, the boy's mother may hold a wedding reception as it is her son who has hurt someone else's daughter. The young couple continue to live with her till a month or 12 months later a reconciliation is effected. The sentiment regarding such a situation is often summed up in the words: 'One must have regard for another's daughter, one must think of what if it were one's own.' Says the *Manukye* 'If a young man and a young woman have clandestine intercourse, the parents of the former are not at liberty to withhold consent to the marriage.' (If the parents do not reclaim their daughter, the marriage in any case becomes valid). The word for elopement is 'steal and run', but the marvellous old *Dhammathats* are kinder: 'If a young woman shall be taken away from her parents with her own consent, let the young man restore her to them three times (that is, expecting her to re-elope each time): as the young woman is consenting it shall not be called theft.'

Property in Marriage

In the absence of a sacramental nature, marriage in Burma has been likened to a social contract or a business partnership. Both custom and law, however, have invested it with more qualities than a purely social contract. Harvey in the *History of Burma* describes its social aspect thus: 'The Burman chose as his wife an equal, to be his helpmate; they shared their daily life, its common toil and interest, their children grew up under the care of an equal man, an equal woman, gaining the benefit of a father's as well as a mother's example (Harvey, p. 210).'

The *Kinwunmingyi Digest* reinforces this aspect of marriage and introduces another aspect of a joint venture; 'It is only when one is the helpmate of the other, both trying to acquire (and garner) property jointly and agreeably that they are well and genuinely matched like the soil and the rain (Maung Maung, p. 48)'.

The law regards marriage as a 'civil and consensual contract, and an institution which creates a status, the incidents of which are quite independent of volition of parties.' (This is to say, despite the ease with which a union becomes valid particularly in the absence of registration or ceremony, responsibilities and commitments nonetheless come with it.)

> Marriage determines questions of legitimacy and inheritance and imposes liability on the husband to maintain wife and children and remain faithful. There is also an additional incident that flows from the contract or marriage, namely the joint interests enjoyed by both husband and wife in the property acquired before marriage. It also leads to joint interests enjoyed by husband and wife in property acquired after marriage (Lahiri, p. 6).

> According to the custom of the country, the wife takes a great deal of trouble in the acquisition of property (ibid, p. 56).

The position of husband and wife regarding this property must be clearly stated:

> It is usual to regard all properties acquired by the spouses during coverture, except inherited property, as belonging equally to the husband and wife (ibid, p. 56).

> Husband and wife are joint owners as well as joint possessors, and the husband is usually deemed to be the manager of the family (ibid, p. 57).

> The joint nature of the Burmese family's property interests is a traditionally strong aspect.

> Names of husband and wife are often coupled together in business affairs, documents are often drawn up in their joint names, whenever

there is an occasion to sue anybody they sue jointly, and are often sued together by their adversaries (ibid, p. 58).

Before noting the salient aspects of property in marriage, I must mention the different classes of property, as distinction is made between pre-marriage and coverture property: *Payin* is property held by husband and wife personally before marriage. When the husband or wife have had a previous marriage, such property is calld *atetpa*, to distinguish it in case there are step-children who will inherit. This *payin* or *atetpa* will always revert to the owner should a division of property have to be made. *Hnapazon* is property jointly acquired during coverture by exertions or by produce of properties held by the couple. It is liable for equal division between husband and wife when the need for dividing arises. *Letetpwa* is property accruing to one spouse (either husband or wife) during coverture either by inheritance or exertion. It is liable to a division of two thirds to the one to whom it accrues, and one third to the spouse. *Kanwin* is that given by the groom's or both pairs of parents to the bride for joint use.

There is also separate property, acquired by one without family help, held and *kept separately*. There is, in addition, the concept of *nissata* and *nissaya*, dependant and supporter respectively, to be applied especially to the condition in bringing property into the marriage, for example, if one brings much (*nissaya*) and the other hardly at all (being *nissata*) or in inheritance acquired. The dependant, when the property is divided, gets one third of the supporter's *payin* (or premarital property) and the *nissaya* keeps two-thirds of it for him or herself. These types of property are listed in a cut and dried manner which must stand out if a division becomes necessary. In practice, during coverture they are merged in joint use. For example, in Hla and her husband Ko Myint's family, a plot of land was bought with savings from his pay alone. The house built on it was financed in good part with sales of her *payin* or separate property. The home, now joint or *hnapazon*, is in her name only. Later, when her mother died, she inherited a certain amount. Part of this went towards the purchase of a new car which was registered in his name, merging her *letetpwa* into her *hnapazon*.

Regarding the definition of *hnapazon* (as from joint exertions, in which equal shares are held) and of *letepwa* (as property from accrument to, or from the exertions of one) in which the shares are only one-third to the spouse who is not involved in its acquirement, it might be asked if, in the instance of the husband alone earning a good salary, this does not make the couple's holdings *letetpwa* rather than *hnapazon*. To this Dr Maung Maung says 'the rule of community goes not by who earns but whether husband and wife prove to be helpmates to each other both in prosperity and adversity; and if they do, then, they shall divide the property equally between them if they mutually desire to separate (Maung Maung, p. 166).'

As Jardine in paragraph 24 of his *Notes on Buddhist Law* (on the Hindu Origin of the Burmese Law) says: 'The ultimate settlement, as might be expected in a Buddhist country, is in favour of individuality and equality.'

Though, in the absence of anything shown to the contrary, the husband is regarded as manager of the joint property, the wife is not deemed to consent to his actions unless he is acting as her agent, and she can sue him if he mishandles a deal, for example if she gave him money to buy land and he fails to do so or to return the money. Again, though his share of joint property is detachable in discharge of his debts, her share is safe from such attachment. U Lun's house is a case in point. U Lun, who was a widower, re-married. He built his house from a mixture of separate and joint accruments after this second marriage and so half of it belongs to his present wife. Subsequently it was found, in a transition of the national economic system, that U Lun was liable to pay the government large taxes. His personal property from his previous marriage and bachelor days was attached, but the house which belongs to his present wife, whose share cannot be attached, was left untouched.

The types of property held by a Burmese family are agricultural lands, houses for residence and rent, shop premises used or rented, small family businesses, vehicles for commercial transport and for personal use, gold and jewellery. The national system does not allow absentee landlordism, nor holdings of paddy lands above 50 acres. It does not allow large business interests either in production or in trade. Large transactions of gold are also against the law but in fact gold is still the traditional form of saving. Gems mined in Burma are also controlled, private enterprise being barred in their mining or trading, but holdings in secret and in the form of simply set jewellery for which there is no restriction (which is legal) are still very common. Burmese jewellery is generally set in 22 carat gold and in simple designs which do not intrude in the calculations of its market value.

One notable feature of Burmese family holdings is that houses of a substantial nature are most often registered in the wife's name, less often in children's names, regardless of the source of money which helped to acquire or build them. In one family of four sisters and one brother who are all married, the sisters' houses, built in most part with joint earnings between them and their husbands are held by each in her name; their brother's house, built in the same way is also registered in *his* wife's name. Just before leaving for USA I needed two guarantors with immovable property to sign my income-tax bond. I had little time at my disposal, so meeting on the road two of my husband's friends out on a walk I asked if they could oblige. 'Oh!' said one in great embarrassment, 'the house is in my wife's name and she is away in Lashio for two months.' The other said: 'We can oblige, but can we do it today or tomorrow at the latest? Our house too is in Mya's name and she is leaving to visit our eldest daughter in three days from now!'

Factors of Conflict

(a) *Polygamy*: In all the *Dhammathats*, polygamy was allowed, and no reversal of their sanction has been ruled by modern law though the society they related to was different. It was a monarchy and for kings the traditions in many cultures prescribes a plurality of wives. The court followed the King on a smaller scale but by its nature, it derived its prestige and power also by adherence to such high-estate concepts. The common people, even then, did not practise polygamy. With such traditions as governed their family matters and the relations that existed between a common man and wife, they seem to have found monogamy more satisfactory. As long ago as 1435, Nicolo di Conti, the first European to wander into Burma, includes, in his description of the Burmese Kingdom of Ava, the remark: 'The men are satisfied with one wife (Harvey, p. 98).' J.F.S. Forbes, writing in *British Burma and Its Peoples* in 1878, says 'In ordinary life a man with more than one wife is talked of as not being a very respectable person.' In 1951 Lahiri, the Indian lawyer from whom I have quoted so much, remarked that though the practice of polygamy is recognized by the *Dhammathats*, 'There is a strong feeling amongst the people against the practice. Burman Buddhists are rather monogamous by nature.' I have an interesting note on this point. An observer, personally interested in the polygamy question, has pointed out the difference between Burma in this matter and Thailand next door, though both would be presumed to have received similar cultural influences. He mentioned that whereas in Thailand some officials have a number of wives, in Burma, an official has been known to be relieved of his post when his desultory polygamy, kept clandestine for fear of social disgrace, was uncovered.

The Shan States of Burma continued to have their traditional forms of administration till 1959. This included a reverence for rulers within old Buddhist concepts, and though many rulers since the thirties had kept to monogamy which suited their ideas better, polygamy continued to be practised widely among the rest of the rulers, and among some officials in their areas. The same can be said for other ethnic areas which similarly retained their traditional political systems under British rule, such as Kachin and Chin.

The 'taking' of a second wife usually results in the severance of the first marriage tie so that only a handful of polygamous unions exist. In such instances, laws regulate the rights and status of wives. Wives are to be treated equally and to their satisfaction as regards recognition, house and maintenance in which case the law regards them as 'equal and superior' wives, entitled to equal shares in the estate should division of inheritance need arbitration. But if a wife lives apart, and has no share in management of the husband's business or in household affairs – and performs no 'wifely' duties beyond receiving visits, then she is considered an 'inferior' wife, entitled to nothing from his estates (Lahir).[18] These are legal terms. Present day usage does not include the words 'superior' or 'lesser' but calls both wives 'parallel wives' in the rare cases where they exist.

(b) *Divorce*: Foreign observers regard divorce in Burma as being relatively easy because the law does not require a process or registration if the divorce is 'by mutual consent'. This must be a real agreement, duly given to the divorce by both sides.

Despite the fact of divorce being easy, there is a much lower rate of divorce in Burma than, for example, in Java and Malaysia where 50 to 60 per cent of marriages are shown to end in divorce, though this is revoked in a good number of cases. Since there is no registration of marriages and divorces here, proper statistics are not available, and personal observations and personal census must be relied on. Fielding Hall says:

> In the villages and among respectable Burmans in all classes of life it is a great exception to divorce or be divorced . . . I have even tried to find out in small villages what the number of divorces were in a year, and tried to estimate from this percentage. I made from 2 to 5 per cent of the marriages . . .

He attempts to explain this low incidence: 'the facility for divorce makes a man and a woman careful in their behaviour to each other.' The incidence of divorce has risen since then. In 1976 two surveys on the same lines as Fielding Hall's were conducted. In Rangoon, Daw Hla Kywe, noted for her contact with a wide range of families of all income levels, was asked by a researcher to name 400 married couples she knew. Once she had prepared a list of these, she was then asked to identify the unions which ended in divorce or which contained previously married or divorced persons or other divorced men and women she knew. Result: Total number known, 330. Divorced cases 31. This means a percentage of less than ten. In Taungni village the rate was found to be even lower. Of the 347 households resident there, Patricia Kingham, an inhabitant of Taungni herself, could, with the help of the headman, find only two separated couples in the year 1978. Socially, divorcees, male or female, never enjoy full esteem. The choosing of auspicious couples free from divorce, for officiating and attending engagements and marriages puts a premium on marital accord. Children of divorced parents have 'smaller face' than others.

In cases where there is an absence of mutual consent, one may see a notice of divorce put by a husband in the newspapers followed by the wife's announcement that there is no divorce and she is still his legal wife. This makes them still man and wife, and if the dispute continues, one can take it to the law. A man or a woman may ask or sue for a divorce on the following grounds: Adultery on the part of the wife if it is proved or if it is admitted by her. Cohabitation on the part of the husband with another woman. Adultery alone on the part of the husband is not sufficient grounds for divorce, unless cohabitation with that second woman follows, against the wish of his wife. Cruelty, both physical and legal. The law recognizes legal cruelty as a cause for divorce – this can take the form of repeatedly accusing the wife of adultery though no proof can be offered.

Desertion also provides grounds for a divorce – by this is meant desertion by a man for a period of 3 years during which he does not correspond or send support, and a period of one year only of such behaviour by a wife.

If such divorce cases go to law regarding division of property it is laid down that each spouse takes back his or her *payin* property, half of *hnapazon* property, one-third and two-thirds respectively of *letetpwa* property kept as separate, each to his or her own. Where there is *nissaya* and *nissata* regarding the amount of *payin* brought in, the *nissata* (who brought in little or none) is entitled to get one-third of the *nissaya's payin* (pre-marriage) property. The division may be affected if either of the parties has been at fault, the guilty party being deprived of his or her share, for example in a husband's gross cruelty or in a wife's confessed adultery, in a deserting partner's clear intention to desert. Custody of children, according to *dhammathats*, allows the boys to go to the father and the girls to their mother and the law, if pressed for a decision, consults the wishes of the children and gives them consideration so that in fact children in most cases, live with the mother, especially when they are young (Maung Maung). The husband who has been manager of joint property is now accountable to the wife for his management, and he can be sued by her for mismanagement even if she is the one guilty of 'marital offences'. When a 'Burman Buddhist is sued not qua husband but qua manager, no wrong done to him in the former capacity can benefit him in the latter! (Lahire)'.

A husband has a positive duty to maintain his wife especially if she has no means of her own. If he takes another wife and the first wife does not wish to share the same house, she is entitled to the above maintenance still, while living separately. If the husband does not give her the means of such maintenance, he is liable for the debts she contracts in the purchase of necessities. For such rights of maintenance the wife can claim under Section 488 of the Code of Criminal Procedure. This code also compels the man to support his children with lodging, food, clothing and education of the minimum standard which convention calls for, till they reach maturity, even if they live with their mother (ibid).

These are the laws. In practice, divorces are more often settled without recourse to them, in accordance with personal circumstances, financial resources, and pressure of elders.

Shwe's husband took a second wife when he was on a new posting. Shwe did not accompany him, staying behind with the children in the bigger town where they were at school and where she usually did some casual brokerage to supplement his modest wages. After intermediaries had made sure the man did not intend to give up his new young wife, both sides put a notice in the paper that the first marriage had ended. Shwe kept on the house bought with their joint efforts, all the possessions in it and the jewellery and cash savings. The man as the guilty party did not press for any of it. She, on the other hand, knowing his modest earnings and knowing that no regular payments could be expected, and not wishing to go to the trouble of the law for such small maintenance, did not ask for it. She kept all five children with her. She stepped up her brokerage activities, and in time got the eldest two settled in jobs and marriages as a result of which they now helped her out with the younger ones.

Aye Aye on the other hand had a husband who was in a lucrative business. She never earned anything or took part in his business, for she had three children to look after and the house-keeping to manage. The house was built out of his earnings, on land acquired through his connections. When he showed persistent unfaithfulness, though he had no other permanent liaison, she decided to ask a divorce with the help of elders. This was achieved without recourse to the law courts. She kept the house, all their possessions and the children just as Shwe did, but she also got maintenance, a sum sufficient to keep her in accustomed style, being fixed by arbitrating elders. Payments were regular at first, then tailed off. When they first tailed off the pressure of elders sufficed to bring them in again. Later as they became even more erratic, advice was given to Aye Aye to economise, to try and earn something and to make do with the occasional payment till the children were settled. (She is still able to live fairly well without recourse to the law). This case shows the pressure which society can exert on a man through purely personal urging and through his fear of censure from kinsfolk and senior friends who might be present, or former patrons. In the U.S. I spoke to a few couples who had been divorced after coming to the country. Two of them confirmed that although the seeds of the break-up had been present in Burma, they would have found it very difficult to have a divorce there because of social pressure to the contrary.

Three of the four cases mentioned above are concerned with a man's deviation towards other women. What about the law regarding adultery on the part of the wife as grounds for divorce? In one known case the wife admitted to being adulterous, was forgiven and remained with the family. The marriage then continued. In another case the woman and her children moved to her own parents' house where the father continued to send support for the children.

Cases of cruelty often come up before the court. In the British days they were often dismissed according to a reading of old law cases (ibid). But nowadays the law is kinder to women. Sein Sein, a young girl who fell in love with and married a boy, a high school drop-out, of poor parents. They had one daughter soon after marriage. Sein Sein had a domestic job in which she continued. Both were very high spirited and they quarrelled violently and often. On one occasion Sein Sein's husband slapped her face, cutting her lip and she ran out to show the neighbours. Soon after this the husband left to seek a job in another town while Sein Sein continued in hers. Shortly afterwards, she fell in love with a Chinese, a chauffeur. Under the present system of making justice accessible to the poor, the government has a pool which lawyers may join. Though these lawyers may, on their own, pursue private cases and charge high fees to clients who are able to pay, they may also be assigned by the government to poorer clients needing legal services. For this they are paid at a modest daily rate by the government and not by the client. Sein Sein was assigned a lawyer. She sued for divorce on the grounds of cruelty and desertion – her husband had been absent for a year and had not sent her any money or even communicated with her. She got her divorce and is now married to the Chinese.

Women at the village level often change spouses when they move to another region. Ma Win Sein and Ko Ohn Maung who both had other spouses fled from a village near Taungdwingyi to our vicinity when they wanted to change 'partners'. Their position in the village would have been untenable especially as Ma Win Sein's husband had been a cousin of Ko Ohn Maung's. They came 300 miles with her four children. Beginning as construction workers, they soon made good and have been farming in a small way, for the past ten years. People come and go between the two places and often create alarm with the news that the husband is coming after his children. The two elder ones are girls in mid-teens and if their father insisted that the new husband was an improper house-mate for them, society would support the father even though he is an alcoholic.

In the case of desertion, there is very little that can be done, especially among poorer people. Ma Ngwe was left with five children about six years ago when Maung Chit, her husband, disappeared. She continued to work the plot of about 3 acres of orchard land which they had, but when the elder children reached school age she decided to come into town and seek domestic work. After a couple of years the village authorities told her she should give up the land if she could not work it and did not live in the village. She thereupon changed her job to casual laundry work so that they could go to the village and sleep in the orchard at weekends. Suddenly Maung Chit turned up again. Ma Ngwe let him live with them for a few months after which he disappeared again. However, she now shows him on her household list as the head of the house, 'absent on a temporary job'. This allows her to get extra rations.

Special Marriage Acts

The only noteworthy legislation regarding family matters in modern times has been passed in order to protect the rights of Burmese women marrying foreigners whose own laws would deny them the rights they could expect from a marriage with a Burmese-Buddhist. During the period of British rule there was a mass immigration of Indians who were encouraged to come over for labour in almost every field of the modern life that the British administration ushered in. Out of a total of over 400,000 immigrants in a year soon after 1927, 350,000 remained in Burma, so there was, every year, a great swelling of the Indian population (Foucar). In 1931-38, there were an estimated 1,099,991 Indian and Indo-Burmese, Moslems and Hindus resident in Burma, of which 724,218 were males and only 375,773 females. 565,909 of these were Hindus, 396,594 were Moslems, and the rest were 'other Indians' and Indo-Burmese. There were also some Chinese immigrants (Christian, p. 342).

The poorer Burmese women, especially in the course of their bazaar trade and contacts, often married the 'foreigners', not knowing the different rules that such marriages subjected them to. The British government's ruling was that a person would be subject to his or her personal law, i.e. a Hindu to Hindu Law, a Moslem to Islamic Law, a Chinese Confucianist to his or her own law, Jains, Sikhs likewise. A Burmese woman 'marrying' a Moslem would find that Moslems are forbidden to marry members of non-deistic religions like Buddhism, unless she made a confession of entering the Islamic faith. She would either find herself not considered married, or even if married after embracing Islam, she came under Islamic laws which, as far as divorce and inheritance are concerned, are less advantageous to women than Burmese-Buddhist Law. Hindus too, of the four upper castes, are prohibited from marrying non-Hindus, thus giving a Hindu's

Buddhist wife no rights as a wife and in not qualifying her for inheritance from her 'husband's' property. A Burmese woman's marriage to a Chinese was also at first not considered valid without a special Chinese ceremony. Marriages between Indian Moslems and Burmese women were the most common and resulted in a large class of Burmese Moslems or Zerbadis, for the Burmese women converted to Islam at marriage.

This large-scale conversion as well as the injustice done to ignorant Burmese women who married foreigners (and then found themselves deprived of many rights) resulted in a struggle to get this altered. The Special Marriage Acts of 1872 and 1923 were passed to safeguard the interests of such women, but still the marriage remained outside the application of Burmese Buddhist Law. It was not until 1940 that a satisfactory Act was passed in the Buddhist Woman's Special Marriage and Succession Act.

This Act brought all marriages which involved women who were Buddhists and belonged to any of the indigenous races of Burma within Burmese customary law. It ruled that if the parties were of sound mind, the man at least 18 and the woman at least 16 (with the consent of both parents if either was below 20) and if the woman had no subsisting marriage tie, with 14 day's notice given to the registrar, or the village headman, the marriage would be solemnized and recorded in the absence of valid objections. If the couple co-habited without marriage and without being registered in this way, the woman or her parents, guardians, brother or sister could inform the village registrar of it. If so, the registrar must summon the parties and urge legalizing of the union. If the man refused to legalize the union, a suit for breach of promise to marry, or for seduction would be brought against him. If the union was legalized it came under Burmese Customary Law for all matters of divorce, inheritance, succession and ownership of properties. If the huband was a Hindu, Sikh or Jain with rights to an undivided family, these rights devolved on his widow and children if he predeceased partition. Any child born before legalization of the union also became legitimate. In 1954, a new Act passed by the independent Burmese Parliament mended a few loopholes. It lowered the ages which made the Act applicable, made a union legal from the time co-habitation started in a form which, if practised by Bumese Buddhist made it a valid marriage, ensured that if a man's religion forbade him to continue in the marriage he must leave to the wife his share of joint property and custody of all the children whom, however, he must support throughout the years of minority, and also pay the wife compensation. It also stipulated that in the case of a woman who is a non-Buddhist citizen of Burma and later converts to Buddhism, the family comes under Burmese customary law and if the husband then divorces her on the ground that his religion now forbids the marriage, she must be maintained in the style of life to which she had been accustomed, is entitled to keep her own property and the children, whom the man must maintain through their minority (Maung Maung).

This Act finally removed any reason for a woman to adopt Islam against her beliefs just in order to safeguard her marital and economic position. If despite this, a woman still wished to and confessed to Islam on her marriage to a Moslem, then the marriage comes under the Mohammedan Law as recognized by the Burma Laws Act.

Children and Inheritance

(a) *Adoption*: Adoption in Burmese society is lightly done, using the general term for adoption which is *mwe-sa*. But when inheritance issues come up, the law steps in with well defined rules.

Those who are entitled to adopt a child must be a major in age, but otherwise, a bachelor or spinster, widow or widower, as well as married couples may adopt a child. For married couples, both husband and wife must assent to the adoption. A monk may not adopt a child. Two people who are not related or married may not adopt jointly. A non-Buddhist or foreign child may be adopted on the same terms as a Burmese Buddhist child. (It is interesting that whereas the oldest *Dhammathats* mention adoption of sons only, the Burmanised *Manukye* mentions for the first time the adoption of daughters.)

Burmese tradition distinguished between adopting with a view to giving inheritance *mwe-gan-mwe-sa*, called sometimes by the Pali term *Kittima* and adoption not for inheritance but out of compassion, *kauk-yu-mwe-sa*, called by the Pali term *appatititha*. In both adoptions the child is treated as the foster parents' own. The dividing line is thin. It consists in the foster parent making a *kittima's* position clear by words and deeds in the presence of reputable witnesses that they intend the child to inherit. Such a *kittima* must relinquish his share in his natural parents' estate, unless at some point he is accepted back by them into the family (Lahiri). An adopted child can be of any age, including adult, but in that case the adult must himself declare renouncement of rights and responsibilities in his original family (ibid).

People's *kittima* children in my own acquaintance always get a full share of inheritance even when other brothers and sisters, natural children of the family 'suffer' because of the extra division. One reads of many cases where the dead person's brothers or sisters have disputed the *kittima's* right to inheritance, but by proving the discharge of filial duties in life as well as in the last illness and death, the *kittima* is usually awarded his or her inheritance.

(b) *Succession and Inheritance*: Burmese Buddhist Law contains the concept of the eldest child, either male or female as *orasa*, 'the child of the breast' who holds a special position in the family. On the death of the parent of the same sex *orasa* steps into his or her place. He or she has vested shares in one-quarter of the estate which otherwise is at the disposal of the surviving parent. When the surviving parent dies, the *orasa* has a claim to a preferential share in that it must be one-quarter where children numer more than four. However, the conception of *orasa* is less and less put into practice, and it may be said that nowadays all children are held to be equal.

Besides natural children there are to be considered the *kittima* and *apatittha* adopted children described above. There is also the *kilitha* child 'begotten in pleasure', a natural child conceived and bred without the parents cohabiting at all. Such a child is not considered illegitimate, but its rights are inferior to the natural, *kittima*, *apatittha* or the step-children (ibid).

A Burman Buddhist cannot make a will because will-making is considered contrary to the rights of natural heirs. There is the tradition of the *thedansa* or death-bed testament. *Thedansa* are not wills at all, but derive their efficacy from the will or consent of the heirs, not of the supposed testator (ibid).

Such *thedansa* are well-known and the agreement obtained by the dying person who communicates his or her wishes to such friends or heirs as can be assembled is usually adhered to. For example, recently a woman on her death-bed, called her three adopted children to her and stated her wish that the house she had lived in, their house in fact, should be sold so that the proceeds could be divided in five shares, three for them, one for a beloved senior nephew who, though he had a family and inheritance of his own, had always shown her love, and one to an attendant who had looked after her and her dead husband. On her death, one of the children bought out the others after the house was assessed, and shares were faithfully paid to the senior nephew and the attendant.

This kind of settlement is far more common than settlements made by law. Usually rough divisions are made and with the help of mutually respected elders in difficult cases, things are settled with no recourse to law. Among villagers with small plots of land which will not bear dividing, it is quite common for some members of the family to have gone out to seek a living elsewhere, leaving the stay-at-home sibling to tend the land, and eventually inherit it. This accords with the old concept of land-ownership. Apart from inherited or court awarded lands there was *dama'u-kya*, 'land belongs to the first axe' (that clears it). It is in accord also with present socialist policy of the cultivator having prior rights to the land he works.

Though Burman Buddhists cannot make wills they may give away property during their life-term. In cases of dispute, however, the law guards against too great a giving away of their assets to the detriment of the children. They cannot give away a disproportionate share to one child for example (ibid). With the tradition of giving to married children as the years pass, the elder children usually recognize what they have received already, and tend to be generous towards the younger in the disposal of the remaining assets after the death of the parent. Occasionally, when a child is guilty of gross misconduct or unfilial behaviour he or she may be disinherited by a notice in the paper. In actual fact, this disinheriting, to take effect in the event of a parent's death, must prove that the child's conduct was grossly unfilial showing enmity, physical attack or such against his or her parents.

Children of divorced parents may inherit from the parent with whom they did not live only if they continued to keep up filial ties with that parent. This inheritance is seldom claimed. Death-bed gifts are also defined as what is allowable, to safeguard the interests of all heirs, but in the last resort, possession is nine points as everywhere else.

Property must descend if it can, and ascend only when there is no correspondingly close issue in the descending generation to receive it, so that it is only after children, grandchildren and great-grandchildren in this order that brothers, and sisters, parents and grandparents, also in this order, can inherit. Having cleared the ground, let us now note the salient fact that Burmese customary law gives inheritance to the remaining spouse when one marriage partner dies, and the children may expect equal division between sons and daughters only when their remaining parent dies (ibid).

Bazaar seller Daw Khiu Su in earlier years

4. The Household: Material Background of Housewife's Activity

Two Rural Families

Ko Aung Nyein and Ma Khin Nyunt come from the Taungdwingyi area of Central Burma. Their families, from two villages 7 miles apart have small plots of land where they grow sessamum and chillies. The region is dry and sandy; though a new dam now irrigates it, and returns are not enough for all the siblings of either family to share. Aung Nyein preferred to seek work in the rice mills of Taungdwingyi, a day and a half away. When Khin Nyunt began to occasionally work there as well, they decided they would seek a new home closer to urban life. As with others before them, they went to the Shan area of Taunggyi, a state capital. Here, Aung Nyein, like other migrants, easily found loading work at the bazaar, or sometimes joined a construction team where Khin Nyunt joined him.

However, soon they found that Aung Nyein preferred a rural base with the different types of labour it offered, so the couple moved to Bogon, a new village of about 20 houses, just 2½ miles from Shwenyaung, the railhead town of the area. Khin Nyunt's brother, Ko Ohn Maung, had already settled in Bogon and had cleared a plot which he now farmed and kept a few pigs on. Aung Nyein, with his help, quickly put up a house of bamboo and thatch. He decided not to clear any land as only distant and unpromising areas remained. He and Khin Nyunt agree in their preference for a job with a salary and with the possibility of changing it and/or having some holiday. Their housing materials cost them about K/100 in 1969. They were always confident and strong. They have four children and Khin Nyunt has a son from an earlier marriage.

Aung Nyein had no dearth of work, either at daily wage rate of K. 4-5 or at a job rate, right through the monsoon or dry weather in the fertile valley which is still being cleared for more fields. Khin Nyunt too, found occasional work here, but she preferred to walk 2½ miles to Shwenyaung which is a bazaar center. She collected papayas, bananas, vegetables, flowers and eggs and sold them in the bazaar. Sometimes Aung Nyein collected bamboo shoots, mushrooms, acacia seeds or shoots or hairwashing bark and other forest-produce. If she had one load, even a big one, she would put it on her head and walk three miles effortlessly. If it was more she would take the bus which runs regularly on Bazaar days or take a lift in an army or other government vehicle. In days between the 5-day bazaar, she would go to houses to wash clothes, or a confection shop to winnow rice, or to a fruit-pickling house to cut crab apples. She enjoyed short spells of hard work and plenty of company. She also made full use of the People's Shop (which later became the Co-op shop).

One of the things Khin Nyunt discovered from this exposure was that, under the socialist system, she had rights. Everyone was entitled to the same quota of goods, regardless of income resources. With seven heads to feed on her house list, Khin Nyunt drew maximum quotas. It is always easy to dispose profitably of those things that are not used. Khin Nyunt kept all her rice, oil, salt, noodles and the occasional textile piece and sold, at high profit, condensed milk, sugar, kerosene, a reasonable amount of soap and matches as well as odd items like sewing thread and sulfa tablets. (These last can be had free, if needed at the government dispensary.) Whenever Khin Nyunt heard of a feast that was being given by anyone she knew she would go to help, do an afternoon of voluntary group work and get in return a full meal, which she took her family as well.

A normal day in Khin Nyunt's family has this pattern: the family rises about six, late by cultivator standards. Someone starts the fire and puts on hot water. They eat left-over rice with a small amount of relish and drink hot plain tea. Khin Nyunt prepares the main dish while Aung Nyein or one of the boys puts on the big rice pot in which 3-4 pounds are cooked twice a day. The main dish may be vegetable with or without a bit of beef or pork from the Bazaar – it may be pulses or dried fish products. They may eat this at home together, or take it along in carriers according to the day's programme. Rolling up bedding which consists of gunny sacks laid on the floor, pillows and shared blankets, is quick work. Khin Nyunt goes off leaving instructions with the boys to sweep the house, fetch water, get firewood, look after their sisters, look for food, and if she is late in returning start the rice pot and pound the chillies. On her return she will hurriedly cook the second dish. On occasion she has returned late with nothing but a packet of roasted bean seeds (*pe-hlaw*). She will quickly mix this with a trace of sesame oil, sliced onion, salt and roasted chilli powder. Everyone enjoys their rice with this crisp accompaniment.

Their budget is roughly as follows (for an average year before 1976);

Approximate income per month

Aung Nyein's field jobs	120.00
Khin Nyunt's sales profits	40.00
Khin Nyunt's service jobs	35.00
Profits from sales of co-op rations	25.00
From son's employer	20.00
	240.00

Approximate monthly expenditure

Rice (co-op prices)	70.00
Oil from co-op and bazaar, 1½ viss	45.00
Salt-fish, chillies, onions etc.	25.00
Meat and vegetables from bazaar	30.00
Cheroots, snacks, small outings	25.00
	195.00

The rest of the money is not really a saving. They spend it on clothes and trips to the bigger towns several miles away to stay with relatives and see films or go to seasonal festivities. They do not follow the peasant's steady tradition of buying new clothes for the New Year and the end of Lent. They buy whenever they can and Khin Nyunt may splurge on an occasional blackmarket purchase of 40 kyats for one *longyi*. She gets some old clothes from her part-time employers. Except for her, most of the family is usually only half-clad or in torn clothes. Their offerings to the monastery are very small and only on the main occasions. For the rest, an occasional offering of foliage or flowers to the framed print of the Buddha on a shelf above their common sleeping place suffices. The older residents who live closer to the land and its fruits consider them improvident but Aung Nyein at 35 and Khin Nyunt at 39 appear not to worry about their future. Their children will grow up, be placed in some sort of employment, which, instead of a salary, will give them their keep and clothes and some cash.

The rural inhabitants who are firmly based on their land regard migrants like Aung Nyein and Khin Nyunt as undesirable aliens. They themselves are hardworking, frugal, religiously oriented. Around Bogon they are of ethnic minority groups – Shan, Pa-o, Danus and Inthas.

Here is a typical family from amongst them, farming in an area near Bogon, where there is a variety of crops. The village is Kang Mong, 4 miles of a dirt track away from the motor highway which runs a few miles on from Shwenyaung. There are about 75 households in the village. Of these, about a dozen fare as well as U Chit Swe and Daw Nang Chaw or work as hard. Of the rest, about 30 households are of middling resources and 30 others are poor, sometimes also classified as lazy.

U Chit Swe has two sons, aged 18 and 21, and a nephew who is slightly older, to help him in the fields with livestock; a daughter of 16 who helps his wife, two sons in their early teens who are at present in a monastery as novices, a younger son and daughter who attend the government primary school in the village, and the youngest child of four who is still at home. He is now 48 and his wife is 44.

Their house has developed from bamboo and thatch to one with a timber frame and a zinc sheet roof. They own two buffaloes for ploughing, two bullock carts for transport of produce and firewood; a herd of twenty cattle and an oil-expeller worked by a buffalo. In the house is a sewing machine and in the garden a latrine, as well as a brick tank to hold monsoon rain water. For the dry months they use water from the common spring. They work a total of 20 acres, which they have cleared gradually over the past twelve years. During the monsoon (from May to October) they plant paddy, maize, chillies, peanuts and sunflower seeds. During the winter, from October to February, they plant wheat, garlic, onion, gram and potatoes.

Khin Nyunt with water pot

Of these, corn and wheat are not eaten by them. After reserving some seed, they sell all they produce. However, from the other crops, a certain amount is kept for home consumption and the rest is sold. Of the two basic needs, paddy is enough for the year's consumption but peanut oil suffices for only half of their needs.

The men clear new plots, dig drains, plough, plant, weed and reap, with mother and daughter joining in at peak planting and reaping time in preparation for the seed and storing of produce. They employ no hired labour. The men and boys handle the oil expeller, the bullock carts and herds of cattle which are not milked, but bred for sale to Nepalese dairymen or as bull calves for draught use.

Besides the variety of crops and monsoon vegetables that grow, their food supply includes more extensively than Aung Nyein's family's does, the foods collected from woods, fields and hedges.

Though 'food gathering' has been classified in surveys of man's economic activity as one step more advanced than hunting and less developed than settled agriculture; it is worth noting that the agriculturists of Burma whose agriculture has been developed for centuries, still resort to a great deal of food gathering as a supplement to their planted supplies. This supplement is not only free, but as it is plucked in season at the right stage of tenderness from an abundant natural supply, it is also delicious.

Woodland foods are the flavour of Southeast Asia. In Burma, knowledge of such foods is the rural housewives love, and gathering them is a major pleasure for her.

Few villagers grow vegetables in their gardens out of monsoon time, but at the start of the rains they put down certain varieties, usually climbers which are grown on bamboo frames and which bear much fruit; the leaves too are plucked for use. Thus calabash, chayote, stone and yellow pumpkin, cucumber, ridge-gourd, snake gourd, carilla or bitter melon, beans and luffa are grown on these frames, while mustard leaves and roselle predominate in the few beds that are tended.

There is honey to be collected round February or March. At this time too there are larvae and pupae of wasps and bees, and *ekote*, the specially rich larva of a beetle. There are insects such as *palu* (termites in winged stage), and *payit* and *bazin-yinkhwe* (crickets and cicada) and *ka-chin* (the big red ants) and their eggs from tree nests. From the paddy fields, especially towards the end of the monsoon, can be collected crabs, tiny fishes and snails. There is of course, fishing and though fishing is generally avoided by Buddhists, cultivators take their food where they must. Hunting is equally demeritorious, (for Buddhism opposes all taking of life) but those who hunt get wild pig, barking deer, partridge, peacock, snake, snipe or sparrow.

For villagers like the Chit Swes rice is still more important than its accompaniments. To them, the quality of rice in its fragrance, taste and consistency is the main luxury in their eating. The counterpart to rice in a Burmese diet is oil, peanut or sesame, which is used in more affluent families to cook a 'main curry' of meat or fish, mixed or unmixed with vegetables.

The Chit Swe family may have one such dish at every meal. The young men fish, catch crabs and insects, larvae and pupae. They do not hunt but occasionally buy a bit of barking deer or meats from those in the village who do hunt. They may buy pork when someone slaughters a pig. They also have a few poultry around the garden for occasional use when a very welcome visitor arrives from afar. Their early morning meal is fried rice, the oil for it being a luxury to all

Burmese. The two main meals with good quality rice usually have some animal protein, fish, meat or eggs, along with their great variety of shoots, and leaves, seasoned with chilli, soybean cakes, garlic, onion and pressed fish products. They have no co-operative shop to rely upon.

Urban and professional housewife with helpers and international-style home

Clothes worn at work are old, and often the men go bare-chested. However, a full set of clothes for each member of the large family is bought twice a year, at New Year and the end of Lent, money from the crop sales being set aside for this, though in 1976 it cost nearly 100 kyats for an adult costume and 50 for a child. They participate fully in collections for religious donation, spending about 300 kyats a year on donations.

Their day begins at 5 a.m. They make ablutions and put on hot water, fry rice from the night before and have it with hot tea. Then mother and daughter start cooking while the men go down to the fields. When the rice is cooked a first offering is made at the altar. The school-goers have their meal and walk to school. At about 9.30, mother and daughter sit down to their meal with the youngest child and then the daughter takes the meal down to the field for the men. The housewife now sweeps the house and clears the garden. The daughter on return, helps her pick up manure and store it under the house. During the monsoon, they weed vegetable beds and then either of them may collect vegetables for the evening meal. In dry weather, they sun such crops as sunflower seeds or peanuts, shell peanuts, take off leaves of corn and husk the kernels for separate sale of leaves and kernels. On some days they go to the spring to bathe and the daughter will wash clothes. At about 3.30 they prepare for the evening meal. And at night, after all else is done, the whole family will sit around working together, men, women and children shelling peanuts, husking corn or preparing garlic etc., for planting.

Their cash accounts are given below. Though they only keep a note of big amounts from sales, they are able to give more details of consumption than Aung Nyein can. Expenditure shows very modest sums for food and general living. It is essential fodder and fertilizers which have increased out of proportion in recent years and these take up most of the money. The family food does not seem rich but to a Burman, a sufficiency of oil and a good quality of rice set a high standard.

Cash from sales of crops: per annum, gross – 1975-76
Corn – kernels	1620.00
Corn, leaves	300.00
Wheat	900.00
Surplus paddy	3700.00
Surplus sunflower seeds	740.00
Surplus garlic	1500.00
Surplus chillies	5000.00
Surplus onion	2300.00
Surplus gram	800.00
Surplus potatoes	4500.00

Consumption costs per month
Rice	No cash expense
Extra oil	65.00
Fish and meat	80.00
Saltfish and pressed fish	45.00
Tea leaf	40.00
Salt	15.00
Soybean cake	26.00
Special fruits and vegetables	25.00
Busfares to Bazaar Day meets	30.00
Biscuits, palm-sugar, etc. for children on return from bazaar	38.00
	364.00 x 12 = 4368.00
Religious donations	300.00
(Rice is also donated, about 200 lbs. a year, Social donations, (novitiations, weddings, funerals)	120.00
Clothes	1500.00
Children's expenses	600.00
	6888.00

Urban Families

Turning from rural to urban we look now at a professional woman. I choose Mya because she is like a great many professional Burmese women in one aspect. Despite the availability of domestic servants and an income because both she and her husband work, she has not relinquished her housewife's hold on the cooking. Mya takes great pains to compose her meals to perfection as often as possible. Professionally trained and with an American University post-graduate degree, she has held her present job for many years. She makes time for marketing on one day a week. She varies her bazaars, choosing a different one as is best for meat, fish, poultry, vegetables or supporting kitchen staples.

On her return home from a long working day in a 5-day workweek, she has a cup of tea with the rest of the family but soon slips away to the kitchen to prepare dinner.

I should explain here that there are three main meals in the day of an average Burman. The morning meal is eaten soon after rising at 5-6 a.m., the second meal comes around 9.30 and onwards. And then there is the evening meal. In between there are snacks of various kinds. Burmese cuisine is a complicated affair and, among women of different classes, is considered an art. Hence, no matter if they are urban or rural, they take great pains over it.

In a sense, the 'level' of the cuisine is the chief determinant of a Burmese housewife's work load. As we have seen, Khin Nyunt, from our first family, spends little time on housework. (In many ways rice, the main ingredient, is a good leveller for everyone, rich and poor alike, eats it in more or less the same form).

Burmese food preparation at the lowest income level, as we have seen in the case of the Aung Nyein-Khin Nyunt family, takes up little time. As the food becomes less simple, the time needed for its preparation increases, till, with many housewives, preparing the kind of full meal that Mya provides daily, becomes the major part of their household work. Some might even spend almost the whole day preparing two such meals but Mya has other aspects of life she wishes to emphasize.

She takes a long walk every morning before breakfast. She can do this because her husband's nephew who lives with them sees, at this time, to the cooking of lunch. Lunch is not as important a meal as dinner. While at work Mya has her maid prepare the ingredients for the evening meal. Mya's husband, Kyo, takes a keen interest in keeping their house clean and well kept. At weekends, he does various small and large tasks in the house. He cleans everything, including the bathroom but, interestingly, he keeps up his male Burmese status by never entering the kitchen. They have a small yard, lawns and some fruit trees and plants. Kyo works here too, watering and cutting the grass.

Before writing about Mya and clothes, her other special interest, I will link up the subject of Burmese clothing in general with the other Burmese in the two families described in the preceding section.

The clothing of a family at low income level still follows a traditional pattern i.e. new clothes for the two major occasions; *Thingyan* (or New Year) in mid-April, and *Thadingyut* (or the end of Lent) in October. The first can be bought with the main harvest money, and the second with the monsoon's earnings and saving. These sets of clothes worn new to the monastery and attendant festivities are kept for wearing on outings till the next set is purchased. Meanwhile old clothes are worn for work and at home, with a further saving by men and small girls going topless, and toddler boys bottomless. Those above subsistence level do of course buy clothes at any time.

Clothing ranks above furniture and house decor or personal hobbies in budget priority. Those with means amass it in quantity and it accumulates over the decades without being outdated. The Burmese still dress in their 'national costume'. The women especially do not adopt international dress, however strong their experience of the foreign world might be. This is partly due to conservatism and partly because they are accustomed to a certain kind of dress. The Burmese woman's dress has evolved as a comfortable and workable habit so that very little need for change has been felt. Unlike some more beautiful national costumes, the Burmese dress has been kept by its wearers as the best all round outfit for use, appearance, comfort and cost. Its basic components are: the 'bodice', prototype of tóday's 'long line' brassiere, fitting and waist-length. Covering this is the *aingyi* or 'jacket' also waist length, which is moulded to the figure and crosses over to fasten down front on one side, Chinese fashion. Tucked into the waist is the *longyi* patterned in colours to match the plainer top. This basic outfit of three garments is most convenient for bathing, changing or dressing, or nursing the baby in public, for visiting the lavatory, or making do with wayside places in lieu of a lavatory, and it serves well enough for sports. It folds easily and stacks into a small space for storing or travel. Its appearance suits the Burmese figure by giving it height and it allows Burmese women to indulge their love of fabric designs. It is comfortable because it is light and cool and easy to sit or walk in. Its low cost is another attractive feature – the *longyi* needs no tailoring and is simply a length of material and the jacket is simple to make. So while so many Asian women have discarded their traditional clothes and taken to Western ones, Burmese women keep to their dress.

The low cost of the three-piece Burmese outfit makes it possible to accumulate large stacks of clothing. Weight changes do not in general affect the fit of the *longyis*, the most expensive item. Mya, like most friends of her age, has many clothes.

Burma's present economic troubles have caused a severe textile shortage. The abolition of private capital has led to the disappearance of shops which used to be stacked high with great range of imported textiles. There is now only a blackmarket offering a small choice at high prices. This, however, does not deter people from making occasional purchases.

An essential adjunct to clothes is jewellery, of gold, and if possible set with gems. Some people see its importance stemming from the old *Dhammathat* injunction to man to give his wife suitable ornaments. Certainly, jewellery was given practical direction in the ear-piercing ceremony, traditionally held for every girl on the verge of her teens like a puberty rite. The first pair of earrings set her status as a woman, and this entitled her to wear jewellery. Burmese women look upon gold as an investment which is their own and which generally appreciates with time. When demonetisation took place in 1964 and the larger denominations of currency notes were made illegal from the instant of the law's announcement, people who held much cash in notes lost the major part in the tax that was then levied on holdings. However, the gold remained hidden and untaxed. Now, with such high inflation, women who own gold can make money and sell their gold at its swollen price of 4-500 per cent in order to make their purchases of property or food.

At work in the kitchen

When Beyan came to work for me in 1967, she was a tall girl of fourteen, determined to make her way in the world. After three months of pay at 50 kyats a month, she showed me her savings of 100 kyats. At her wish we went down to the bazaar and got her a pair of earrings. Over the next few months she bought a sarong and two jacket pieces from the blackmarket, but soon after that she was ready again to buy jewellery. This time, she got a ring for 120 kyats. Not long after, her mother Ma Win Sein who lived in Bogon, came to ask for money. She suggested pawning the earrings and Beyan sadly agreed to do so. We went down to the pawnshop outside the bazaar. They gave her 50 kyats for the pair. Beyan was, as I have said, determined, and she spent nothing during the following month, so we were able to redeem the earrings with a little help from me for the interest. This was small, as it was a government pawnshop. Such state pawnshops have been set up all over because of the widespread pawning of jewellery against loans which private shops or moneylenders were considered to have charged usurious rates. Everyone does not have Beyan's determination, and the usual stories of pawned jewellery are not as happy as hers. Many have no access to a state pawnshop or prefer to go to a private lender if they are ashamed of entering a pawnshop.

The higher income groups rarely fail to add to their jewellery. Burma has rubies, sapphires, jade and pearls of high quality; also olivines, tourmalines, zircone, aquamarines, garnets, spinels. To these are added imported gold and diamonds though these last are now rumoured to be mined in Burma as well. Social changes have not diminished the role of jewellery. New trends have merely changed the styles and class of owners so that while many sell out their jewellery to survive, many others of a new elite acquire it, and goldsmiths continue to thrive.

Ko Tin Hla, a jeweller I know, has a house and shop that can be said to be a good example of a traditional Burmese joint enterprise between husband and wife on one hand, and between home and shop on the other. The couple came to Rangoon 25 years ago when there was an influx of people into the capital a few years after independence. Rangoon had been a city chiefly of British rulers, and Chinese-Indian business interest. The Burmese were barely in evidence. The small number then dwelt mostly in quiet western sections past which the Hlaing River runs and over which the Shwedagon Pagoda looks down.

The Tin Hla's rent the ground floor of a small wooden house. The end room is the shop. Some of the apprentices have worked for him for 15 years. Along the inner wall of the room are ranged some armchairs and in one of these Ko Tin Hla's wife Ma Than Nwe sits to receive clients. She has also started a side business by offering to dispose of visiting clients' unwanted pieces of jewellery to other clients, thus earning a commission.

Their business has prospered and now Ma Than Nwe has hired a maid to take charge of housework while she sets up a stall in the Bogyoke Market alongside other displays of attractive gold and gem jewellery. She has 4 children who are now able to take are of themselves although they are not yet earning. The couple's upward social mobility has been very rapid, from early days when Ma Than Nwe used her spare time to make base-stoppers for cheroots.

A Trader Family

Of the many wealthy traders who live in the traditional Buddhist-oriented style of house I will now describe U Tun Wa and Daw Than Than, if only because their house and family show a transition which may gradually change this life style to a non-traditional one. U Tun Wa is known to be rich largely from the cheroot business which employs about 50 women rollers, who used to be housed in the back of their house and paved yard. It has now been moved to a separate plot of land across the back lane of their house. This is one of the changes I have noted as transitional in their life style, in contrast to the large cheroot leaf broker house described in Chapter VIII. The other transitional feature is that the several sons and daughters have been trained and work in the various professions. Two daughters are doctors, one son who has graduated as an economist helps with the family business but the daughters practice medicine full time.

The Work Load and Sex Roles

In the low income families, the majority of whom are agrarian, the burden of housework sits very lightly on the wife. Meals are simple and there is little cleaning to do. Children of both sexes from the age of about six onwards can and do help in the housework.

The husband too helps by collecting firewood, carrying the children or cooking the rice, apart from doing the gardening and building chores. In urban areas, when the man goes out to work, he may do the household shopping.

At this income level the wife has to help with the subsistence-input as well. With cropwork, gathering food for sale, trading or handwork – as the first 2 case studies below show – housework in itself may in such cases be a very small part of the woman's work in the home. This comparative lightness of the woman's domestic burden has been remarked upon by Mr Nash in his study of village Burma in 1960.

When we come to the middle and higher income brackets the picture changes. Meals are fuller, the house larger and there are more possessions. The children go to school and therefore are unable to help in the home. The husband is seldom self-employed. But, at this level, housewives often have the option of hiring domestic help.

Of households surveyed, the figures are as follows:

Income in kyats per month	No. surveyed	No. with hired help	No. with relative helping
less than K.300	56	0	39
K.300 – K.800	58	12	42
K.800 +	36	26	23

The table here shows that the majority of housewives have relatives living with them to help with the housework. This is often true even of low-income families.

A later chapter deals with domestic service as a profession for women. However, in the table below we look at households who have either relatives or domestic help living in the house.

Help for the Housewife – Hired hands or resident relatives (figures refer to number of households with relatives or hired help out of a total of 50 in each area).

Area of survey	Wife's relative	Husband's relative	No. with relative or hired hand	1 hired hand	2 or more hired hands
Yezin Village	7	5	38	0	0
Country Town	17	9	17	13	8
Capital Town	16	5	21	8	8

I also note that even when there is domestic help, the housekeeping at these levels involves many hours connected with food preparation. The trips to bazaars almost daily for fresh foods, long waits at the co-operative shop, the cleaning of supplies, the pounding, sprigging, cutting and cooking for the several dishes daily; then the turning over, sunning, airing and further cleaning of foods for storage, the fires that need fanning, the water to be conserved or carried, the various economising chores that are done to beat ever-increasing prices. All this takes hours to do, yet there are very few complaints about the injustice of a woman's lot in having to do all these tasks. Many women who spend time thus, regard it a part of life, and see it as their natural lot.

Because the hours spent in housework have become such a way of life for the majority of women, Burmese women have evolved their own ways of work. To make kitchen work less tiring women do not stand and work, rather they sit at the low round family dining table, which can be lightly rolled to any spot, indoors or outdoors. The stones women use are often portable and can be moved to the floor – this makes far less toing and froing between the table and the stone. By not having to stand all the time many Burmese women manage to avoid varicose veins, an illness many western women are subject to.

The Burmese woman's conservatism is visible in many small things, even with utensils, although these are now made of new metals, she prefers her old ones.

In general, the Burmese woman seldom feels that her commitment to domestic tasks is denying her the chance to work at an alternative and more fulfilling or more creative responsibility. Sex roles are totally accepted and with the woman as house manager, this very acceptance is, in a sense, a statement of an equality in which for every male participation, there must be a corresponding female participation and vice versa. Down the ages the proverbs echo this complementary, equal and fair juxtaposition which sets for every sphere of life a 50-50 basis.

Aung Nyein and Khin Nyunt
dressed in their best

Is it danger to life or limb?	Then 'Man rides the raft, woman gives birth to the child.'
Is it labour?	Then 'Damsel one load on head Stalwart one burden on shoulder.'
Is it demerit to be incurred in search of sustenance?	Then 'Man the hunter, woman the decoy trap setter.'
Is it sustenance itself to be sought?	Then 'Husband climbs the toddy tree. Wife cooks it into jagaree.'

So, for the house there is *ainshin* – house owner or lord, whose equivalent here is *ainshinma* – house owner lady, whose responsibility is the management of the house. The term *ainshinma* is translated as a housewife. A Fillipino informant states that this term of housewife in the Philippines has the connotation of the woman being 'only a housewife'. This attitude has not yet reached Burma where *ainshinma* with its concomitant adjective *pi-pi* means 'as befits a houselady' in dignity, and complete mastery of her responsibility.

Management of Finances

It is by now well known that in countries of Southeast Asia, such as Thailand and the Philippines the mother of the family is the treasurer. In Burma too this tradition is still strongly observed. Where wealth is still held in cash or gold it seems natural that woman in whose care the house is, should be the custodian of it. We have seen one of the woman's duties is to 'keep the treasure bag secure'. Crops above subsistence production are sold, often beyond the village, by the husband but the norm is still that on return from market he entrusts his earnings to his wife for safe keeping. Banking and credit facilities are still not used except by a very small section. In trade, the wife or daughter who is more tied to the shop is the obvious banker. She can be seen presiding over the till. The salary system did not interfere with such a tradition. I remember clearly that on payday, my father would walk home behind his office *peon* instead of in front of him as usual. The *peon* carried on top of his basket of files, a string-bag full of money – father's pay! As soon as they got home where mother would always be bathed, dressed and waiting in the porch, he handed the bag to her with a flourish. He rarely had need to handle money. Mother made all decisions in consultation with him and all payments including items outside housekeeping such as school fees, help to relatives and clearing our accounts with shops. Now when salaries are paid directly into a man's account he may, for his wife's convenience, get the money out and hand it to her in cash. Later she may hand back something for cigarettes and casual expenses. The following table shows this kind of control still prevails in the villages.

Household Finances
(Figures refer to the number of households out of 50 in each area).

Area of survey	Wife earning salary	Wife self-employed	Wife decides spending	Husband decides spending	Joint decision in spending
Yezin village	6	27	50	0	0
Country town	24	10	41	3	6
Capital town	30	3	25	0	25

Healthcare within the Family

Burmese health care is compounded of the use of Western techniques where they are available, and there are varying degrees of reliance on indigenous methods and systems. Though people have learned to take advantage of modern medicine and health care they have not given up the traditional household dependence on old ways and, to a great many, the old systems are still the only ones available.

Facilities are now provided solely by the government. Christian and other missions and voluntary bodies which had set up privately endowed hospitals, creches, and dispensaries have now turned them over to the government whose scheme of socialist medicine provides free service to the people. Under this scheme in 1973, there were 410 hospitals with a total of 24,769 beds in the whole of Burma, staffed with 2868 doctors and 4199 nurses. There were also 1546 private doctors who were not attached to any government facility. The largest towns like Rangoon, Mandalay and Taunggyi have specialist hospitals, the smallest hospital towns like Shwenyaung have 16-19 bed general hospitals with facilities for simple surgery. In even smaller centres, there is usually a health assistant who prescribes and dispenses medicines, gives injections, treats simple ailments and a nurse who is a midwife as well. The assistants and nurses work at epidemic control, spraying or reporting of cases to larger centres. People from villages have learnt to go to the nearest hospital in emergencies such as snake bites, illness during epidemics, difficult labour and for emergency surgery. At these hospitals free care is given in both outpatient clinics and wards and this includes major surgery and intensive inpatient care. There are now no longer private and public wards – the former have been abolished. In general, hospitals do not provide food and patients often have their relatives bring in food from home. Even Ma Khin Nyunt, when she was in hospital for her baby, would instruct Aung Nyein and the children to prepare some rice and a bit of fried fish to enjoy 'a touch of home' while in hospital.

Villagers are now growing familiar with modern medicine to the extent that they ask for tablets by name and tend to demand injections. Town people are even more used to prescribing medicines for themselves. Since supplies often run short, they stock up. Good-natured Burmese doctors knowing how handicapped one will be if the shops are out of stock of medicines, readily write prescriptions for precautionary purchases by healthy people, so a middle-income housewife's medicine chest may be stocked up not only with fever and cold alleviates but with sulpha and penicillin preparations, pills against diarrhoea, and even stronger drugs like terramycin, streptomycin etc.

This short description of modern facilities available to the housewife is given as background against which she still resorts to indigenous methods of family health care. Indigenous methods may follow one of two lines of treatment: by food or by herbal remedies.

Certain foods are prescribed as suitable for good health and there are specialists who can be consulted on this.

The housewife does not always call in a specialist for treatment. The system parallel to food prescription is that of *beindaw* or herbal remedies and of these, various well known specifics are stocked in every household. Best known are *yetsa*, a digestive powder, *shabutsay*, or small pellets for sore throat or chest congestion; *ngan-say* or fever specific; *thway-say* or a red powder for a variety of ills ranging from faintness, palpitations to a cut on a lip where non-edible medicine cannot be used. These are only a few of numerous brands on sale for all kinds of illness. These simple remedies are used by housewives because they are harmless and have no side effects.

The housewife knows the lay person's law about the effects of food she cooks, as well as common plants that are available and can be used as medicines. Foremost among such plants is the betel-leaf. This leaf is so useful medicinally that a spirit or *Nat* is believed to reside in its center while an ogre resides at its base and a celestial *deva* at its pointed tip.

Some plants that the housewife knows for effects on the system are food plants commonly used. For example, she knows that *mezali*, pickled bamboo shoots, coriander and *danyin* cause drowsiness, in the same way as other foods such as hilsa fish or coconut milk may do. Such foods eaten in too great an amount will surely cause heaviness in the neck and head regions. Certain foods she cooks regularly like *dandalun* leaves for soup, she knows will relieve high blood pressure, so she cooks these more often if someone in the family needs them. Similarly, *danyin*, known to benefit diabetes, can be served often if needed.

Other plants which the housewife knows for medicinal use may not belong to common food vegetables. Such leaves as *kyet-le-san* to prevent high blood pressure or *kyaw-paung-ta-taung* are boiled to a stock formula.

Besides resorting to such use of beneficial plants, the housewife stocks other well known and dried aids, such as a bit of wild goats horn, a piece of python's bile sac or bark of the tamarind tree or the *akyaw* tree. She keeps a tiny round mortar shaped liked the cosmetic bark grinding mortar and on this she grinds any of these dried aids with water to produce a cream for applying to inflamed eyelids, boils, abscesses and cankers.

There are a special set of mysteriously effective remedies called *say-me-toe* ('Quick fire remedies'). Such are the raw bile sac from chickens cleaned in the kitchen, or the dried stomach of porcupine powdered, which I have tried with success for asthma.

Another system commonly resorted to by the housewife is that of massage. At all times people may complain of '*nyaung-ta*' which may be translated as being tired 'from strain'.

In conclusion, it may be stated again that the housewife uses all the common means at her command, combining them to make sure of alleviation.

One aspect of family care the housewife does not neglect is the provision of horoscopes, unless indeed the family is too poor to heed this traditional and still strong practice.

Leisure and Social Aids

The Burmese woman's leisure activities may involve reading, if she is literate. However, the most enjoyable part of her 'leisure' is often when she combines work with pleasure. As when she goes to the shops, she may meet her friends and spend long hours talking to them. When hawkers come up to the houses they often stop for some tea and a chat. Children often play outside the houses while their mothers watch over them and talk at the same time. A woman goes round in the afternoons, with a child astride her hip, meeting friends and socialising. On the family's free days or times she will of course go with them to the cinema, the pagoda, a night bazaar, or the neighbourhood's current festivity where she may also help. Her leisure life is very much determined by her immediate community and there is little room in it for formal organizations or meetings, self-improvement lectures or consciousness raising courses outside the community's activities.

In such household visits, food and drink are always served but it should be noted that alcohol has little place in Burmese society as a whole. There is the Buddhist fifth precept against intoxicating drinks and even if precepts are commonly broken, this one is observed by a large number of people. Burmese society does have other mild and totally acceptable stimulants, which are always served to guests. One such is betel.

We have seen the importance of betel in Burma's Pagan period (11-13th century). A recent observer L.A. Peter Gosling has remarked that today, Burma, more than other Southeast Asian countries, has retained betel-chewing. In almost every house, you can find the box of lacquer or silver, with the top tray of ingredients and under it the pile of fresh green leaves to make the quid. *Pa-o* cultivators who walk bare-foot to Taunggyi Bazaar Day still carry in their shoulder bags the nut and leaf, their lime paste, in a small box of brass or silver. Urban families on the other hand may not have a betel box in the front room but may send out to the corner cigar booth for prepared quids to follow a meal or to serve to visitors. Their quids may contain tobacco, cloves, bits of orange peel, aniseed or a potent muskie for connoisseurs. Besides the many medicinal qualities of the areca nut, (from *Areca catechu*) and the leaf (*Piper betel* vine) and the quid as a whole and when not used in excess, stimulates with alkaloids and nicotine, benefits the gums and teeth from the astringence, promotes salivary flow and refreshes the mouth especially after a meal. In the bazaar, piles of green leaf and tubs of lime soaking in water are sold at one end, by women. At the other booths, trays of nut and other ingredients for the quid are found in front of shelves packed tight with varieties of cheroots – the light Burmese cigars which pervade Burmese life more than betel does.

The old observers who commented on the great foot-long inch-round cheroots of Burmese women also noted that a nursing mother would place a lighted cheroot in her baby's mouth to pacify him or her while she turned to other tasks. While I can't claim to have seen this I do know that cheroots play an important part in the lives of Burmese women. The cheroot industry is predominantly a female one and a detailed note will be found on it in Chapter VIII among the economic activities of women.

The third widely used stimulant with a traditional symbolic importance is *lepet* or tea-leaf pressed in a silage treatment. It was customary to eat *lepet* in recognition of the occasion which its appearance marked, such as in a law suit, in a marriage ceremony or divorce deliberation. The parties concerned ate *lepet* to mark agreement of contract. Today it still makes its appearance everywhere.

There is also the ubiquitous pot of green tea. It is found to be the best thirst quencher in hot weather and its use is so constant that it is called just 'rough hot water'. From tea grown on the eastern hill slopes the best leaves are plucked before the rains in May, taking only the tenderest pair from each twig to give choice brands called *Shwe-phi-mo-lut*. These are the four chief 'supporters' of the long periods that Burmese spend together, gathered in homes or in public places.

A Rural Family of the South

In this final section I give an account of one more rural family. The other two rural families described belong to the same inland region bordering on foothills. Here, we move further South to the sea coast and in a personal account link up rural and urban which intertwining is still a graceful feature of Burmese life. The family also show a self sufficiency of supplies in the eloquent omission of accounts in the detailed description given me by its eldest son who in urban life is very conscious of prices, expenditure and saving.

The family works a smaller holding than the Chit Swe's of Section II but has more cash to spare. Perhaps it is because they live in a more fertile region, with more rain, richer crops, proximity to the sea and its products, as well as to a big and prosperous town.

They live in Pienkama village, situated three miles away from the small town of Mudon which again is 24 miles from the big town of Moulmein at the mouth of the Salween River at the northern end of Burma's long southern coastal tail. Car and rail connect the village with Mudon and Moulmein. There are about 350-odd houses in that village. The poorest are of bamboo with *inn*-leaf roofs, some with leaf walls which are cheaper than bamboo matting. The middle income uses timber for posts and maybe for flooring and walls, with leaf or *dani* thatch roofs. There are also brick and mortar houses, both old and new, with zinc roofs.

U Tet Kalaw and his wife Daw Yee, like the rest of the villagers, are Mons. Aged 41 and 40 respectively, they married early and have six children. The eldest Maung San Kyaw, after finishing at primary school, went to Mudon for secondary school, then to Rangoon for higher education. Daw Yee's mother, a village girl, married an official of importance in her first marriage, and went to other parts but she returned later to the village and raised a second and rural family. It was to Daw Yee's half-brother, who assiduously kept his village roots alive from his urban professional background that San Kyaw went. There he attended high school and university; now he is a graduate with a job in Rangoon. The second, a son, aged 23, after passing primary school continued with farming, married and now lives independently. The next, a girl called Ma Aye Than, now 20, was, when she was 16 and had passed middle school, sent to the uncle in

Rangoon to stay and take a professional course in tailoring. She is now back in the village as a leading dress-maker. The next girl aged 12 is going ahead in the fifth standard and the youngest aged 6 is just beginning school.

The family works ten acres of rice and glutinous rice. They consume about one-fourth of the crop, pay a hired hand with another of it and sell the rest for cash. The hired hand and U Tet Kalaw do the ploughing, transplanting, weeding, reaping and waterditch work, with help from wife and children only after their (the latters') work is done. The wife, sometimes helped by daughters, does the household tasks, chief among which is cooking. She may help in the fields. She also sells in the bazaar the vegetables and fruits plucked by the children and sometimes, leaving her daughters to care for the house she goes to other smaller villages, selling fish products as well as a herbal remedy (*Thway-hsay*) for which she arranges for the ingredients from town and mixes her own formula. Salting, pressing, fermenting, and drying of fish and shrimp is an activity that nearly every house in this village takes to, apart from agriculture. This area with its proximity to seabeds and good fish supplies is one of Burma's chief sources for these products.

The family eat well because of the abundance of good natural resources. They buy very little of what they eat. Their consumption of rice is two *tins*, 240 pounds a month. Cooking oil is what they have to buy but they use only one *viss* a month, very much less than the cultivator family up north. They have a wealth of leaves and vegetables from gardens and woods. Besides common garden vegetables, they can also get such leaves as *kyet-tha-hin*, tamarind, acacia, *badatsa*, mango, *taw kokko*, *kaukkauknyun*. There is little reliance on chicken, pork or beef. Fresh fish and other seafoods, together with the processed and salted fish relishes are the staple protein foods; in addition there are foods from the hunter's bag. This area is also the orchard for Burma's most delectable fruits: durian, mangosteen, rambutan, pomelo, pineapple, banana, jackfruit. At the time of the village pagoda festival at *Tabaung* (March), the family often has several visitors who come to stay with them. This is a common feature of Burmese life and both husband and wife join together to make their guests welcome.

5. The Household: Family Care and Life Stages

Childbirth and Early Infancy

I am reminded of an observation often made by foreign writers at the turn of the century on Burmese birth practices. They remarked that a woman in Burma aged ten years each time she had a child. I recall this in order to contrast it with the prevalent Burmese saying: *ta-tha-mway, ta-thway-hla*, 'one child born, one blood change into more beautiful'. In other words, childbirth makes a woman bloom.

Pregnancy is normally much desired. Children are always welcomed as blessings – gem sons and gem daughters who give joy, act as vehicles for the fulfillment of parental duties, and give affectionate support in old age. At a wedding or engagement the elders called to officiate must be couples blessed with more children than one and preferably of both sexes. This underlines the strong wish that the coming union may result in children. If pregnancy proves difficult, a child may be adopted.

Pregnancy often sits lightly on many women. There are few taboos and much indulgence. You can eat what and as much as you like. You may interpret dreams to show possible reincarnations of relatives. The circumference of the *longyi* makes it easy to wrap around a distended middle, and no attempt need be made to disguise your weight. Obviously you carry 'body's burden', obviously you are a 'child-carrying mother'.

Pre-natal care is given by hospitals and clinics in towns. They are used readily by urban women of all classes as well as by some from outlying villages. Once a woman registers, she can have free examinations and advice are given. She calls this 'entrusting her belly'. She may entrust it instead to a trained mid-wife in private practice in the neighbourhood, preferring to have the baby in her own home. Trained midwives can be found in villages also – some of them are on government postings. There is also someone called *let-the*, or 'hand-operator', who is more common among the rural sector but can sometimes be found in urban areas. She may be used by those who have no access to a trained midwife. Having entrusted her belly, the pregnant woman also registers at her co-operative shop in order to be eligible for special rations of cloth and other necessities.

The child can be born either in the hospital or at home. In a home-birth with a local midwife, the birth minute is recorded, the cord is cut, (turmeric powder is rubbed on the cut), the baby is cleaned, bathed and swaddled. There are no strong preferences for a boy or girl, although some people do prefer a male child. Many women are anxious if a first child is born on a Saturday, for that means that the mother will have a difficult time in bringing up the child. The 'afterbirth' is taken out of the house and buried to the east of it. This is called the *chet-myok*, 'burying of umbilical cord' and one way of asking 'Where were you born' is 'where is your cord buried?' That is the place to which you will surely be drawn to.

The birth chamber is called the *mi-nay-khan* 'stay by fire' room. It is the building of fires which used to stretch the whole length of the mother's bed two feet away to drive out noxious vapours and to provide heat. Often bricks were heated, wrapped in cloth and applied to the mother's pelvis. Turmeric is still rubbed all over her body, staining the bedclothes a bright orange. Those who do not like this will often swallow turmeric powder moistened and made into little balls with salt. It serves to contract the uterus and aid the expulsion of afterbirth tissues. When baths are taken, leaves which give heat such as eucalyptus can be boiled in the bathwater. A steam bath may be taken by getting under a mat canopy with a big pot of this steaming brew or by sitting on one's haunches over baked bricks and pouring water. A packet of sesame is rubbed or a stick of pine resin is lighted and held for sniffing in order to clean the nasal passage. After her bath, the mother will cream her skin with the ground bark of special fragrant and heating woods, *taungtangyi* or *meikthalin*. She will cover herself with a blanket in the hottest weather in order to get up a good sweat.

The new mother is treated with great solicitude as having 'tender new blood'. Diet control is important for her. To encourage milk flow, hot soup made from grilled fish, with a lot of garlic and pepper is given several times a day. The root bulb of lotus is also eaten in soups for the same purpose. This root bulb is most useful for pregnancy as well as new motherhood. It induces conception, and also helps towards normal birth. Hot and sour foods are avoided, as well as 'cold' foods like cucumber, cabbage or bananas. To avoid diarrhoea in mother or infant, the safest are dry foods, like rice with fried or grilled fish or saltfish, though in the latter case fish with markings on the skin is avoided. The new mother's abdomen is tightly bound with yards of cloth to keep it taut as well as to hold the womb in place, particularly for those women who must go down to the fields shortly after childbirth.

No other rituals are observed by the women, rural and urban. The growing infant continues to be kept snug, swaddled, sometimes weighted down with a pillow over the chest to add to this sense of being encradled. The mother takes the child wherever she goes as nursing in public places is perfectly respectable, even in urban settings. Initially, the child sleeps in a soft, small box of porous bamboo or cane weave placed in bed beside the mother. Later he or she will graduate to a cradle, for which there used to be a celebration to mark the cradle-placing (*pakhet-tin*). This cradle may be of stout cotton blankets swung from the rafters and is as snug as the bambo box. A ceremony which is still observed with more or less formality by all classes of people is the *kinmun-tat* or hairwashing of the month-old infant.

A neighbour's house

Breast feeding on demand continues for nearly a year, though in some instances, milk powder or condensed milk may supplement or substitute for the breast. Boiled rice, which is fed at an early age, is still first chewed by mothers (particularly village women) before being given to the infant. Plantains are given but many families withhold eggs which are supposed to cause the infant to forget his or her past existence about which the child may well speak when it is able to talk.

A charming story attaches to a baby's smile. It is said that jealous spirits taunt the baby and say 'your mother is dead'. But the child, having been at the mother's breast, knows this to be untrue and smiles joyfully at this secret knowledge. And when the child cries, it is said the same jealous spirits, more cunning this time, say 'Your father is dead'. And the child not yet knowing the father believes them and cries.

Post-Natal Care

The government gives free post-natal care at the established hospitals, and also maintains 'Lady Health Visitors' who visit new as well as expectant mothers. These health visitors report such cases as need assistance of any sort. Most towns have a voluntary Maternity and Infant Welfare Organization whose members raise funds, make periodical visits with the health visitor, dispense milk powder, help needier mothers with gifts of soap and cloth for baby wrappers and diapers.

When Hla Win's mother Ma Khin Nyunt first came from her distant village to our town of 80,000 souls, she lost no time in discovering that under the government's socialist system she had definite rights to well-marked-out quotas of goods and services. Similarly, at the hospitals she knew her rights in all the outdoor patient clinics and always managed to get pills, lotions, elixirs, injections and dressings of all sorts. She hated staying home, loved walking and at the slightest sneeze she would pick up or drag the child right off to hospital. Despite this her family had a rural base and they went and settled in Bogon village as described in the previous chapter, but when two years later, her husband Ko Aung Nyein got the offer of a livestock and orchard job next door to us on the outskirts of Taunggyi town, Ma Khin Nyunt expecting a child, and drawn once again to cinema houses, urged a move back.

Once in town, Ma Khin Nyunt 'entrusted her belly' to the local women's hospital, and went for regular pre-natal checkups. After the baby was born, she did not make any special effort to care for him but simply added him on as a new member of her family. Nonetheless, the child was so handsome that it won a prize, thus enabling the family to have an evening out.

Family Size and Planning

Table showing size of families in Taungni Village.

No. of families	Total no. of children per family	No. of mothers under age 40
3	9	1
5	8	2
3	7	1
7	6	4
9	5	2
4	4	2
6	3	2
3	2	5
8	1	6
2	0	2

Total number of households in Taungni Village – 347
Number surveyed: 50 households adjacent to and nearest the bazaar quarter.

The table shows the average family size to be 4.46 children. Further investigations revealed that 37 children out of the 223 born to these 50 families have died. This leaves the actual size at present at 3.72.

Traditionally there is no known or acknowledged method of family spacing. The best known and most widely practised method is the continued nursing of one child to inhibit conception of another. There is also the belief that powder ground from the hard seed of the *gonyin* creeper, licked with salt every day, prevents conception. Foreign researchers in other cultures of Southeast Asia have collected lists of vegetable foods eaten as contraceptives, but I can find no corresponding information from Burmese villages. Villagers are less credulous than rural folk elsewhere and do not mention anything that is not effective. Villagers say that after they have had many children (five or more), the husband and wife 'sleep separately'.

Abortion, except for medical reasons which involve the need to save a mother's life, is definitely seen as criminal, and is forbidden. But secret abortions are to be heard of now and again; girls often attempt to induce abortion by drinking concoctions containing alcohol, ginger and purgatives. In actual fact people at the village level are quite casual about this; if despite trying to prevent it a woman still gets pregnant, she doesn't worry about the danger of getting an abortion and often just goes ahead and does it.

The hospital's post-natal care may extend to advice on family planning. So far there are no government measures for family planning. For those who have the means to buy from the open market, sometimes treated as blackmarket, there are doctors who do not feel it against any rules to insert the loop on request. Special consideration is given by a hospital board for contraceptive surgery. While some men from the upper income bracket find it possible to get vasectomy done privately, the government makes sterilization for women available without charge. Maternity hospitals prefer to do this at the time of childbirth. Sanction is granted in cases where the mother has already had four or more pregnancies or where her health should be spared from having more. It cannot be given on grounds of poverty and inability to feed any more mouths, but must be for health reasons only. This is the stated rule but actual practice is another matter. Ma Shan, who has five children told me of the 'operation' which will prevent her having any more children. 'It was quite easy. I got a letter from Ma Ma June and the doctors did it for me.' I asked her if the decision had been an easy one for her.

> Oh yes, so many people are doing it now. It is not so easy for them as it was for me. They had no one to help them like Ma Ma June, so they had to undergo examination by strange doctors whom they had to pay K.50 or K.100, before they could get a letter like the one I got free and easily, because Ma Ma June knows how poor I am.

There is actually no religious or cultural bar to family planning and if the government decides (as it is now believed to be considering) to put such a programme into practice, there will be a ready response. Burma has a population of 30.1 million (estimated by the 1974 census), with a growth rate of 2.3 per cent Her birth rate is 32.0/1000, her death rate 10.9/1000. The infant mortality rate used to be quoted as one of the highest in the world, but great progress has been made, and recent years show this decrease in the rate:

Infant Mortality Rates for 1000 Population

1962	1963	1964	1965	1966	1967	1968	1969	1970	1971	1972
139.3	121.8	130.9	109.3	88.77	66.50	65.8	65.0	62.8		59.0

Socialization of Children Before Puberty

The growing Burmese child begins socialization at a very early age by working, playing and generally participating alongside adults in the adult activity of the time. No child activity is devised specially for the child. He or she imitates or joins in some other way in whatever the adults have to do in the course of their own activities.

Whether it is carrying the baby astride on a tiny hip or peeling and cutting vegetables, kindling the fire, plucking produce, whittling bamboo, or buying and selling, the child in imitation alongside the parent or older sibling contributes to the family's labour input. This, however, does not mean that children are not shown any indulgence. The trip a mother makes to the bazaar is a focal point in every child's day, for she will bring back all kinds of snacks and delicacies. When she returns, each leaf-wrapped parcel is taken out and unwrapped with the child's eager co-operation, and the reward is well worth the waiting.

There are simple toys for children and boys and girls within the family, as well as in the immediate neighbourhood, play freely together before puberty. Extended family relatives and neighbours are free to take close interest in loving as well as reprimanding the children, and despite the occasional quarrel likely to arise between friends and neighbours from such a free relationship, this reinforces the rounded, communal world in which the child grows up.

The child's training begins early. When Cho Cho came to stay with us, she brought her three-year old daughter Aye Aye Nyunt. Cho Cho was, at that time, separated from her husband and this made mother and daughter all the closer. While the mother sat at the round kitchen table getting the meal ready Aye Aye Nyunt with a knife in one hand and a potato in the other practised cutting. Her potato cutting did not help much in the kitchen effort but she was happy to do it. When she was out in the garden and she was able to water the flower pots with a small can or even wield the hose-pipe. When they plucked flowers for market she plucked too. More important, she could be sent up periodically with baskets of the adult's plucking, to deposit on a low table bringing back the emptied baskets for uninterrupted plucking. Sweeping, picking grits from the rice, or shelling peanuts, work-play kept this 3 year-old busy and happy with no time to ask for this or that. The return of the bazaar basket every alternate morning was her high point of delight. As each kitchen packet was unwrapped and its contents deposited in the correct place, she called it out like a lesson. Then when her packet of titbits was opened, she jumped away with it, no more a kitchen help but again a mere 3-year old.

Khin Nyunt's five year old was often seen with the family baby astride her hip, while the seven-year old shouldered a pole and two water-cans her father had found, and chopped flowers and leaves and seeds.

There is among children, a great identification with the family's needs, as there is with its enjoyments. Children are also very close to relatives and neighbours. By the time a child is 12, he or she is trusted to get light fuel and water, cook the rice, pluck leaves and fruits within easy reach of the light pole, pound curry ingredients, make a tasty relish, wash and sweep, mind the baby, make cosmetic bark cream, use a catapult and make simple sales and purchases. Till they are about twelve, boys and girls have pretty much the same training in the majority of families, and they play happily together. School sits lightly on them. Attendance, especially among poorer families, is secondary to family needs and in the neediest cases dropping out is common. In higher income families, however, school is taken more seriously.

Up to the age of twelve or thereabouts, there is only a slight divergence in tasks and skills learnt by boys and girls. It is only after twelve that this divergence becomes more marked. We will look at the girl's world first.

Socialisation after Puberty – Girls

For girls, the tasks learnt earlier continue, while the sense of responsibility for household needs, especially with higher income families, increases. Feminine deportment is also instilled. The girl is taught to be well-groomed, to walk and sit in a 'feminine' way; she must not show open preference for boys' company, she must not go anywhere alone without a definite objective, she must always have company, even if it is only younger siblings. She takes on tasks such as putting jasmine offerings at the altar, carrying flowers to the pagoda, or laying out her father's clothes. With girls in higher-income families these tasks increase as food preparation becomes more elaborate and sewing clothes, comparatively absent among poorer families, is included in the mother's responsibilities. The girl must also learn the family business if there is one, for example, trade in textiles or jewellery or timber or cheroots. She is often the 'Keeper of Keys'. The bond between her and her mother is thus very close, in a practical as well as an emotional way. With her father there is a strong emotional tie but his touch is light.

Home for an average girl comprises the family and fond relatives, visits in the family group to houses of friends and relatives; picnics with them, outings to the pagoda, snack-eating, cinemas or local stage shows. And all this is often done in close company with other girls – relations and friends. There is coming and going between each other's houses including at meal-times, as well as cinema and shopping expeditions, outside of home-helping hours. The girl will study but if the family cannot spare her services for long, eventually she will drop out. (The drop out rate is indicated in Chapter VII). There are several careers open to her – these can be in business, in teaching, nursing, government jobs etc. Marriage is not thought of as an impediment to career plans.

Teenager ready for ear-piercing ceremony

Besides school and home, girls in villages and up-country towns also have a community life, which is described in Chapter XI.

This world of the growing girl is encompassed by the deep beliefs common to most Burmese Buddhist people. She believes in the world of unseen spirits all around her, especially in nature, but she also believes in the safe refuge afforded her by the Triple Gems of the Buddha, his Teaching and the *Sangha*. She is regarded as attractive physically, no less than in other attitudes, when seen at such devotions. Prayers mean supplication not necessarily for Nirvana but for another life after death, with more beauty, more wealth and reunion with loved ones.

In short, she lives thus, by the affection and esteem which are bound in with her place in the family, and in the opinion of relatives and neighbours. This guides the apparent behaviour of almost every girl to some extent. If ever her instincts pull her in a way which endangers that place she will often stifle such instincts. The girls who fail to do so are very much in a minority though they are now on the increase. Most feel they lose too much by breaking away. The average girl expects such a conflict to occur in her life only if she is so unlucky as to fall in love unsuitably. The limitations which surround courtship for her have been described in Chapter III. Meanwhile she does not share any secret thoughts she may have. She does not tell her parents. It would be disrespectful to discuss such feelings with them. If the time comes when she has to slink out to a meeting against their wishes, it would be more respectful, more like a good daughter, to keep it secret from them than it would be to boldly let them know she had disobeyed them.

The teenage period for a girl was traditionally marked (around the onset of puberty) by an ear-piercing ceremony, which gave her her first pair of earrings, symbolising her entry into a woman's world and ending her days of careless play in the company of boys. Now, the ceremony is not always held. Some families, however, still keep up the ceremony as part of the showy social accompaniment of a boy's novitiation celebrations. Both ceremonies may be regarded as puberty rites.

Onset of Male Puberty – Novitiation Ceremony

Before going on to the adolescent male, I pause to take a look at the events which mark the beginning of adolescence of both girls and boys. This event is a most important life stage especially for the male child. It is the novitiation ceremony by which a boy enters, even if for only a symbolic and very short period, the life of a novice monk in a monastery of a family's choice. This is for the family, the greatest event. It gives the parents a highest accruement of merit towards their future existences by their act of giving their son into the refuge of the *Sangha*, even for a short period. For the boy it reaffirms his great *kan* (good fortune) in being born as a male human being, in which form it was that the Buddha attained his Enlightenment. The *shinbyu* symbolizes renouncement of the worldly luxury of his life as a prince in order to enter the path in which he eventually found the way to deliverance.

The ceremony falls into two parts. The first, denoting the princely status of the *Buddha*'s family background, provides the boy with finery and a show where he is the center of attention, and is accompanied by a great feast. The second, which marks his entry into monastic routine gives him a taste of the discipline, ascetic and religiously oriented way of life. The preparation of the essential part of the event gives him at least a small measure of literacy and memory training.

Within these essentials of a *shinbyu*, the actual ceremony can vary according to the status of the family. It is an event for which people borrow money and clean themselves out in order to have it on a full scale. However, those parents who cannot afford to do it at all can give their sons to others who are either childless and wish to perform the novitiation for someone or who wants company for their sons in a big ceremony.

I performed this ceremony for Ko Aung Nyein and Ma Khin Nyunt's sons. On the evening of the ceremony we went in a group of seven to the little pagoda beside the monastery, and there the father shaved the boys' heads while donor and mother held a white sheet to receive the hair. This was followed by a bath, after which each boy donned a plain white *longyi* and went into the monastery. We seated ourselves before the monk, and after our prostrations the boys held up the robes that had been bought and asked in set words they had learned, to be allowed to wear them and enter the Order. This was granted. With the aid of the monk, they put the robes on and we left in order to make preparations for next morning's meal which I had arranged to serve at the monastery to a few monks and guests.

When my neighbours Sao Tha Tint and Saw Myint U held their celebration they made a full-scale show. Three sons were to be novitiated and two daughters to have their ears pierced.

On a dais at the head of the main pavilion, the three young boys and girls were in court dress with faces powdered white and a sequined and spired head-dress surmounting their raiment of silks and satins. They sat leaning on big satin embroidered cushions. In front of them were big silver bowls, one containing white *pareit-kyo* (sanctified yarn), one more in front of each child put ready to receive gifts. The guests came in, sat and were served with trays of tea-leaf salad, cheroots and hot tea. They sat and chatted and then went up in turn to make their greeting. They took a circle of yarn, slipped it over the wrist of each child to mark their gift and put an envelope with a small amount of money into each bowl provided. They were then led to the other pavilion and served a full meal.

6. Women in Religion

Doctrinal and Historical Background

Buddhism broke through the caste barriers of its Hindu homeland. Caste had maintained the status and function of people within the groups into which they were born. It reserved sacramental offices, and spiritual knowledge especially to members of a group determined by birth. Buddhism, teaching that each individual's fate equally with another's, governed only by the individual's own actions, during previous incarnations for this life, and during this life for future incarnations, opened religious learning, holy exercises, and spiritual advancement to all who might seek them.

It is of special interest to examine what place women, who undoubtedly held a very subsidiary place in the Hindu system, found in the teachings of Buddhism. Did they have the same opportunities as men for religious learning, and for acquiring the spiritual rewards towards their future incarnations?

Essentially, yes. Any deed done by a woman to further her spiritual account is equally effective as one done by a man. Meditating and dispensing boundless goodwill, chanting of *suttas*, keeping of the precepts in less or greater number, *dana* or giving in the building of a pagoda, a monastery, in the ordination of a novice monk, in offering alms to the *Sangha* or Monks, and food to laity – all these whether done by a man or woman will equally send him or her forward on the path of spiritual progress.

This path's final destination, the deliverance or cessation from the cycle of lives (with the pain of their impermanence, sufferings, illusion) can be won only by obliterating desire for life and all its worldly bonds. The way to do this is to leave home, become a houseless one, concentrate on the eightfold path and deny the bonds of family, property, love or striving. A woman may follow this path but in practice it is often harder for her to deny what must be denied to enter it, and experience has shown that there are far fewer women than men who have chosen this path. Moreover, a woman is, in some ways, considered a distraction for men who have chosen this path. Once she has entered the path however, there is no bar to her achieving deliverance. Thus Nirvana can be won in the woman's state. Gotami the aunt of the Buddha, collected 500 women of like mind and prevailed upon him to allow an Order of Ordained Nuns, just like the Order of Monks or

Bikkhus, the *Sangha* who had cut off the bonds of worldly life. Against his fear that the presence of Nuns would distract the *Sangha*, the Buddha, with the pleading of his disciple Ananda allowed the Order of *Bikkhunis*. In this Order many nuns are said to have attained *arahatship*, the state of being ready for deliverance. *Psalms of the Sisters*, (*Therigatha*), which is part of the Pali Canon of Buddhism, records these triumphs.

The fact of women being admitted to the *Sangha* was a triumph in social progress. Straight out of the hearth which bound the Hindu woman's world, these Buddhist sisters could leave the drudgery and escape restrictions, share an 'intellectual communion of the religious aristocracy of the *Ariyas* (Coomaraswamy)' Though technically appointed junior to the *Bikkus*, 'it is equally clear that, by intellectual and moral eminence, a *Theri* might claim equality with the highest of the fraternity (Rhys-Davids, p.26).'

In the centuries following the death of the Buddha, however, the Order of *Bikkunis* declined, and eventually disappeared. When this happened exactly is not certain. In Burma, in the Pagan Period of the 11th to 13th centuries, the nuns mentioned in inscriptions were, according to Luce and to Than Tun, ordained *Bikkhunis* or *Rahanmas*. 'Even in the Church they could become fully ordained nuns. One rose to be a bishop (Luce (iii) pp.95-6; Than Tun, pp.37-47)'.

In his article *Social Life in Burma*, Than Tun makes reference to *Bikkhunis* of this same period. These *Bikkhunis* enjoyed the same veneration from the laity as *Bikkhus* did, for they had been ordained as male monks were.

Although women are admitted into the Sangha, it would not be wrong to say that men are given greater veneration. This is not only because they have turned their lives in the direction of deliverance, but also because they are men doing so – men with the *pon* or potential glory residing in them. The male *pon* is given recognition without rationalization in religious attitudes all over the world. Though Christian doctrine teaches the equality of the individual soul, man or woman, for spiritual grace, Christian sects have in practice denied women the offices of holy sacraments, and of hierarchical rank, authority and veneration. In Buddhism this conception of a male glory is rationalized in remembering the characteristics of Future Buddhas as given in the *Introduction to the Jataka* (part of the Pali Canon).

> A human being, male of sex,
> Who saintship gains, a Teacher meets,
> As hermit lives and virtue loves,
> Nor lacks resolve, nor fiery zeal. (Warren, p.33)

This has set the seal on the conception of greater veneration for a man. It has made the idea acceptable. There has been no questioning and revolt such as has just resulted in the admission of women to the ministry in the Episcopal Church and the denial of them to that of the Roman Catholic Church. The Buddhist concept, on the other hand, has sustained greater veneration for the male *Sangha* who have continued in unbroken tradition of ordination. The *Bikkhuni* Order, unfortunately, died out. Added to that was the fact that the bonds of life made it comparatively difficult for women to seek that path. Still there is the small minority who do seek it, and after the disappearance of the Order of *Bikkhunis* we find some Burmese women still exercised their right to leave the duties of hearth and home in order to tend to their spiritual advancement in a houseless life, even without ordination. Thus there are 'nuns' today as there have been through the centuries. Here is how a foreign scholar views them.

> There are, in some Asian countries, ladies who live in a 'nunnery' and wear a type of 'robe' but they are regarded merely as what they are in fact, very devout laywomen striving to live the holy life. There is no reason why they should not succeed in this, and many do, but since the Order died out, there is no means of reviving it to correlate with the Order of monks (Maurice, p. 91).

The Burmese have no need to apostrophize the terms used for such devout women. 'Nun' is merely an English word. Burmese refer to them as *Thilashins*, Keepers of the Precepts. They address them as *Saya-lay*; the male term for Teacher or *guru* suffixed with *lay* meaning junior. While many today grudge them a whole-hearted accord because they feel their presence near monasteries a distraction to the monks, the *Thilashins* have no doubt played their role as teachers in past centuries. The two sections following will deal with *Thilashins* today. Here I end the historical background with a note on their influence in the reign of King Mindon, the last great king of Burma (1825-1878).

As a prince, Mindon had often listened to the preaching of two famous *Thilashins* Saya Kin (Saw Monyin, p.496) and Saya Mai Nat Pay. When he became King, he went to invite both to come and teach his queens religion as well as manners. Mai Nat Pay was the daughter of a master mason. She decided she could not change her abrupt and rough way of speech to suit a court, so she decided to stay on in the forest, at *Mingun Gugalay Gyaung* (Vale) near the *Dhamma Thera* Vale where she eventually built a pagoda which is named after her to this day.

Saya Kin, 10 years younger than her, was 45 then, and agreed to come on three conditions, which she thought necessary to ensure her freedom from the chains of court life. She would sleep in no tiered roof residence, she would receive no titles nor medals, and no 'alms money' was to be given to her. She herself chose various places to stay in and 'people must come where the shade is' to hear her, under the trees of Sagaing across the river, east of the *Shwegyin-taik* or near Mandalay Hill in the capital, and most of the time in a monastery built '500 fathoms away from the nearest house' to the north of the palace in the royal city. The court and other women came to her for instruction to learn how to read the scriptures and to write, for Pali grammar and Buddhist philosophy. Children were brought along for disciplining. Court and commoners became *Thilashins*. King Mindon was most appreciative and, as a mark of veneration for Saya Kin, he had his younger daughters cut off their hair with great pomp and ceremony in order to become temporary *Thilashins* under her tutelage.

As years passed, Saya Kin raised pupil *Thilashins* to take over the court instruction in her place, and finally returned across the river to the Sagaing hills and woods, where her ties with the bodily life became very light. She would sit to meditation at 8 p.m. and not rise till the pre-dawn alms food was brought to her. Passing the young *Thilashins* still asleep then, she would say in her soft voice as they remembered all their lives 'Oh, the young girls are sleeping. Get up girls, get up.' Ethics, Calmness and Wisdom were the qualities people saw in her. In 1878 while practising *Vipassana* she passed away. King Mindon, when he heard the news was greatly affected and he had her ashes put in a tomb so that he could pay his respects to them.

Nunneries Today

Today there are 'colonies' of *Thilashins* up and down the length of Burma. It is difficult to get exact numbers. Like monks they are not registered and in many cases may be shifting in numbers. A book on such colonies called *Thilashin Sasana* written by a monk using the name of Yeway Tun has, unfortunately, not been published. In a later work which was published – *Thilashin Thamaing* (1964) – gives a figure of 8753 *Thilashins* in Burma in 1961.

The word 'Nunnery' is merely a convenient English equivalent which refers to the residence of *Thilashins*. The Burmese word is *Gyaung*. It is a word that is used to mean a quiet nook, especially a secluded hollow or cave surrounded by woodland. Such a site is chosen for meditation, and the hills in its vicinity are often crowned with pagodas and monasteries. The word 'monastery' in Burmese is synonymous with school. It is *Kyaung*, and so to call the residence of the *Thilashins* a *kyaung* would not be wrong, though 'monastery' may not be as applicable. Some Burmese translate *Gyaung* as vale, with poetic connotations of a remote retreat in mind. Cloister is perhaps more generally applicable, to urban as well as woodland centers.

The chief centre of *Thilashin* cloisters is Sagaing, across the Irrawaddy from Mandalay. The river which is over a mile wide here, is crossed by the Ava Bridge. Across the river from Mandalay, Sagaing appears with rocky cliffs and ridges above a sandy plain. Pagoda spires and monastery roofs in ascendant tiers crown these ridges, and in them are caves and hollows which have through the ages enticed all those in search of tranquility.

There are over 100 *Thilashin* cloisters in Sagaing. A notable one is the *Thitseint Gyaung* situated on a ridge overlooking the river with towers and spires surrounding it. About 50 *Thilashins* are here. Unlike the majority in other cloisters, they get enough alms from relatives without going out to seek and they can therefore concentrate more on studies and keep a strict timetable.

The *Hkaymaythaka Gyaung* with most *Thilashins* also has the distinction of housing the first one to win the title of *Dhammacariya* (Teacher of the *Dhamma*) in the scriptural examinations held annually. These examinations are open to monks, *Thilashins*, men and women alike and a note on them will be found at the end of this section. The cloister is exceptionally magnificent and has a huge central hall of two stories, its pillars gilded with gold-leaf. It too is noted for its strict rules. All over Burma, there is a current use of loudspeakers which broadcast without let-up, night or day, during the religio-social *dana* (giving) celebrations. Sermons and chanting are broadcast loud enough to benefit a distant neighbourhood and keep all thoroughly awake, but in between the sermons come music and announcements. This takes place even when the celebrations are held in monasteries or pagoda precincts. At this cloister however, such celebrations are strictly forbidden. The nuns themselves observe a very strict routine, the infringement of which is punished by impositions of shoulder loads of water cans, up to 60 loads for repeated back-sliding which, if not corrected, ends in expulsion.

In the *Ayemyo Gyaung* with about 65 *Thilashins* is a noted scholar with the rare title of *Gandakayaka*, Treatise Writer. Her work, *Nibbana Pawasathanikyan*, has become a religious best seller running into several editions. Further up on the river is Mingun, famous for having the second largest bell in the world and what was in 1900 the largest pile of brick masonry in the world. This is the pagoda temple which was to have been 450 feet square, and 500 feet high. It lies now, only partly finished, 450 feet square and 165 feet high, with great cracks running down the brickwork base due to an earthquake. It was built in the early 19th century when the power of Kings to command armies of labourers was on the decline. Despite this awesome gloomy reminder of the vanity of endeavour Mingun has a repose, which bears out the promise seen from downstream. Backed by woods, a riverine strip contains other graceful pagodas, on hillocks, resthouses, a home for the aged and about 30 *Thilashin* cloisters housing a total of 400 *Thilashins*. Best known among them are *Ariyameggin Gyaung* from which Daw Dhammacariya has passed an examination in 9 scriptural treatises, at one sitting and *Sharpin Gyaung* which has the first *Thilashin* to pass all three grades of the *Patamabyan* examination.

Monywa, in this stretch of plain, Webu right across at the eastern foothills, Prome and Shwedaung further south on the great river, are some of the cloister colony centers. In the delta to the far south, Twante among the mudflats has a cloister holding 100 *Thilashins*. Moulmein at the mouth of the Salween to the southeast in Mon country has, among others the *Khemayama Gyaung* to which a Nepalese girl eager to study Buddhist scriptures came and in 10 years passed the *Dhammacariya* examination. Qualified to teach the *Dhamma*, Ma Thudhammawadi is now back in Nepal with a Mon *Thilashin Dhammacariya* who helps her spread Theravada Buddhism there. In 1964, there were four girls from Nepal studying there, brought by the reputation this cloister has for successes in the *Patamabyan* and Pali examinations.

Rangoon has about 100 *Thilashins*. They take care to avoid the cosmopolitan and political taint ascribed to some Rangoon and Mandalay monks, having little contact outside the cloisters. Except for going out for alms, the *Thilashins* believe that they can achieve as much detachment in these urban centers as the vales of

Sagaing would have afforded. Most famous of the cloisters is *Nyanasari* or *Myanaung Kyaungtaik* with 120 *Thilashins*, with a name for both *pariyatti* (study) and *parapatti* (practice). Modern education in other subjects including English is also taught by lay teachers. This cloister is the best endowed having a great central hall donated at a cost of K.250,000 by two rich men. It has also had *Thilashins* from many countries coming to study. Buddhist girls between five and ten years of age come to this monastery to spend summer vacations, don the Thilashin's garb and take on her routine. They are trained in basic Buddhist deportment and duties, such as presentation and offering of almsfood, of votive water, of flowers, as well as the asking for precepts, taking of precepts, prayers and *suttas*. This not only gives them religious instruction, it is felt to be a training in graceful manners which makes their speech elegant.

A smaller Rangoon cloister, the *Aye Nyeing* also had two Nepalese sisters who came over to study and work as *Thilashins* and have now returned to Nepal where they have started an orphanage, the *Yasodhara Vihara* (Yaway Htun).

What makes a *Thilashin*? It has been stated earlier that *Thilashins* are not ordained nuns in the way that men are ordained as monks who have to follow 227 rules of the *Vinaya* or monastic code, after ordination in a ceremony which has come down in unbroken continuity since the time of the Buddha. The *Thilashins* however, are Keepers of Precepts – in a special way.

All lay people 'take' the five precepts, that is, they recite them and hope to keep to them. The five are to refrain from killing, stealing, sexual misconduct, telling of falsehoods and intoxicating the mind with alcoholic drinks. On special holy days like the significant full moon and new moon days throughout the year, with the quarter days, added during Lent, lay people may take in addition to the above five, three more precepts: not to eat after midday, not to use cosmetics nor to enjoy song and dance, and not to sleep in a high, big and luxurious bed. The *Thilashins* generally observe the eight precepts which devout laity do only on special days of sabbath. As a rule, they observe them for each day and throughout their lives as *Thilashins*, but every day is a fresh undertaking, and there may be slight modification. Some of them who go on the alms-round for example might not be able to observe all eight on those days. Others who do not want for alms can and do observe ten precepts as the monks do. This includes a ban on handling of money and the splitting up of the bans on cosmetics and song and dance into two separate precepts for greater emphasis. There is no dividing line in this matter of the observance of precepts between the very devout householders who might extend their sabbath observances beyond Lent, and the *Thilashins*' commitment throughout the year. But the *Thilashins* signify also their break with the lay life by shaving their head, wearing a special garb and moving into a cloister though residence in one is not a compulsory part of their code.

The garb consists of an 'earth-stained' light brown sarong called a *khawut*, an apricot coloured tight-sleeved jacket with cloth buttons in front called a *letkyat*, a calf-length gown to be worn over this called the *kike*, a length of cloth over one shoulder and under another arm with ends brought together, called a *ko-yon*, and a folded cloth worn on the head or held over one arm called the *kaung-tin*. All garments are of cotton received white and dyed by the *Thilashins* themselves, except in the case of natural brown cotton. The cloisters require an entering *Thilashin* to have four such sets of habit, as well as a razor, umbrella, slippers, box, rosary, bedding and tray (for receiving alms). She should also have some pots and pans. To become a *Thilashin* with this initial equipment cost about 100 kyats in 1964, and therefore poor girls who enter with the idea of getting food and shelter in a congenial life still need sponsors to start them off. In the matter of subsistence there is great contrast between the monks and the *Thilashins*. Monks are offered cooked food such as rice, fish, meat and vegetable accompaniments, as well as prepared fruits and desserts. They are also offered uncooked food on many occasions, either by individual households going to the monastery with offerings, or by a communal gathering together of rice, oil, and other supplies with great celebration and fanfare. There are associations such as Buddhist Associations and Rice Donating Groups who see that collections are made to keep the monasteries supplied.

Procession of meditating women

Thilashins are never offered prepared meals but only uncooked food. There is no ceremony about such offerings, and though enough alms are usually ensured, they often have to search for them. Some cloisters, either by having *Thilashins* with rich relatives, or some eminent scholar whose reputation attracts zealous support, get alms more easily than others. The majority depend on the *Thilashins* themselves going round twice a week to receive rice and other supplies from householders who give because it is a meritorious act, higher than giving to laity but not equal to donating to a monastery whose monks are regarded as following a purer path and who serve the cause of religion by keeping this way alive.

Regarding this great difference in status between monks and nuns, it is worth noting that the comment made on *Thilashins* by a male writer in *Thilashin Thamaing*, alleges invidious discrimination:

> Although the *Thilashins* have no privileges, they do not hanker for any. Throughout the ages, from the days of absolute monarchy to now, they have never cried out for their rights. At *Thadingyut* (end of Lent) the Prime Minister himself gives almsfood to a thousand *sanghas* (monks); the *Thilashins* are not included. During *Tazaungdine* the *sanghas* are given a double set of robes; the *Thilashins* are not remembered. Again on Independence Day 100 *Sanghas* are given uncooked alms. Yet not a thought about *Thilashins*. The *Thilashins* however, do not raise one voice. They certainly are not 'the crying child (who) gets the milk' (ibid).

A Thilashin has the option of leaving a cloister at any time she decides to return to a householder's life. This return, even as a monk's return, carries no ignominy or difficulties. But the status in law between a monk and a *Thilashin* is different. A woman's legal status is not affected by her becoming a *Thilashin* as a man's is when he becomes a monk. Whereas a monk who enters a monastery with the intent to remain there for life loses claims to family property, with the rule that ordination causes cessation of ties of relationship, and divestment of property, *Thilashins*, not being ordained, do not cease to own or possess properties. Their ties of relationship are held to exist (Lahiri, p.352).

There was one time when *Thilashins* formed an association to protect their interests. That was when rice lands were being nationalized in 1954. It was declared that lands belonging to *Thilashins* would not be exempted from nationalization, unlike the 'religious lands' as *Thilashins* were not fully 'servers of religion' (*thathana wunhtan*). This made the *Thilashins* react. Not so much because of the danger of losing their lands, but because they were said to be not truly servers of religion. Here again, a note alleging invidious discrimination of women's interest was sounded: Was it because (directing sarcasm at worldly monks) they did not mix with ordinary people so much, did not meddle in their affairs, did not take part in politics, did not stand for parliamentary elections like some *yahans* (monks) and did not exercise the right to vote in elections that they were not classified equally as 'servers of religion'? Who indeed were the true servers of religion in the light of this difference in participation in worldly affairs?

The All-Burma Association of *Thilashins* successfully settled the land issue and other problems and has been kept going as an association since.

Something must now be said of the activities within the cloisters. The first thing which visitors remark on is the meticulous care given to the grounds, buildings, resthouses and shrine areas. There is fastidious cleanliness, and the altars are always full of flowers, food offerings, and fresh water. Cooking is an important part of many *Thilashins*' mornings as they not only cook for altar offerings and their own food, but also for monks in the nearby monastery if there is one. Preparing and offering food for monks is one of the meritorious acts open to all, and *Thilashins*, like fully lay men and women, will not neglect this means of acquiring merit. Some colonies receive old people and care for them. Though the care of the aged is most predominantly a family concern in Burma, there are the cases of poor or kinless old. Daw U Zun who became a *Thilashin* in middle life was a pioneer in such work. In many towns she founded homes for the poor and old and her original Home for the Aged, founded in 1927, in Mingun, the site of many cloisters, is still flourishing.

Such cloisters also care for orphans. The *Zeyathiri* in Toungoo was started by two *Thilashins* who found four orphans needing care. They started to clear land themselves, went round for alms and struggled on till 3 years later, they had 25 *Thilashins* and 18 orphans in their care. Their work which they did not view in terms of a separate tradition of social welfare was first appreciated by the police force of the district. With the urging of the police commissioner of the time, U Ba Thike, every policeman in Toungoo district, put in ten pyas (2 cents) each month from his pay. This not only made all the difference to the *Thilashins*' budget, it also encouraged town and bazaar to support them.

Girls are another concern of *Thilashins*. The Buddhist Girls' Home in Mergui was started by a *Thilashin* Daw Haymaryi of Moulmein when she also started the *Khamayama Taik*. There are now 60 girls being cared for by *Thilashins*, with the support of town and the government social welfare department. The girls range in age from 6 to 16. They received schooling from primary through high school, but during one vacation or another they become *Thilashins*.

The idea of missionary work among non-Buddhist people in the hill areas which are Burma's outer rim was mooted more than once, and especially in the early 1960's, but it has not succeeded. The *Thilashins* prefer to seek their spiritual advancement in an environment which is already Buddhist.

The time that remains after such 'extra' activities, as well as their normal duties such as care of altars, buildings and kitchens is spent in studies, prayer and meditation. The importance of distinguished scholars in the reputation of cloisters has been noted already. Studies include Buddhist literature, scriptures, treatises, commentaries, philosophy, Pali grammar. Advanced studies are, as among monks, only for those who are dedicated to them. Such *Thilashins* in fact enter this life because their early taste of religious learning leads them to seek deliverance from life's fret and striving. These studies have been given such emphasis in the *Nyarnasaryi* of *Myanaung Kyaung* in Rangoon for example, that women have come to it from many countries to pursue them. *Thilashins* from Nepal, Cambodia, Vietnam, Thailand, Japan, Switzerland and England have come there, where their photographs are hung till today.

Though the majority of *Thilashins* may not progress far with such studies, those who do, enter the annual examinations. The highest examination open to *Thilashins* is for the title of *Dhammacariya* (Teacher of *Dhamma*). (By 1965, the number of Thilashins who passed the *Dhammacariya* totalled 123.) The rate of success in this examination was 9.9% in 1975.

The ordinary scriptural examinations held yearly are called *Patamabyan* at three levels of Junior, Mid and Senior. The figures in the table below indicate (a) the proportion of *Thilashins* to monks, (bearing in mind that there are probably more than ten times as many monks as *Thilashins*) (b) the nature of the studies where many who register fail to get ready in time, but the ratio of women who fail thus to sit is less than that of men and (c) the low rate of success for both monks and *Thilashins*.

Examination data for 1975.

Examination aspirants		*registered*	*sat for*	*passed*
Patamagyi	Yahans and novices	2488	1921	303
(senior)	Thilashins	132	111	10
Patamalat	Yahans and novices	3206	2360	560
(mid)	Thilashins	149	129	17
Patamange	Yahans and novices	5124	4098	1338
(junior)	Thilashins	203	158	52
All	Lay men	2	2	1
examinations	Lay women	1	1	1

It is considered that *Thilashins* were a more thriving institution during the days of monarchy, that they declined throughout the colonial period, that only now are they on the upswing again, not only in numbers but in scholarship, discipline and greater activity, and that the appreciation of their status is also rising. Though Burmese society is less pervaded by outside influences than in most other countries of Southeast Asia, the conservative element sees the manners and morale of girls in much need; they feel that girls have become rough and crude in manner and deportment, slack in morale, and woefully ignorant of their Buddhist learning. They turn to *Thilashins* as a major corrective influence and there is some movement even from the upper echelons of fashionable society to give them greater regard. Here are some personal histories to cover a wide range among *Thilashins* and indicate various reasons for joining the cloisters.

Some Personal Histories

I begin with two village girls who grew to be the most distinguished scholars of this century.

In 1975, Daw Marlar Yi was 95 years old with her faculties clear, her health sound. Her long life has been devoted to learning as much as to teaching. Born to villager parents in Khattiya in Nyaungdon Township, she attended a village school together with her sister. At 17, swept by the desire to devote her life to study of the scriptures she went to Sayadaw U Ponnya of Thamein Tawya Monastery, received the ten precepts and became a *Thilashin*.

She now began a long period of study. She learned *Pali*-based religious writing from the presiding monk. Next she spent 6 years studying under her cousin the renowned *Dhamma* lecturer U Zanita (sein-za-ni), then with other teachers at Rangoon and Pyapon for two years at each place. During this time she was also under the tutelage of *Tayanka Sayagyi*, who had won the title of *Yazaguru Egga Mahapandita* three times. Next she spent four years in the cloister of Thayaing Village in Shwebo district up in the north. Then she meditated at *Sagaing Guni* for another two years, at the same time learning the higher level of commentaries or *Atthagahta*.

In 1931, at the age of 46 she finally built a cloister the *Thameikdawdaya Gyaung* on the Sagaing Hills. There, she began the teaching which continues till today. She started with 7 *Thilashins*, and today there are over 100. In 1945, she began holding examinations in grammar, vocabulary, poetry and philosophy. About forty of them would pass in a year. They were rewarded with cloth for their robes, from 5 yards to one bolt, according to their grades. Meanwhile she continued her search for self-improvement: seven years meditation training with *Mahagandayone Sayadaw*, further to Seikkun village in Shwebo district, and another period with *Sayadaw* U Kawthala. She went wherever there was someone to instruct her further. In 1970, at the age of 90 she handed over her administrative control of the Cloister to her neice Daw Haymaryi and two others.

At 95 with her eyes, ears, and teeth functioning well, her face unlined, drinking lime juice and offering up or giving away half of every fruit she opened before she would eat it, Daw Marlar Yi was still reading books on *Vipassana* by the *Mahasi* and *Mogok Sayadaws*; she was the only woman member in the examinations on Buddhist Literature, and her clear memory often reminded fifty-year old pupils of things they had forgotten (Saw Monyin pp. 508-11).

Daw Dhammasaryi is another scholar who began her studies by attending the village school. After she passed elementary school, her parents trained her in a salesmanship at a silk stall in the bazaar. She was a pretty girl and did well in the bazaar, but as soon as she came home, she would pick up the book her father had put down (*Satuyetkha*) and start to read. The works of Theingaza Sayadaw impressed her so much they filled her with a yearning to be free of the cycle of birth and death. She determined that one day she would become a *Thilashin*, devoted to this path. When she was 16, she asked permission to do this but her parents refused, her brother emphatically saying he did not wish to be called 'the *Thilashin's* brother'. Nevertheless she went with some friends to a Mingun cloister where after a year of observing and performing religious duties, she became a *Thilashin*. She studied Sanskrit in Mandalay, and while there, met a monk who, it is said, for love of her, left the monastery and became a layman, though still a devout one. But Daw Dhammasaryi took no notice and went ahead with her *Thilashin's* life.

She later went to Sri Lanka with monks who took a gold cube for holding the Sacred Tooth there. Sri Lanka had no *Thilashins* but she was able to spend two years there studying Singhalese. When she returned, she became a teacher of monks as well as *Thilashins* who wished to learn the scriptures in that language. She wrote a book *Thissawadi tika* and her sermons were famous. One eminent Abbot, Nyaung Sayadaw, is said to have asked someone if he had heard Daw Dhammasaryi preach, and when the reply was 'not yet', he answered: 'Then you are still far from attaining *Nibbana*.' She died in 1971 and was buried at Mingun (ibid, pp. 499-502).

We now come to another long-lived and famous Teacher Daw Nyarna Saryini, daughter of a rich landowning family. Her father was a Circle Headman, which during Burmese monarchic times, was a hereditary office, recognized by royal appointment and marked by special symbols of office such as a red umbrella, guards, a more elaborately roofed house. Daw Nyarna Saryi was the eleventh child of such a Headman in charge of a circle of villages in Myanaung area. Her brothers, given modern university education were already filling official posts in the British administration when, at the age of 16, she asked her parents' permission to become a *Thilashin*. Three times she was refused, her parents crying and saying that a youngest daughter should look after her parents when they get old. She replied that she would benefit them more by being a *Thilashin* but they would not hear of it. So she enlisted the help of a maid in fleeing the house. As told to the writer Saw Monyin, she planned with the maid for nearly a month.

Only when I told her that a *Thilashin's* existence is truly rewarding did she agree to help me. I left a note for my parents saying 'I'm going where I shall be free from the slavery (of attachment). Please forgive me.' I showed my aunt where I kept the diamond earrings and bracelet which I always wore. Then I asked the *Nat* (Spirit) to help me free myself from the captivity of lust.

At the break of dawn when I heard the owls and koels calling, I got up, and after cutting off my hair, donned the *Thilashin* robes which were dyed and ready. Then I left with my cousin for Daw Wi La Thi's school. You have to cross the *Indaing* forest which is 1½ miles long. I did not know the way but I heard a bullock cart in front and followed it. At the school it was morning but no one dared to shave my head for me. My uncle U Kyaw Ya, who was a magistrate was very powerful and had a fiery temper so the *Thilashins* wouldn't even lend me a razor. In the end, my cousin borrowed one and shaved my head for me. Myanaung Sayadaw said 'well done!'

My parents, having discovered my absence, arrived in a bullock cart at 8 p.m. in tears. They telegraphed to my brother U Hlaing Bwa at college but he did not come. My Inspector brother from Lashio, U Kan Gyi came at once. When my parents started crying in front of Ingyin Myanaung Sayadaw, he comforted them and said wasn't it a happy thing for a sister to be a *Thilashin*? When they came to me I said: People do not understand the doctrine about conception and life. Thus they crave for living.

When my father heard that, he said no more. He retired from work and after entrusting me to the school, he immediately began a new building for it. After I received the title Mai Nyarna Saryi, and about one month after I adhered to Sayadaw Wilathi, 20 girls joined as Thilashins.'

So Mai Nyarna Saryi got what she had longed for which was to be immersed in religious books. She went through study and training as the two *Thilashins* described above did, like them choosing the place where a Sayadaw, whose teaching attracted her, taught. When she entered for the *Partamabyan* examinations she won first prize in the senior level.

In 1930, at the age of 31, she returned to her native Myanaung to found a new cloister. In 1947, she started yet another one in Rangoon in the famous *Myanaung Gyaung*. There she started with 60 Thilashins whom she had trained. Recruits joined from all over Lower Burma, from Twante, Maubin, Pegu, Moulmein, Myanaung and Rangoon. Her examination results were impressive and she became known as 'Teacher of 500 *Thilashins* and more'. It is at her nunnery that girls from other countries have come to study Buddhism and small girls spend vacations in learning Buddhist duties as *Young Thilashins*. She was very strict with her rules of writing and diction. She was also a tireless questioner and many monks avoided her lest she ask questions to which they did not know the answers. She composed poems and songs for various religio-social occasions, often spontaneously. Once, while on a boat up the Irrawaddy to Bhamo on the China border, she sang about her fellow passengers, a monk with a young boy Nga Chit, making amusing rhymes on his name. In April 1976, at the age of 90, she died. Her funeral was crowded with people and banked with religious offerings. Her pupils carried her casket and put it on a flying *Nat* (Heavenly Spirit) horse (ibid, pp. 512-18).

These are some among the distinguished ones. Let us turn to some of the large number of *Thilashins* who did not pursue advance studies but find a different refuge within the cloisters. Daw Nyar Na, in a cloister adjoining a monastery in Rangoon, was a village girl known as Ma Ngwe, who attended the monastery lay school for boys and girls at the age of six. When she was twelve she lost both her parents. Her nearest relative was an aunt who was a *Thilashin*. Ma Ngwe went to live with her as a *Thilashin* herself and, from that early age, has known no other life. She is now 68. Her earlier days included studies but at no level approaching examinations. Now those studies are over. She gets up at 5, cooks rice, offers it at the altar and prays. She then serves food to the monks living in the monastery close by. She cleans up, sweeping the monastery inside and out, helps others prepare the mid-morning meal, and after the monks have eaten, has her own meal; all this to be finished before midday.

The period following this one used to include some studies for her, but now she gets the long interval to rest and pray. At about 6 p.m. she retires to bed with a rosary on which she repeats *Anneiksa, Dokkha, Anatta* (Impermanence,

Suffering, No-soul) or recites the nine attributes of the Buddha. She has friends in the outside world who visit her from time to time, and she gives them spiritual solace when needed.

My cousin Tin Tin has her favourite *Sayalay*. Tin Tin is forced by weak health to live a retiring life but is full of interest in her more active relatives. If any of them are in trouble Tin Tin tells her *Sayalay* about it and usually returns with some counsel which is acceptable as from one who lives with the doctrine and has time for reflection.

Sayalay, like Daw Nyar Na, has found a home and sustenance, as well as a life which has raised her to a measure of esteem and given her spiritual solace.

The death of one's parents is a common reason for girls becoming *Thilashins*. Not only is home no longer the same as the loving daughter used to know it, but the impermanence of life strikes her consciousness and turns it towards the doctrine that bases its teaching on a recognition of that very fact. Daw Gonmaryi, who became head of a Sagaing cloister, had been studying in a Roman Catholic Convent in Rangoon for seven years when she lost her parents. Though her elder sister was by then running a flourishing shop and wanted her to share in it, she was too stricken to accept anything but the *Thilashin's* life and entered it.

Up till 1959, the Shan State of Burma used to be ruled by the traditional system of *Sawbwas* (subject to a central authority). Hsipaw State was about the richest of these states. It was close to Mandalay which had been the capital of the last Burmese King till 1885. Hsipaw regarded itself as the successor of the courtly tradition and kept alive many of the splendours associated with Buddhist kingship. The ruling prince till 1928 was Sir Sao Khe K.C.I.E. He was not only knighted by the British, he retained more traditional forms of a kingly status. He had a total of 24 wives, some earlier and some later. Of these wives, 5 including the *Mahadevi* (chief one) mostly in their late thirties or early forties became *Thilashins*. They did not go to a cloister but remained within the *Haw* (as the royal residence is called), observing eight to ten precepts and absolved from the necessity of conjugal and domestic service to the prince, able to read, meditate or pray with shelter and sustenance provided by the ex-husband who could make no objection at this renunciation of domesticity in favour of a religious life. They were henceforth addressed as Sao Mai Khow (the White-clad Royal Mothers). One of them, Nang Kham Ong, had a daughter who became the *Mahadevi* (and only wife) of the heir, later ruler of Kengtung State, the biggest and most remotely situated of these Shan States. She eventually went there to live and there, I knew her as Sao Mai Khow in 1940. She lived in a small house beside her daughter's big one and was completely detached from her daughter's stormy concerns with state and family. To her grandchildren she was just like anybody's grandmother.

Though missionary work among non-Buddhist hill peoples could not be organized, one or two women who, in a small way, ventured into new paths (including such work) deserve mention. Fifty-year old Ma Weikzethi, after passing the *Dhammasariya* examination got a degree after much effort and now among her *Thilashin* pupils are other ethnic groups such as Palaung, Shan and

Khaku Chins.

One thousand miles up from Rangoon, in the furthest northern little town of Putao, local residents of Kachins, Shans, Yawyins, Lisus and other ethnic groups know little about Buddhism. A small group of Buddhists in Putao decided to find a teacher for them and found one from the southern most tip of Tenasserim. Sayalay Dhamma Saryi, after a high school education, had taught school for a while, and had also taken training as a nurse at the hospital in Mergui. In 1964, hearing of the need in Putao she went all the way up, and is now teaching men and women meditation, as well as Buddhist basics and secular school subjects to children from the surrounding ethnic groups, up to a middle grade level (Yaway Htun).

Finally there are the girls who become temporary *Thilashins*. Two girls I know did so, for a few months, one to get over an unhappy love affair, and the other on the eve of a seven year move abroad for a dental surgeon's training.

Among young parents I know, perhaps Ko Soe Khin and See are the most 'stylish'. He is a surgeon, she an economist, and both are fond of good clothes, food, house furnishings and garden. They have three daughters, aged 4 to 9. With all this the Soe Khins spend part of weekends at the meditation centre which is set in a pear grove near the hospital. It has little chalets separated by the pear trees from a central hall which has a most resplendent altar of gold and glass mosaic. In the summer of 1975 when I last saw them, the Soe Khins were preparing to make little *Thilashins* of their three daughters along with 15 other little daughters of friends, and to 'give them a sound Buddhist foundation of behaviour'. The girls were looking forward excitedly to the prospect. I could picture them solemn in the dignity of apricot robes, important with the shaving of heads, tripping with small trays of offerings to the altar, changing water, changing flower vases and prostrating themselves after doing these offerings, straightening up and with eyes closed reciting the passages they had learned over raised hands. These are offices which as adult women they will do all their lives and it is expected that investing them with this experience will add considerably to the devotion with which they will continue them in later life.

Women in Lay Religious Life

We now look at the involvement of women who do not renounce their homes but are active within monastery and pagoda precincts to a more than ordinary degree. They make more than a normal Burmese housewife's effort toward their spiritual progress.

The *Thathana Yeiktha* is one out of many meditation centres in Rangoon. On an average day in 1976 it showed the following classification of persons practising *Vipassana* Meditation: *Sanghas* 73, Male *Yawgis* 35, Female *Yawgis* 99 (interviewer). The term '*yawgi*' (which is a Burmese rendering of 'yogi') takes the meaning 'ardent effort' from the word. It is applied to lay-people making such an ardent effort. Of the 99 female *yawgis*, about one third are *Thilashins*, the rest are women who have not made a break with home. They spend anything from 2 weeks to six, living in cells at the Centre, receiving instruction daily from one of the monks under the system, instructed and guided by the *Mahasi Sayadaw*, whose scholarship, sanctity and progress in spiritual exercises is famed. The regime at this and other well-known centres is very hard. No meal after midday, sleep for about 6 hours only each night, and unremitting concentration on breathing, walking and every physical act. Problems and difficulties are discussed with the guilding monk each day. Encouragement is given to persevere despite many starts which appear almost hopeless at first. Those who go through the course speak of acquiring ability to discount their worries and to do with little sleep or food, all resulting in a wonderful feeling of lightness, exhilaration and achievement.

Such a strict system is followed by other famous centres in Rangoon and in other towns such as Prome, Mogok, Sagaing, Mandalay and Kyaukse. There are less well-known centres in other towns too and people may go to them for less prolonged meditation. In Taunggyi, for example, a town of about 80,000, where there are 28 monasteries, seven of them have meditation centres. A large number of people, men and women go to these centres for short-term spells, others at regular morning sessions perhaps, of about an hour following a sermon. Only occasionally, when able to dispose of business and household affairs, they make a continuous stay in one of the cells. My sister-in-law Sao Van Tip, who died very recently, was one in a group of five friends who regularly went to the Mingun Monastery's centre. They choose to go there because they like the Sayadaw's way of guidance. They take turns to give a *dana* meal to the monks and about 50 to 60 people once a month, and for this they help each other in the cooking and serving. Four members of the group are married women with responsibility for family and households, but they are all aged above 50. Sao Van Tip is a widow with no family responsibility but she is hampered in her meditation programs by ill health which the cells in the Centre, not being weather-proof, tend to aggravate. The Sayadaws recommend that one be in good health when undertaking meditation. Recently, before her death, she had donated, for K30,000, a new cell within the Centre precincts which would be warmer for her. Though she had hoped to meditate there herself, it would have benefited others who can continue to use it. She did this despite straitened means, by selling jewellery for which she no longer had a taste.

The families of women who go to the meditation centres must get along without them for the time. Among our friends is a wife who keeps bad health at home, for the most part, but feels quite well when she moves into a centre as she does for about a month from time to time. Her husband considers these moves worthwhile. He thinks the influence of religion, the quiet authority of the Monk as well as the meditation itself is responsible for the good effect. He himself is keenly religious but confines his meditation to morning visits.

Another husband, who is a Christian, has a younger wife who has a taste for meditation now and again. During her spells at the monastery, he looks after the home and their family and he cycles to the monastery every day with the morning meal in a food carrier.

The term *yawgi* is sometimes applied to women who choose to dress in plain dark brown clothes cut in the usual style but add a scarf (to their habit) which crosses their shoulder and chest and goes round diagonally. They feel the garb is a reminder to discount vanities.

My cousin Daw Kyi Kyi and her two daughters would wear such clothes when they kept Sabbath during which Daw Kyi Kyi refrained from marital relations. When one of the daughters Mya Mya Win became a doctor and was posted in Mandalay in the vicinity of Mandalay Hill with its pagodas and monasteries, she still followed the habit of wearing *yawgi* dress occasionally. During Lent she would keep sabbath for forty nine consecutive days, living only on fruits meanwhile, as she did her medical work. All the money earned from her private practice during such times she devoted to the repair of pagodas, monasteries and steps up the hill.

There is another person called the *hsoon-ama* or alms food sister of monasteries. This is a woman who undertakes the care of a monastery of monks though she lives outside it, usually nearby. One such, at the Mahagandayone Monastery of Mandalay not only sees to the almsfood, but runs a press for publishing the scholarly treatises for which the monks at this monastery are noted and she also markets the publications.

A connection of mine, Daw Su Su, who has never married, is the *hsoon-ama* for the Dhamma Medini Monastery in a quiet corner of Rangoon. The monks here came from the Mon area of Bilin towards Moulmein and the small group of devotees of the presiding monk, headed by my aunt and mother and other relatives, welcomed them, to be regarded as the focus of their devotions in the metropolis. The *Sayadaw* had all the virtues of the life they associated with their home of forests, waterfalls, and a historic tradition of being the first centre of Buddhism in Burma. While my mother and my aunt, a spinster who lived in Thaton and intrepidly managed our rubber estates in a lawless area outside the town, were foremost in donating buildings at the monastery's founding, Su Su was the best fitted to run around for the functions held at the monastery, which was small but well known for the exemplary lives of its monks. It is also noted for its gardens, shady walks and trees, shrubs, wells and buildings standing in grounds of bare swept earth at once restful when you enter through the solid walls.

Su Su is now 59. After finishing at high-school she managed a textile stall in the bazaar with her mother, a widow. I still remember the stacks of cotton prints in those days when our country could afford imports from India, Japan, England and Czechoslovakia. Her pleasing speech, broad smile and quick ways made her business prosper. Mother and daughter had built a solid house just outside the monastery, acquired a car and all the household goods they needed by the time the national economy changed to a state system and all such stalls lost their business. The Medini Monastery meanwhile grew in buildings, which are still modest for the monks, but include now an assembly hall for public gatherings. Gradually people came to entrust the arranging of their feasts to Su Su. Today she keeps a rose and orchid nursery to be at home as much as possible with her old mother, and does a little quiet brokerage on the side. She recruits young men for the service of the monastery. They attend school in shifts, cook, clean and wait on the monks in their spare time, some sleeping in Su Su's outbuilding and some at the monastery.

Nuns carrying alms food

Su Su goes to bazaar for food supplies. She personally sees to the cooking of the 5 a.m. rice gruel for 130 monks, and the morning meal of the *Sayadaw* and 10 senior monks who do not go the round to receive alms. For the big meal of the main body of monks, some cooking is done at the monastery to supplement what is received on the round. Money is Su Su's responsibility. There are regular donors who give her a monthly contribution, and for the rest she or her boys do house to house collections from those whom they get to know among the crowds that attend the monastery functions. In a normal year, about 60 functions are held at the monastery – novitiations mostly, but other *dana* offerings also. Donors used to give Su Su their money, stipulating the menu they desired, but in 1978, supplies were so difficult nationally that she asked for foodstuffs to be sent directly and she just did the cooking and organization. Some of these functions cater for about 700 people besides the monks. At the end of Lent is a big robe-donating ceremony called *Kahtein* (Pali: *Kathina*). In 1975, she collected about K25,000 towards this. Robes are offered to 150 guest monks as well as to the 130 at the monastery. Full meals were offered for two days to these monks. Formerly, all of the laity who came would have been given the full meal too, but due to hard times they were this year served only a rich semolina and coconut confection, and tea-leaf salad with tea. Gates were open to all and no limit was set to their sitting for hours over this hospitality.

Perhaps the most spectacular instance of women organizing such large-scale *dana* took place in 1954-56, in a great wave of national religious fervour that swept the whole nation with the holding of the Sixth Buddhist Synod. In the history of Buddhism since 2,500 years ago, synods to correct the scriptures, had been held five times only. The first in *Sattapani Cave* in Rajgir, Bihar, North India 3 months after the Buddha's death in 544 B.C. The second in *Vesali* (also in Bihar) in 433 B.C., the third at *Pataliputta* (present *Patna*) during the reign of Emperor Asoka, and the fourth in *Aloka Cave*, Ma-la-ya village in (then) Ceylon where, for the first time, the resulting corrected Scriptures were inscribed on palm leaves instead of remaining an oral tradition. The fifth Synod took place long centuries after this, in 1871 in Mandalay, Burma and its resulting texts were inscribed on marble slabs, each one of which was enshrined in a separate structure in an impressive array of 129 such shrines called the Royal Act of Merit. There were many errors in inscribing and a new Synod would in addition to correcting these, use not only this edition as a basis but also other sources such as from Sri Lanka, Thailand, Cambodia, the Pali Text Society of England and Commentaries. Nomination of noted scholars from monasteries all over Burma was called for and goodwill missions sent in advance to Buddhist countries to arrange for their scholar monks' participation. And this time all the results would be printed and distributed all over the world.

A great Cave was built in a suburb of Rangoon. Within its rough hewn exterior, a deep well seated the laity. Ranked above them in raised galleries, and a high front dais, were ranged the yellow-robed Sangha. A pagoda, dormitories for 25,000 monks, an Ordination Hall, a Buddhist Studies University, a Library and a tree-planted park surrounded this Great Cave. The Synod began on the Full Moon day of Kason (May 17, 1954) and ended on the same day 2 years later, on the 2500th Anniversary of Buddha's enlightenment. In the 6 days of ceremonies which marked its triumphant conclusion, people held celebrations of flag-flying, chanting, offerings, feastings, drums, conches blowing announcements, while in the Cave messages from all over the world and addresses were given by people from Sri Lanka, India, Bangladesh, Germany, Vietnam, Nepal, Japan, Sikkim,

Thailand, Cambodia and Indonesia.

In an event of this national size it was a group of dedicated women carried most of the burden.

The Prime Minister's wife Daw Mya Yee headed an association called the *Withaka* to take care of the duties involved. She was joined by wives of government servants in Rangoon as well as devout women from all over the country, taking turns throughout the two years to help the nucleus of association members. For two years they organized the feeding of the Text Committee of 500 monks, and for 5-6 months at the end, this extended to food for over 2000 monks. The food was always of excellent quality, the serving almost ritualistic. This included early dawn breakfast and therefore entailed late night duties of preparation. They also undertook the collection of funds. Daw Nwe Nwe Yi, wife of another minister took a group of men and women all over the country to find donors for each full set of the *Pitakas* when they would be published. They also organized the novitiation ceremonies for 2,500 novices to mark the 2500th anniversary of *Theravada Buddhism*.

They were not merely domestic servers at the Synod. In the cave they formed their own aisle alongside the men, and in reading of laudatory chants, and pouring of libation water, their leaders Daw Mya Yee, Daw Nwe Nwe Yi, Daw Nu Yin and Daw Kyi Kyi read and officiated, in turns, with the most devout laymen.

Giving, to religion, and alongside that to laity is the most stressed aspects of being a Burmese Buddhist, and each householder tries in small ways or according to their means, to practise this. Among them all I must tell here of my friend Daw Kon, a specially blessed giver who constantly worked, with success and happy energy to earn the means to give, then gave it with the greatest fun to her community. She raised a family of seven children, and when the elder ones reached university age and had to live in Rangoon 460 miles away she started a freight trucking business, arranging some children to settle in an apartment at one end and she in the family house at the other. She always obliged people more than business terms demanded. She would squeeze in extra parcels here and there without charge. This won her friends and swelled her business. Like every pious householder she rose early to cook early morning offerings to her altar which on the top floor of her substantial house was a lavish one. Beside it in a corner was an image of the *Nat, Suasate* Spirit of Learning, given offerings with the hope of help to her sons and daughters in their examinations. In addition she cooked four pounds of extra good rice everyday, and without missing a day that she was at home, she would be standing in the street with the steaming basin. A long row of monks and novices, bright orange robes in pale light of dawn came by at this time. They paused as they saw her, lifted the (alms) bowl lid with downcast eyes, as she with bowed respect, spooned in a portion into each bowl.

When her two youngest sons had their novitiation ceremony, it was already bad times for everybody but she belonged to the considerable number who felt that just because of bad times their *dana* should be more lavish and bring much needed spiritual life. She had a *mandat* or huge pavilion constructed by professional *mandat* people from Mandalay. Its bamboo posts, its rippling roof, were surrounded by eaves and door decorations all mounted with intricately cut metal painted to look like silver and gold. A dais was provided for the monks and novitiates, the rest laid with carpets for public, musicians played at one corner, and neighbourhood boys and girls served cheroots, tea-leaf salad and tea all day long to whoever went in to sit. The preparations were watched over for days by such visitors. Nearer the day her offerings to the monks were displayed – rice by the sackful, oil by the ten-gallon tin, other dried food supplies, robes, towels and numerous small items. Invitations were sent out, more to announce than to choose invited guests, for all would be free to come. Besides detailing the events for the ceremony, and stating the Nirvana oriented aim of her husband and herself in such a deed, the invitation card listed their donations up to date. This announcement of *dana* to make people rejoice (and to state in the libation ceremony that you wish to share the merit from it with all) is of course the extreme opposite of hiding your light under a bushel and not letting your left hand know what your right does in the way of good works.

Ma Kon's list included pagoda precinct wall sections, pillars and ceilings, monasteries, resthouses, stone benches, bridges and roads all the way from Sagaing till Taunggyi and its environs.

Three years after this big event she was still as busy laughing and travelling as ever when terminal cancer struck. The whole community took turns to visit her in a special downstairs bedroom prepared to facilitate this. She would have died happily in this environment, but an effort to go for more treatment in a bigger place had to be made by a wildly hoping family. So she was in a cancer ward, far from the religious influences she lived by, far from the comfort of neighbours, in a big city that was not hers.

At this point, a man who had tutored her son for a short while heard of her condition. He tutored thousands of students and among the thousands of his parent population he felt special warmth for Ma Kon, who had lavished expressions of gratitude on him. He went to the hospital and invited her back to his home. 'But *Saya*, your house is new,' said her son. 'Mother is going to die and you will have a death and funeral marking your house so soon after building it.' No matter. Ma Kon was moved there, and now expressed her wish to offer robes to monks; to hear their sermons and holy chants. He arranged it all, and even on a stormy night at 2 a.m., the *Sayadaws* still came. She was at peace. She grew strangely remote from worrying about her business or seven children or husband. 'Mother doesn't give us a single order or suggestion any more. It was she alone who was the whole business and family manager. But she doesn't seem to think about it at all.' On her last day she closed her eyes and told them to 'Keep good and well, I'm going to Meiktila to hear the doctrine further.'

The houseowner sent word of her death to all his thousands of pupils, who, not knowing her, still came. She had a huge gathering which could hardly have been bettered by the crowds that would have walked behind her in her home town. Just before her coffin was lifted out, thirty *Thilashins* arrived. They sat around her and chanted the *Dhammasetkya*, the Sermon of the Wheel of Law, which tells of all the recurrent cycles of existence. As her coffin travelled to the cemetery, they accompanied it with continued chanting. Her family followed, but they were no longer her children, as she was borne on the waves of the *Thilashins'* chanting to realms outside the human span.

Nat-Kadaws — 'Spirit Wives'

I now come to a topic which Buddhists of my background find quite irrelevant to women's activities in religion. This is the role of *Shatmans* or spirit mediums. It is a topic that has engaged the attention of foreign sociologist studying Burmese Buddhist culture. The whole subject of 'Spirit worship' in Burma is given by them a significance which appears to the majority of Burmese Buddhists to be unduly stressed. The Burmese who take this view do not agree that spirit worship plays a large part in the consciousness of the average Burmese. The Burmese from whom the foreign sociologist must get his information, however, are the ones committed to such spirit worship and so his findings are certainly true of their cultural life.

It is necessary to make a distinction when in the English speaking world, the meaning attached to 'Religion' may be a human being's conception of his or her relation with the universe. This would certainly include Burmese practices in spirit cults. To the Buddhist, Buddhism is named with the term *Sasana*. This is not a general term like religion. it means the way to deliverance as preached by *Gotama Buddha* and while a belief in the existence of spirits called *Nats* is not denied, practices in propitiating or invoking their help do not advance one on the path of deliverance as shown in the *Sasana*. There is no doubt that the spirit cults with their strong sense of supernatural presences, their music, dancing and manifestations of possession make a strong appeal to a section of the Burmese as well as to the foreigner in search of local colour.

The central figures in such proceedings are the women believed by devotees to be possessed by spirits of whom detailed accounts can be found in the writings of Melford Spiro or the late Dr Htin Aung. Here, I will only note that traditionally and up till very recently, such women were not regarded as quite respectable. The liquor they have to consume, the dances they perform while believed to be possessed by the male *Nat*, the generally modest nature of their patrons, the smallness of the fees they earn either in cash or in kind made them a poor lot compared to the great occasions connected with the *Sasana* as described elsewhere in this book.

Ready for meditation

7. Education, Training and Some Social Problems

Traditional Background — Schools without Women

The organized schooling of women in Burma did not begin till after the successive British conquests of 1824, 1852 and 1885. A system of education did, however, exist before then. Though it was not for women, a brief examination of it, with a look at such education of women as could be found, will be useful. It will reveal the traditional Burmese concepts of education, which, persisting into the present, influenced the use of facilities as they became available. These concepts also guide the Burmese adoption of modern forms of instruction today.

It is well known that Burma had a system of monastery schools since the earliest centuries of its history. Reference has been made in Chapter I to the *Pyu* kingdom of the 7th to 9th centuries A.D. when girls as well as boys attended monasteries for learning, though it is not clear whether they had separate 'monasteries' or not. In any case, the inclusion of girls in the system was not to be found by the time of the Pagan period in the 11th century. Monasteries teaching boys continued in unbroken tradition during all the intervening centuries, and the word 'monastery' is exactly the same today as 'school'. Both are *kyaung*.

The monastery was set apart from the village on a secluded site. However, it did not function so distinctly from the home as later lay schools did. It was an extension of the home's spiritual and religious life, and the focus of its social events. To it, on days of offerings, came all the family including babies, the old, and girls.

In this setting, boys learned the alphabet and spelling, trying them out with texts such as the *Mingala Sutta*, the list of thirty-eight blessings of mind to achieve, and the *Singalovada Sutta* which enumerates the duties of human relationships. Those who remained beyond the age of 20 with the aim of joining the order would go on to the *Abhidhamma*, the *Vinaya* and the commentaries. Though religious in content, their lessons embodied the national culture in the poetic and literary training it gave. They were taught some arithmetic. The secular arts of astronomy, astrology and medicine could be learned but the pursuit of these was not considered fit for monks. There were also the necessary devotional formulae of observances to be memorized, and homilies on proper conduct to listen to. Domestic tasks and physical exertion were part of the training. Boys swept and scrubbed floors, waited personally on the monks and were at their beck and call. They fetched water and helped in kitchen tasks and cleared the garden.

At seasons when work in the fields was at its peak, boys could go home to help – in this way also monastery training was not divorced from home interests. Its end result had to produce villagers who would be acceptable residents in accord with other villagers and who would continue to relate to the monastery and support it.

Girls' Education Prior to Organized Schools

The above was the system for boys. What about the girls? There was an underlying assumption that while boys needed education for the religious life, girls did not. The few girls who did feel an impulse towards the religious life had to find their own way as described in Chapter VI in the cases of women who became nuns. These nuns in turn taught the daughters of court and well-off families. Besides this, there were some lay schools in towns for girls. Howard Malcolm in his visit to monarchic Burma in 1830 tells of such schools (Malcolm). Apart from nuns and these few and far between schools, girls could become literate through private contacts with other literate relatives and friends, male or female. My cousin U Lu Pe Win, now aged 77, tells of various female elder kinfolk he knew and their ways of getting an education. I quote his communication to me about them. Although they were born just over a century ago, their ways of acquiring learning cannot have been very different from the way other women did in previous centuries in this society where the traditions have changed so little. 'Your maternal aunts Daw Lon and Daw Toke never had their formal schooldays. They were taught the three R's and Buddhist Burmese books by my father's neighbour, the learned *Pali* scholar, Saya U Po Yin.'

And another case – here the intertwining of female responsibilities for the household and family with Buddhist female education, so repeatedly to be seen, must be included.

> My cousin Daw Lun Yin did not have any chance of schooling because her father died two years after the birth of Ma Hta Myint, his youngest daughter. Naturally the eldest had to look after the two younger sisters and at the same time help the widowed mother. Fortunately for her, paternal relatives who were learned maids of honour to the then Queen used to come down to Rangoon thrice a year on business and while staying up with her, taught her. She lived for 65 years as a widely read Burmese poet. A book lover and collector, mostly of rare publications and out-of-print texts that she was, she left behind half a dozen steel trunks brimful with leather-bound books.
>
> My mother in Moulmein never had the chance of attending school.

She learned the 3 R's from her spinster aunt who taught her both prose and poetry, as well as the bookkeeping and correspondence for the timber trade of my maternal great-grandfather U Kyi (Kaung, p.96).

These accounts refer to the last days of the Burmese kingdom just before the final British annexation in 1885.

Early Schools and Female Response to them

Since annexations before 1885, lay schools for both boys and girls had begun to be set up. They were induced to do so with grants in aid from the government. A report of 1869, lists the schools in Lower (British) Burma then as follows:

	Number	Pupils
Monastery schools	3438	43773
Lay schools	340	5069

A government report of 1867-70 shows that of the 5069 pupils only 1231 were girls (*Reports on Public Instruction in Burma*). Why, in the light of the traditional equality and activity of Burmese women in life outside the religious that we been seen, were girls so slow to take up the new facilities offered?

Two reasons come to mind. First, that the new schools though no longer associated with the monastery which was the boys' sphere, were still divorced in aim from women's spheres in active life. They offered teaching in subjects not regarded as educative, either in the traditional Buddhist sphere of religion or in that of fields or markets. They offered teaching which was seen as training for males for posts in the service of the new rulers and their trading companies – in clerical posts or teaching, land survey, law, police or the lower rungs of general administration. This was not considered relevant to women because though women had been active on behalf of the family, no tradition existed as yet to go to work for a salary paid by an outside employer.

Second, with the diminishing of the monastery's influence on village and especially town life, there came a hiatus in boys' education and discipline. It was felt that school was almost a necessary substitute for boys who no longer got their training in a monastery. Girls on the other hand suffered no disruption in their old training at home in religious observances, altar duties, household care, family trade and accounts, together with the literacy they acquired from relatives and neighbours.

It took time, but other aspects of education did later make their impact. The school system came to be a part of the amenities of life. And gradually teaching became a profession girls could aspire to. My mother, born in 1886, was the youngest of five daughters. Her elder sisters, as mentioned above, did not go to school though they were the daughters of a famous Mon and Pali scholar, U Shway O, but were taught by an equally learned neighbour. Mother, however, went to school and in the fourth and final year asked her father to let her go to the bigger town of Moulmein to attend secondary school. Family opposition put an end to her pleas but when the results of the government-supervized fourth standard examination appeared, she was posted as a scholarship winner. Her father relented and gave in. He put heart into her brave venture by sending with her, two younger sons and another girl, his eldest granddaughter, to keep her company in the big town and new school, a Baptist missionary one. In Moulmein they boarded with her elder brother who had already become a junior government official, and by 1905 Mother had completed her high school work and taken her teacher training, returning to Thaton to work as a teacher. In the year that she had been born, an educational census taken of the whole kingdom which had just become British, showed the recruitment of girls to be just ten percent of boys in primary schools. By the time she went to Moulmein they were twenty percent in primary and over twenty-five percent in secondary, and by the time she graduated the percentage had risen to thirty percent in primary and again over twenty-five percent in secondary schools.

This rate of rise in the female school attendance continued slowly and steadily for the remainder of this pre-war British rule period. Figures below show actual numbers:

		1885-86	1895-96	1905-06	1915-16	1926-27	1935-36
Primary	Boys	133408	101477	121369	167563	Not available	Not available
	Girls	13347	20006	42816	79769	86435	138157
Secondary	Boys	7170	16072	37562	89860	Not available	Not available
	Girls	1711	4738	9692	33034	61842	73871

According to the above table, the number of boys rose from 133,408 to 167,563 in 30 years, from 1885 to 1915. The number of girls rose from 13,347 to 76,967 in the same period. Girls took 50 years to reach in 1935 the number of boys attending the first schools set up in 1885.

It seems suitable at this point to recapitulate the types of schools which took in these pupils. In the Annual Report of the Education Department in 1927-28 quoted by U Kaung in *The Beginnings of Christian Missionary Education in Burma* the following types of schools are revealed for the year 1927-28:

Institutions directly under Government supervision	104
Institutions under local Education authorities	82
Institutions privately organized and aided by Government	6676
Institutions private, unrecognized and unaided by Government	17730

The first two categories are schools set up by the Education Department of the

Government or by local municipal authorities, and were mostly co-educational schools and in urban areas. The third category included Christian and non-Christian schools set up in villages as well as towns, vernacular and Anglo-vernacular co-educational and separate sex schools. ('Aided' included some monasteries). The last category was mostly monastery schools (Kaung, p.42).

Mawn, newly graduated from nursery school, pictured with primary schoolmates and Amara, now a *mujo*

Apart from the question of government aid, and without going into differences of curriculum, education can be seen to be provided by three streams other than the government. First, in the monasteries, though the *Sangha's* status, organization and powers were greatly weakened by the change from Buddhist monarchic rule to British colonial rule, schools remained in existence and in part provided schooling to girls as well as boys. When the British first annexed a part of Burma, the first Chief Commissioner, Sir Arthur Phayre, advocated giving books, and including simple science, geography and history in the curriculum, as well as arranging supervision by a culturally competent staff, thus utilizing a system respected by all, instead of setting up a new system. This attempt to adapt monastery education was only partially successful in the early years, as many monks resisted supervision and the imposition of conditions that interfered with their views and objectives. Lay schools were therefore given encouragement. Here the second stream of private effort is seen in indigenously organized lay schools both before and after the nationalist movement gained momentum. Such lay schools in pre-British times would have been set up by men or women 'for merit' and were free, but when the British government started to encourage education, this tradition changed and education had to be paid for. In 1874-75 the government offered double grants for girl pupils, and in these early years 'The Lay School, presided over by a Manager or Manageress, was intended primarily for the education of girls.' In the schools of those years girls stayed, like boys, till they were 12 or 13 years of age. Boys then went to monasteries and girls stopped, or if they could afford it, continued with a tutor.

At first such schools had no conscious nationalistic bent. With the growth of Christian missionary schools however, many Burmese efforts were directed towards fostering traditional cultural values and teachings. The elder brother with whom my mother boarded in the years 1898 to 1905 was encouraged by his English friend, Commissioner Bernard Houghton, to start lay social work as a Buddhist. With the increasing importance of secular life over the monastic influences, Buddhists should increase purely lay activities, since the Christian missions were already setting up schools, hospitals and dispensaries. He thus started the U Yan Win school and founded the *Buddha Sasana Society* which in turn founded the *Buddhaghosa High School*, both of which schools survived with their original names until incorporated into the nationalization programme in 1964. Such schools in various parts of Burma were the forerunners of a nation-wide nationalist movement which took its inspiration from the promotion of Buddhist religion, and expressed itself in a demand to have more say in the moulding of educational policy. The landmark of the nationalist struggle was indeed the Boycott of 1920, when school and university students protested against the type of future university education laid down for Burma by the British. And one result of the successful boycott was a proliferation of national schools, for girls as well as boys, in which a more nationally-oriented education could be given in place of the colonialist values bred in the government and mission-sponsored systems. This meant incorporating the cultural richness of the native inheritance in history, legend, poetry, prose and religious writings and substituting Burmese history for British and European.

At this point it is as well to ask what the aims of a nationalist-oriented education involved, so that one can assess the trend of Burmese education for girls as well as for boys. One important influence which these national schools meant to counter was that of the Christian mission schools. From as far back as 1721 the Roman Catholics had tried to set up schools and had suffered reverses.

It was only after the British conquest that they and the American Baptist Missions saw a survival and growth of their efforts. The earliest 'lay schools' were undoubtedly set up with an evangelistic purpose and though this should have disqualified them from the terms of government grants in aid, aid was in fact given them. These first schools were the barest of efforts, with a newly converted teacher in charge and only cursorily inspected by the overworked missionaries themselves. Unlike the indigenous efforts where teachers had at least their cultural knowledge to impart, these converts often had to feel their way blindly in teaching a new philosophy. But with time and persistent training the schools soon thrived, and by the time my mother received her education at the Baptist English Girls' High School the school had acquired a name for itself. The early evangelistic efforts soon proved unsuccessful as far as the majority Buddhist Burmese population was concerned. I quote another family note from my cousin U Lu Pe Win, whose father, founded the two private schools mentioned earlier in Moulmein. This time he writes about his wife's education which took place in the 1915-1925 decade.

> Ma Ma Lat attended an Anglo-Vernacular missionary middle school for girls in Pegu. Just as my father had to write his Buddhist Cathechism (*Boddhabatha Amay-aphyay*) to counteract the Christian teaching which your mother had to learn, Ma Ma Lat's father kept her busy learning Ten Great *Jatakas* and '550' Lesser *Jatakas*, all under the supervision of his niece who was a nun. To look after her invalid widower father, Ma Ma Lat had to leave school in the middle of her Fifth Standard. She had to read repeatedly for the hearing of her ailing parent the *Jatakas*, the biography of the Buddha as recorded in *Zinattha Pakathani* which is virtually the bible of the Buddhist in poetic prose by Kyithe-lay-htat Sayadaw of Shwedaung, the favourite author of your mother. Furthermore she had to read over and over again the Burmese translations of biographies of the *Theragatha* and *Therigatha* (brethren and sisters) to emulate the example of Buddha's female disciples, if not all the members of the Sangha under the guidance of her father. She also had to do day to day commercial correspondence and accounts in connection with rice-milling, timber-milling and timber-trade.

Missionary schools began to curtail their evangelistic efforts on this main unresponsive mass of the population, and concentrated on raising the educational standards of their schools. By the end of the nineteen twenties they controlled 4/7ths of the Anglo-Vernacular education which, as it included a knowledge of English, would produce the ruling section of the educated. Besides this they had vernacular schools in villages, a teacher-training programme and even a University Studies level in Judson College. They survived and grew again after war and Independence, adapting themselves to changed social conditions, until with the nationalization of all private schools in 1964 they lost their identity. In the missionary school that I went to, we were taught British history for five years by a rabid Irish nun who surpassed even the Burmese nationalists in her depiction of suppressive British rule. There was no proselytising of non-Catholics in the school. They did not participate though they attended chapel and other services; often lively Buddhist girls would join in orisons during a procession, with jocose Burmese phrases shouted under cover of the Latin litany, rather than walk along silently.

After Independence, with the surge of a new national spirit and a feeling in every walk of life that the common people would now move to the center stage, school-going received a new impetus. Not only were more schools set up very rapidly (especially after 1962 when the target was 1000 new primary schools each year) but the recruitment of girls increased more markedly. Today's situation may be gauged by the 1973 figures which are the latest full figures I have been able to get.

	Boys	Girls
Kindergarten	497,188	473,902
First Standard	414,077	384,490
Second Standard	342,292	310,259
Third Standard	279,759	233,502
Fourth Standard	210,415	154,260
Primary School Total	1,743,731	1,556,422
Fifth Standard	145,505	98,540
Sixth Standard	107,048	63,011
Seven Standard	91,144	60,112
Eighth Standard	72,464	51,573
Middle School Total	416,161	273,236
Ninth Standard	49,431	35,076
Tenth Standard	48,134	38,637
High School Total	97,565	73,713
GRAND TOTAL	2,257,457	1,903,371

(*Source: Author's personal correspondence*)

Looking at the figures for just 1973 it might be noted that the decrease, though greater for girls in the Primary and Middle sectors, is not so between Middle and High sectors. Girls who manage to continue into Middle school generally go on to High school as much as boys do.

The State School System

State schools numbered 17899 Primary and 1741 Secondary in 1970. In these schools buildings are usually provided by the state. Sometimes one of several structures making up a monastery may be used and the grounds of the monastery can be treated as playgrounds for both boys and girls. The lay teachers go in and perform all the teaching and supervisory duties just as in any other school. The monks may walk by or walk up and down as part of their regular meditative exercise.

Since the nationalization of schools, has produced a nation-wide uniformity, it might serve to describe one school and assume that the general description is applicable to other schools in Burma.

The State High School in Taunggyi, in the 1930s, had a dynamic woman called Daw Khin Thein as its Principal. She did not do much teaching, but she would spend time walking around the school and looking at various classrooms to ensure that traditional methods of imparting knowledge were maintained. One of the important features of Daw Khin Thein's school, and this is common to several other state schools, is the kind of links it maintained with the community. Whenever there were weddings, festivals or functions of any sort, the school teachers and students would prepare decorations, food etc., for them. And they would often be present at such gatherings to hep with the work. The school had a fairly fully academic curriculum as well, and students therefore received a multi-faceted education.

The number of boys and girls in Daw Khin Thein's school was as follows. The figures below also show the relative success achieved in different fields by male and female students.

Relaxing at the pagoda

	Total	Boys	Girls
Number sitting for Standard VIII	272	194	78
Number passing Standard VIII in Science Stream	91	58	33
Number passing in Arts Stream	6	5	1
Number sitting for Matric Exam.	356	255	131
Number passing Matric Exam.	75	49	26
Distinctions gained	31	20	11

Figures are for the year 1976.

Teaching Staff

Teaching staff is largely female in the State High School described earlier. Figures of staff for the whole of Burma show Heads and Teachers who are termed Senior Assistant Teachers for grades in High Schools, Junior Assistant Teachers for grades in Junior High School (called Middle School grades here) and Primary Assistant Teachers for elementary standards from I to IV.

Teachers	Male	Female	Total
High School Heads	335	199	534
Senior Asst. Teachers	3090	4578	7668
Middle School Heads	791	205	996
Junior Asst. Teachers	6562	6327	12889
Primary School Heads	12735	2457	15129
Primary Asst. Teachers	23022	24009	47031
Total	46535	37775	84310

(*Source: Author's personal correspondence*)

These figures show a preponderance of women teachers in the High Schools as well as in Primary Schools, but Headships of schools continue to be held more by men.

Luyechun (Top Student Awards.)

In order to encourage students to become good all-rounders, the Government has instituted certain merit awards. These are open to boys and girls. I give below the figures, for a few years, of male and female students winning awards from High School grades.

Year	Ninth Standard		Tenth Standard	
	Male	Female	Male	Female
1964	72	29	39	10
1966	32	21	35	18
1968	32	22	33	17
1970	37	15	39	12
1972	31	20	44	7
1974	44	9	39	12
1976	36	17	39	12
1977	30	21	34	17

(*Source: Author's personal correspondence*)

Youth Training and Corrective Schools for Girls

A few special schools called *Technical Schools* set up with foreign help and well-equipped with machine and other workshops exist in three big towns for the recruitment of boys aiming to set up in businesses of small-scale skilled work. Girls do not qualify for such schools. Below will be found a mention of courses given to girls in other skills. These would be dismissed by feminists elsewhere but within traditional Burmese society they still have an economic value for the women.

Leaving this type of training aside for the moment, we turn to the sphere of youth training which is regarded as very important by the present revolutionary government, and is given to both girls and boys.

It starts with 1) *Teza Lu-Nge* which means Youth Power. Those who join (usually children of 6-10 years of age), are guided in their meetings to be friendly and helpful towards each other, to take an interest in their school activities, to be well-mannered and exemplary in dress and behaviour generally. 2) *Shay-Saung Lu-Nge* means Youth's Vanguards. Aged 10-16, the members of such groups are expected to oversee the training of the younger group mentioned above. They must be conversant with the national aims of the state towards a socialist ideal, notably the economics of socialism. They are expected to be among the more exemplary students and must take their cue from the senior and third movement. 3) *Lanzin Lu-Nge* – Youth Who Follow the Way. Aged 15-25, these youth provide the link between school children and the Burmese Socialist Programme Party, which is the official party in the one-party system of the Union of Burma. These *Lanzin* youth must be ready to help in patrolling the neighbourhoods which now set up their own system of '*kin*' or watchguards to help keep law and order. They help at all times in the government's need for economic stability. They volunteer for census work, help in preparations for elections from village, township or divisional levels to the National Assemblies and Councils. They were especially active in sounding out the public's wishes when the new constitution (adopted March 1974) was being drafted, amended and finally consented to by a nation-wide referendum. From the ranks of this movement are expected to come the hard core of good cadres for the Party whose progress must be regarded as the national progress. Girls as well as boys are encouraged to join. The movement was set up by a Central Committee on 4 August, 1971. It is estimated that members number 220,651; about half of these are girls (BSPP, (ii) p.266). At the present time, more than at any other, the government is trying to involve schoolgirls and boys in national efforts towards growth and sanitation. Such efforts are publicized regularly on national radio. In the sessions featuring student help in special high yield paddy production, village construction, town cleaning sessions or anti-illiteracy campaigns, the broadcasters usually consist of two high school girls and two high school boys discussing the projects they have worked on and what they have learned from them.

Chatting on campus

On 28 October, 1973 an all-nation Congress of *Lanzin* Youth was held in Rangoon. 1239 delegates from parties all over the Union attended of whom 418 were girls, and at the Congress assembly in Aung San Stadium an estimated crowd of over 100,000 youths were present, the first time in Burma that such a large assembly of youth collected (ibid, p.266).

Youth training is also carried out in the Red Cross. This movement has become very popular. In colonial days, Boy Scouts and Girl Guides were greatly

111

encouraged. As everyone knows, however, these movements had their origins in such excellent empire-builders as the Baden-Powells, and this did not appeal to the spirit of Burmese nationalists. To let them die a natural death in the independent decades created a void in youth training. The government therefore welcomed the growth of the Red Cross. A niece, a university student who is much to the fore in the movement, informs me:

> About half the school pupils join the youth movements but nearly everyone joins the Red Cross. We have a month's full training in the beginning and this is not only First Aid but also basic army training (author's personal correspondence). Their normal activities are neighbourhood cleaning (roads, drains, and overgrowths), help in relief work for disasters after floods, storms, fires and bad accidents, blood bank and general liaison with the *Lanzin* Youth.

I would now like to look at another aspect of training for women. This is corrective training. My requests for information on this subject brought two replies, each different from the other. One consisted of sets of figures by a government employee, who gave a list of different types of homes run by the state and specified the number of women in each institution. The other was a fourteen page letter from an old friend, Daw Tokegale, who has devoted her life to social service. Given below are summaries of both:

According to the official note, there are three types of institutions run by the Social Welfare Department. These are:

1. Training schools for adult women (meant for the correction and care of convicted prostitutes).

Year established	Location	Capacity	Present intake
1960	Rangoon	100	112
1963	Mandalay	50	50

2. Girls Homes (meant for girls under 18 without homes or guardians)

1964	Rangoon	120	85

3. Training School for girls (meant for girls under 18 who have been convicted of certain offences. One such school is located in Rangoon and it has a capacity of 150.

Apart from these institutions the Social Welfare Department gives annual grants to the Girls' Homes run by voluntary organizations in the following towns: Mandalay, Toungoo, Moulmein, Amherst, Kyaiklat and Rangoon. The main purpose of all these institutions is to equip girls with skills which will enable them to earn a livelihood.

Of the 908 girls cared for by the Girls' Home in Rangoon during the past ten years, 129 have been put back on their own feet, 71 have become government employees, 18 have got jobs with the production co-operatives and 40 have got married.

As a part of its preventive measures the Social Welfare Department has been conducting training courses in domestic science for women in all 14 States and

Divisions of the Union.

In addition, two courses at the Instructors' level have been held at the Thamaing Social Welfare Service Training School where a total of 60 women were trained.

Subjects taught at the Training School for Adult Women

Rangoon.   Sewing/Tailoring; Brooms/Fans making;
              Food Preservation (Pickling) Laundering.

Mandalay.   Sewing/Tailoring; Basketry; Wool knitting;
              Food Preservation (Pickling); Laundering.

Subjects taught at Girls' Home, Rangoon
Weaving; Tailoring; Food Preparation (Cookery); Book Binding; Broom/
Fan making.

Although the Training Schools for Adult Women in Rangoon and Mandalay were opened originally for the purpose of The Suppression of Brothels Act, the Mandalay school has so far been unable to take in any convicted prostitutes due to lack of space. Of the Rangoon institutions only 29.33 percent of inmates are those convicted under the Act. Only 10.66 percent come from homes where the girls lived with their own parents. 26 percent came from homes with so-called 'adoptive parents' (actually they were unpaid domestic servants), 20 percent from homes of relatives.

The Social Welfare Department hopes to increase the capacity of the Rangoon Training School for Adult Women to 150 during the financial year 1977-78, and the Mandalay Training School for Adult Women from the present capacity of 50 to 150 in 1978-79.

Daw Toke Gale began life as a teacher and later became a social welfare officer. Her work previous to this had entailed extensive tours of villages and smaller towns to visit schools. She was happy in her new job. Here is what she wrote to me in answer to my query about corrective institutions for girls.

The Director (U Aung Min) placed me with the first assignment of opening a Women's Home – an open institution, in Civil Lines, Court Road, Mandalay, as an administrative officer. The cottage system, as learnt at Paramatta, Australia, appealed to the Director, and with the full consent of the Ministry of Social Welfare, was first introduced into this new institution. It has one double-storied building, housing 10 inmates upstairs, with two single cottages behind it, each cottage, with one house-mother and ten girls. The warden appointed was an experienced elderly ex-teacher from Myoma High School, and there were three assistant wardens, who were also vocational teachers during school hours. Girls were under 21, and are unconvicted girls, sent by the Voluntary Social Welfare Agencies, foreign Christian missions, and some by the police station. Girls admitted to this institution are largely orphans, a few waifs and strays. The inmates are taught cane-work and sewing, given primary education, and do gardening in the evenings. Every care and protection is given. Medical attention is regular. Parents of the inmates are allowed to come and visit them twice a month, and if possible, once a week. Their *recreation* being motion pictures in the institution, once a month. They are also made to participate in outdoor games, like basketball, *htoke-sii-dow* skipping, etc . . .

I was then transferred to the Home for Convicted Girls at Natmauk, Rangoon. There are two separate buildings, one for the girls under thirteen, and another for the bigger girls – all have been charged for sexual offences – some are prostitutes, all come from broken homes. These girls are first tried in Law Courts and Juvenile Courts, after being arrested by the women-police. When found guilty, the girls are kept on remand for about two weeks, awaiting the visit of a medical doctor and a psychiatrist. The girls are medically examined by the doctor. After they have been admitted to the Home, girls who are found to have venereal diseases are kept in a separate room till fully cured – then only they are allowed to go to the dormitories to sleep in the company of other girls.

Girls fourteen and under sleep in a separate dormitory, in order to avoid the night devotion at the altar. (Bigger girls in one building; the younger girls in separate groups under the supervision of some wardens who are on duty every day. At 8.00 p.m. they go to bed. They are all lined up at 7.30 p.m. for their night devotion at the altar. (Bigger girls in one building; the younger girls in another building – sleep, eat and play differently. They are never kept together.) Under their supervisor, girls in each building consisting of 50 to 60, go up to their dorm, change their day-worn clothes, all ready to sleep at 8.00 p.m. Each deliquent girl's movement is carefully watched and corrected. This convicted home is well staffed, with experienced middle-aged women. The warden dines with the girls in the dining hall sometimes. She has to watch them when they are lined up, before and after meals. Everyone is silent, without a whisper.

Social Problems – Homosexuality and Rape

Female closeness which in the West is often taken to imply a lesbian relationship is, in general, accepted by Burmese society as natural companionship and affection between women. Unmarried women particularly, seldom go out alone. Most do not care to sleep alone in a room. In the absence of a husband, therefore, a woman may choose a friend to keep her constant company. They will always be invited together, they travel on holidays together, share the same bedroom and generally are inseparable. It may be asked whether expressions of physical affection occur between such female couples. Very often they do, particularly among young girls in dormitories. Once the girl marries, this kind of close friendship with female friends continues, but changes in character. There are very few cases of women becoming permanently, or even on a long-term basis, becoming involved with other women. I know of only one such case where a woman became permanently desirous of a female companion for life. In later life, she chose a married woman whose family were old enough to be left on their own. The couple now live their chosen life, and although they are thought to be rather odd, they are not ostracised.

Rape: The incidence of rape, on the increase everywhere in the world, is mounting in Burma as well. In law, sexual intercourse with a minor is classified as rape even when, in the case of Hindus in Burma the victim is the childwife of the man. Child marriage does not exist among the majority who are Burmese Buddhist, as will be seen from existing laws noted in Chapter III.

As in the West, one burden of proof which lies on the women is to show her non-consent to the act. However, according to Burmese law any 'preliminary' assault before successful rape is also classified as a male crime in outraging the modesty of a woman. In a public crowd, any contact such as pushing, pressing, pinching or slapping any part of a woman's body, if it is resented by her, is actionable against the man. The sentence for rape varies from 10 years imprisonment to life.

Prostitution is criminal. Street-walkers are hardly ever seen but the Suppression of Brothels Act makes brothel keepers criminal.

Adult Education in Rural Areas

To raise literacy has long been the dream of nationalists, and with Independence, the Parliamentary Governments set up and encouraged a Mass Education scheme that sent organizers to be resident in villages, and by liaison with radio and school personnel, to 'widen people's eyes', into political consciousness of socialist and national unity.

However, the outstanding activity in this respect belongs to the post-1962 Revolutionary Government years when, especially around 1971 under the stimulus given by the personality of Dr Nyi Nyi, then Deputy Minister for Education, there was a great push in the literacy campaign, using volunteer University students during summer vacations, getting district after district taught the 'Three R's' and getting results which won Burma the Mohamed Reza Pahlevi Prize of 1971.

When British rule first brought Burma into the British Indian Empire, notes were often made on the high degree of literacy that prevailed compared to the other Indian provinces. Here are some figures:

	Literacy Rate per thousand		
	Male	Female	Average
All Burma	560	165	368
Burma Proper.	600	182	397
Bengal (India)	180	32	100
United Provinces (India)	94	11	55
Bi har and Orissa (India)			8

During the days of elitist education, villagers suffered a setback in their literacy. The figures below illustrate this. The high incidence of illiteracy they showed before the campaign started, so many decades after what should have been a progressive and modern administration, are, in the light of the high traditional Burmese literacy, dismaying enough not to need comparison with other countries.

Meiktila District 1969 to 1971

Township	Population	Illiterates			New Literates		
		Male	Female	Total	Male	Female	Total
Meiktila	126,817	1,498	22,559	24,057	1,437	21,961	23,398
Mahlaing	77,183	1,415	16,579	17,994	1,388	16,173	17,561

(Above data applies to persons aged fifteen to fifty five years only).

Young people played a large part in the literacy campaigns, particularly in attempting to bridge the gap between rural and urban. I give here the story of one such worker, a young woman called Tin Tin Wint.

Tin Tin Wint, 28 years old, is one of five sisters. She is also a member of the *Lanzin* Youth group who are trained for active membership in the Burmese Socialist Program Party. Normally she would have to wait until her fourth and final year of her Zoology studies to go on a field trip in the Shan States. However as a *Lanzin* Youth member she entered the list of volunteers in the literacy campaign during the summer vacation of her third year at the university.

Together with hundreds of other students she was given a week's intensive instruction in teaching adults to read as quickly as possible. After this, the volunteers left for different parts of Burma. Tin Tin Wint's group of about fifty boys and girls boarded a special launch in which the elders and project organizers of Pa-an had come to escort them to Pa-an. Pa-an is the capital of the Karen State, one of seven ethnic states within the Union of Burma.

The morning after their arrival, the volunteers were divided into groups of four with two boys and two girls being assigned to respective villages where they would teach. Tin Tin Wint and a girl from the Shan States went to Ye-tha village where lodging had been arranged for them.

Tin Tin Wint had thirty women of various ages to teach, and she used the village primary school building. Her friend taught under the shade of the palms. The classes were joined by some literate young men of the village who volunteered as assistants to continue the work after the visiting teachers left.

Teaching was slow. The villagers were Karens with little Burmese but, as one of the aims of the campaign was to promote union between peoples and interchange of urban and rural spirit, success was remarkable in the quick and eager friendships struck between the girls and the villagers. Wherever the girls went they were received with smiles and welcoming cries of *Salamu* (meaning Teacher). Mats would be rolled out, pillows quickly put down and cups of clear tea with saucers of fried pea-nuts or slices of fresh coconut laid for them. In their spare time the girls helped villagers who, in their rest from cultivation during this month of April, made rice noodles and packets of sweet glutinous rice with banana slices. In this way the girls, too, learnt something from the villagers. Their hosts also tried to teach them the traditional Karen dances, and for Tin Tin Wint, although she had not learnt to dance, the glow of friendliness remained vivid in her mind.

8. Women at Work: Traditional Roles

The largest sector of women's work belongs to agriculture. This is so common a theme in Southeast Asia that it's mention instantly evokes the picture of women in rice paddies of plains or swiddens of hill-clearings bending at peak periods of sowing or reaping. This is especially true in Burma where paddy planting girls and paddy pounding girls are romanticised both in poetry and in dance.

However, this chapter on Burmese women's economic activity begins not in the vast emerald carpets of Burmese rice but in small stuffy urban kitchens. Here, women and girls work in a profession which now has its own status in wage-earnings, as opposed to earlier times when domestic labour did not count as work.

New Status for Domestics

I begin with Ma Thee because her story is the story of so many Burmese girls who work in towns and return annually to the green fields, thus combining a rural and an urban existence.

Ma Thee, 26 years old, comes from a village in the region of Moulmein, Burma's third most important city at the mouth of the Salween, to the southeast of Rangoon. One of Asia'a longest rivers, the Salween, though it rushes swiftly through scenic ravines in the Shan highlands for most of its course, slows down as it approaches a great and calm sea-mouth. From the ridge behind the town, you see this vast expanse of water, in which the islands appear to lie dreaming. Ma Thee comes from the largest of these islands, Bilukyun.

She was orphaned when she was 5 or 6 years old. Her only living relative was her old grandmother. The village headman offered to take her to Moulmein to place her in domestic service and said he would ensure her earnings were sent back to help her grandmother. However, he secretly sold the child to a family of Chinese for a sum which he kept to himself. The Chinese treated her shamefully, keeping her head shaven, an old method of humiliating and breaking the girl's spirit, chastised her with painful punishments, and sent no money to her home.

When the grandmother became ill, the other elders of the village, seeing she had no one to tend her, went to Moulmein in a group. Ma Thee's employer refused to let her go home with them, so they complained to the neighbourhood elders, who, knowing the situation, pressurized the Chinese to let her go. After her grandmother died Ma Thee once again went into domestic service in Rangoon.

After her grandmother died, Ma Thee returned to Rangoon in search of work. Not, as yet, having established a network of contacts, she had to use the services of a broker. The broker is usually a woman who comes to villages especially to collect girls in order to 'place' them in various houses for a small fee. Through the broker Ma Thee found employment with a Sino-Burmese family from whom she learnt much. When they had to move, they placed her with some of their relatives who trained her further. In both places Ma Thee's situation was a happy one. Her employers treated her as one of the family and, in return, she worked extremely hard for them. In the course of service with the two families, Ma Thee married, had a child, and was widowed. When the child was born, Ma Thee's mother-in-law sent her daughter to care for him while Ma Thee worked. But her being there meant that Ma Thee had to work harder in order to be able to feed another mouth. Her employer thus suggested that she send her sister-in-law back and bring the child with her when she came in to work. Often, while Ma Thee worked, her employer's daughter would look after her baby. Thus, she was indeed treated as one of the family – and this is often the case in Burma.

Selling vegetables in the bazaar

Very often, girls and women who work as domestics do not go through brokers. Sometimes they set up their own networks and news of possible posts travels through the network. Sometimes one girl will recommend a friend, or a particular family she knows of. This is a more satisfactory arrangement than going through brokers. Girls in such situations often prefer to do domestic work than to find any other kind of employment. The pay is 80-150 kyats a month and board and lodging are free. This compares favourably with the salary of an elementary school teacher or a junior clerk who get roughly 150 kyats a month, with nothing else thrown in. Girls and women in domestic service have to observe a few formalities such as sitting on the floor in the living room of the house, and being respectful towards their employers. But these small things aside, they often have the run of the house and are free to join in the family conversation.

Remnants of Old Low Status

These domestic servants then are quite a different breed from the maids of my childhood five decades ago. Then they were usually poor relatives placed in a big house to get training and hopefully be settled by the employer into a good marriage. My mother who used to have four or five such girls did manage to get one married well to a clerk of my father's but this was not always easy. In some households, the girl's parents would visit once a year or so and be well entertained and given presents as well as a good sum of money before they left. This made it all the more important for the girl to work well.

A few houses here and there still keep maids at the old and rather poor rate of about 35 kyats a month, with only a few days off, and not much time out. Sometimes they are termed 'adopted daughters' to explain the lack of a full salary. Some of these underpaid girls give surprisingly devoted service and rarely think of leaving.

Ethnic Origins of Domestics in Big Towns

The current influx of Mon girls into Rangoon is a recent phenomenon. Earlier, Karen girls came in large numbers from the delta regions in search of work. Many of them found work with the newly developed bourgeoisie after the British had left. The Burmese, therefore, welcomed Mon girls when they began to arrive.

Mon girls, however, do not go further north than Rangoon. Up country, people have to find other girls. Though these come from many rural areas, a distinctly noticeable stream comes to a hill town like Taunggyi from Kayah, a hill region of some ethnic groups related to the Karens. A lot of them used to come to work at a dispensary set up by Roman Catholic nuns. This was on a farm run only with female labour, to feed the orphans and incurably afflicted people from the neighbouring villages. The Kayah girls who came there were sturdy farm girls, largely from the Padaung peoples who had become Roman Catholics. When the farm and centre were run by an Italian nun, they concentrated on livestock in order to enjoy milk, butter and eggs. When the Italians went home and a Padaung nun took charge she sold the livestock and raised field crops with excellent results – corn, cauliflowers and cabbages. The contribution of women in agricultural families is described in the life routine of the Chit Swe family in Section II of Chapter IV. This can be regarded as an agricultural family typical of rural families all over and I need hardly say that female labour in this form still prevails all over in Burma. The girls at the dispensary farm mentioned above did all the rough work. They were given Italian names: Justina, Eugenia, Bernadetta, Constantine, Amelia, Germina, Louisa. Louisa stayed with me three years before finally going home to get married. Unlike Ma Tin Aung and others who took their annual leave to enjoy the Thingyan Water Festival at home, Louisa went in December, to have Christmas at home, but even more important, to help in the reaping as her family never used hired labour. The girls were not meant for domestic service in people's homes – they preferred farm work. Sometimes when a poor Catholic died without leaving any kin to bury him, the girls thought nothing of taking hoes and digging the grave. On their way into town, they often stopped by to collect Louisa. If there was any job to be done, for example the time they found my tree trunks only half-sawn by men I had hired that day at great expense, they sat down and sawed much more without trace of sweat or fatigue. They were a reminder of how hard women work in hill regions. In the state of Tawngpeng, for example, it is they who pluck the tea leaves, just as far down south it is women who pluck the green leaves of the betel vine.

In the rice regions of Lower Burma, women's work with paddy does not end with the harvest. I know one family rice mill at Pegu 54 miles north of Rangoon, which used to hire about 100 girls at a time to transport paddy from the huge mound outside into the mill. The women used baskets which they carried on their heads, all walking gracefully and easily in a long line. From the paddy that was milled the rice was received into jute sacks which the girls lifted onto a pair of male shoulders.

Women in the plains of Burma carry heavy loads on their heads – this leaves their arms free for anything else they need to carry. Among the hill peoples women use their backs by weaving baskets with a strap that lies across the forehead and suspends the basket on the back. Pa-o women in the more westerly Shan States carry their produce to and from market in this way as they toil up slopes looking bowed and overladen. Women in the more easterly Shan States use a shoulder pole like men do in the plains. Two separate and fairly light loads hang from each end of the pole. This method of load carrying is used by Thai girls also.

A Burmese woman's head can manage quite bulky and heavy loads requiring only pads of cloth coiled into a ring to cushion them. She sits on her haunches, then someone else places the load carefully till a balanced position is obtained, and she rises straight up. I have seen women carrying an extra load in one hand also as they walk along.

Selling votive wares at pagoda stall

In Chapter IV we have seen Khin Nyunt going to sell on bazaar days, swaying gracefully along the road till a passing truck or bus gives her a free ride. But the best feat I've seen this slender woman perform occurred just outside our gate when sacks of bran brought in a hired vehicle by her husband, Aung Nyein, and another man, were dumped beside the road. The driver of the bus said the climb up the driveway through which they had to enter the plot next door was too steep for his old bus to attempt. The two men including Aung Nyein, Khin Nyunt's stalwart husband who used to carry much heavier sacks of rice on his shoulder, tried moving the bags manually by gripping two corners each and walking sideways as they pulled. They went no more than a few yards when their arms gave way and they had to drop the sack. At this point Khin Nyunt came by on her way back from town swinging a basket by one hand. She saw what was happening. Sacks of rice are carried on male shoulders only if they can be lifted on to them from a height by two other men. 'How useless you both are,' she said, 'Come on, give me a load.' She sat on her haunches and the men put a sack of bran squarely on her beautiful head. She rose straight up without disturbing it in the least and then walked in her usual graceful fashion straight up the road to the gate and from there to the store shed where she flung it down. The size of the bag was 2½ by 1½ feet and it was filled to the very top.

Women can be seen carrying loads on their heads in towns at construction sites. At such places there is usually a mason who is regarded as *Saya* or master by

Chorus dancers rehearsing

the workers. And then there is a gang of about two-thirds women and one-third men. Sand, lime and cement are poured on to a cleared patch of ground under the mason's instruction. One man gets a shovel and, while water is poured on, he mixes the mortar. It is very hard work and as one man tires, another takes his place. Meanwhile women carry bricks from a pile to the mason's work spot. Small pans, round and shallow, are filled with about ten bricks and lifted on to each other's heads. They pick their way along the half-finished work and sink to their haunches when they reach the mason who helps put down the load. As soon as the mortar has been mixed to the mason's satisfaction, the women go to it and the shoveller fills each pan which is delivered in the same way. The work-site is generally a merry scene where men and women work easily together. Food carriers collect on one side and a lot of back chat, innuendo and laughter goes on. The mason ignores the occasional pause to smoke a cheroot. The tea kettle is going all the time and this clear green tea is drunk when the workers gather together in the shade.

Construction labour rates, however, differ for men and women. It used to be two and a half kyats per day for women and three for men. Quite often the workers come in families. No complaints are made about the difference in wage-rate as the male job strains the arms a great deal while the females carrying small head-load pans are not regarded as hardworked.

123

At devotions in great pagoda

Bazaar Trade: Bazaar Seller Daw Khin Su

Headload carrying starts with women hawkers who, in small villages without a bazaar, walk from house to house with trays of fish, vegetables or leaves plucked from lake-shores and wayside trees and shrubs. This is the simplest form of food selling which, as we have seen in Chapter I, has been for centuries the women's special sphere.

Ma Khin Su is the daughter of my mother's cousin. She married a poor man and remained poor. When I was about 15, she joined our household where there were 4 girls helping my mother as maids. She was senior to them. Being slightly older than the children of the family and sharing a blood relationship, she called us by name and my parents as Uncle and Aunt. She was tall with heavy brows and a fiercely affectionate nature and a cutting vulgar tongue on occasion.

My mother did not need so many helpers. Knowing Ma Khin Su's superior skills, she arranged for her to go and help her niece who was married to a doctor and had small children. In that family, Ma Khin Su became a very close relation both to parents and children. Years passed and I lost touch with her. War came, I got married. War ended. I went to set up home in far-distant Loimwe, the Hill of Mists, where the British had built a station for their Frontier Service officers to oversee the administration of Kengtung State, my husband's family home. My own family had had a rough and poor time during the war and as it took 4-5 hard days driving from out of Loimwe to reach Rangoon, I felt very cut off. On one occasion, in 1947, we drove down to visit them. As we crunched up the stately palm-lined driveway, we honked loudly. And at once several heads popped out of the rooms to see if it was us. But was it bathtime? All of them, my 3 sisters, a cousin and a maid were all bare shouldered with longyis hitched high up above their bosoms, as they are for communal bathing. I noticed one particular pair of shoulders. It was Ma Khin Su. She had come there to offer her services to me as, according to her, because I was married, she thought I would need help. She came, and she received the children at their first jump into existence. She cooked superbly, antagonised our other domestics. But we could go thousands of miles away and feel assured the children were in loving and capable hands. As they grew older, she got bored. Her services to us were not vital. She wanted to sell things in the bazaar, to chat, to work all day, to handle money.

To present Ma Khin Su's true life vividly enough, I must digress and describe the background in which she chose to work.

A head count on main Bazaar Day in Taunggyi showed a total of 647 women sellers of fresh foodstuffs sitting on a patch of ground along the main aisles which run through the enclosure outside of the roofed sheds providing booths. This count could be made only in one section of the bazaar, comprising about a third of the total ground space utilized in this way. The majority of these women sellers are villagers who have walked about four or five miles with produce, some of it from their own house gardens. As soon as they arrive at the bazaar gates, they are met by women who form another section of these 'seated sellers'. These are women who live in the town or on its outskirts and do not like agriculture enough to be able to find their own produce. They do like selling, however, they are willing to keep at it all day in contrast to the villagers from more distant homes who want to walk home at some time soon after noon. These villagers are therefore willing to sell their produce at wholesale rates to the more urban sellers who risk being left with some of the perishable stuff on their hands by the end of the day. Terms between the two types of women are strictly cash, and the poorest of the urban section must seek a loan to pay. They, in turn, get this loan from a woman of means who lives close enough to the bazaar for herself or one of her daughters to go round it several times during each bazaar. Both interest and principal are to be repaid at the end of each such day, and a loss of good faith means no more loans another time.

Taking a bath

Ma Khin Su belonged to a higher economic for she had access to greater resources. She secured a booth as other women like her did, but as we shall see later, she chose to sit on the ground with her goods in baskets beside her. Bazaar Day exchanges are swift indeed, and there is a great deal of trade going on in every inch of space available for it. Added to this rapid turnover, throngs of housewives come despite the inconvenience of having to push and shove their way.

To enjoy this to the full and to add another dimension to her trade, Ma Khin Su gave up her booth at which she would do only desultry business four days out of five and for which she would have to live in Taunggyi. Instead, she followed the 5-day bazaar circuit in four centres at distances of ten to twenty miles from Taunggyi and took her place on the ground like the poorest of sellers. In regions of the 5 day bazaar system, every 5th or Bazaar Day is special. At each center of this bazaar she sold fish and shrimp products which she knows best and of which the best comes from her home region of Thaton, near Moulmein way down south.

After doing the bazaar circuit for a year or two with Taunggyi as her base, Ma Khin Su moved 11 miles down to Shwenyaung which lies in an upland plain with roads leading to three or four other centres which she judged as the better circuit because their products included more variety. She used the trips to these centres not only to sell but to buy up the produce (such as lentils or potatoes or garlic) of that immediate environment cheaply. A strong reason for choosing Shwenyaung as a base is that it is the railhead for the railway right down to the plain to Rangoon and the rich Moulmein areas to the southeast of it. From there Ma Khin Su's sister, a widow who lived by this trade bought, packed, and sent by rail continuous supplies of fish products. Once a year, just after the monsoon, when clear skies make a favourable time for processing such foods, she herself took the train down to Thaton, where, with fish bought cheaply, the sisters salted, sunned and put into pots large quantities of such foods, ensuring the cheapest and best quality in this way. As people got to know the quality of their purchases, Ma Khin Su in a short time attracted a large number of customers. She greatly enjoyed taking in hundreds of kyats on bazaar days and felt no fatigue from working long hours without a soft seat or back to lean on. She used jute sacks to sit on, and sat surrounded by several bamboo baskets, in which her produce was tightly packed. When the government first started People's Shops at the beginning of the present Socialist Program, it was hoped that these shops would sell essential foods to the public at fair prices. But they were unable to compete with the traditional bazaar sellers. At one point, the news went around that the government, realizing the bazaar women's worth, wished to utilize the talents of the bazaar sellers and pay those of them who came forward a salary of 100 kyats a month to sell the onions etc., which government stocks would supply them with. I visited Ma Khin Su at this time. Three friends of the same profession were with her, discussing this news as they repacked their products. 'I will enter her', said Ma Khin Su, pointing to the girl adopted as a daughter by her sister and very much loved by her, but in Ma Khin Su's eyes a lazy and useless girl. 'I must leave myself free to do quick buying and selling', she said, 'so she might as well earn that 100 since she can't make profits on her own initiative.'

At the start of her trading career, as I have mentioned earlier, Ma Khin Su managed to get a stall in the bazaar. Such a stall has to be bid for and is a section of about six feet round the sides and along the aisles of a big roofed shed. For a town like Taunggyi where Ma Khin Su began this enterprise, the bazaar is an enclosure about a quarter mile square. Every day this enclosure is open from dawn till nearly dusk. At night the various stall holders lock up their wares if they have lids or doors to their storage closets. Security is provided but the main deterrent is the harsh justice which will be meted out to the thief by the bazaar sellers themselves, just as in the village. This bazaar functions every day of the week except the really big religious days when the meat stalls shut down after announcing abstention for two or three days duration of the feast. Daily sales are reasonable but sporadic, and a person of Ma Khin Su's temperament would find the long hours of such daily waiting at the stall tedious compared to the rush and bustle of the five day bazaar.

The five-day bazaar system is an ancient institution in these northern parts of Burma. Marco Polo, travelling through these parts bordering on China and Burma in the 13th century, remarked on a regular bazaar to which hill peoples from the surrounding higher regions walked down. The description holds true of bazaar meets in the Shan States of today. The Shan States used to number a total of 33, ranging from big states of 10,000 square miles or more, ruled by Sawbwas, to middling, or tiny sub-states like Namtok the tiniest, of 14 square miles, administered by a revenue collector. Each of these states had a capital town set in the plain of rice-fields. The ruling family was usually Shan, of Tai race, which established its power by winning this rice bowl. On the hills around, other ethnic groups such as Pa-O, Lishaw, Lisu, Kaw, Lahu and Palaungs live in smaller communities. These peoples plant a variety of crops ranging from indigo and cotton to opium, mostly in the north-eastern regions. They traded their produce for rice, salt, kerosene and matches. They wear very colourful clothes which, to observers, became a part of their identification. This happens at five day intervals in every state capital town.

Selling dry stores in bazaar

The bigger states also held bazaar meets in a few bigger towns besides the capital. All capitals held their bazaars on the same day, and other towns within a radius of about 25 miles held bazaars on days in between. Even in a cosmopolitan town like Taunggyi where there is a bazaar every day, Bazaar Day is noticeable. The swell on every 5th day, with country folk, fresh produce and 5-day-oriented town-wives makes its own hum. It is in the smaller centres however, that bazaar day is most conspicuously a Fair. On the days in between bazaar days, the smaller bazaar centres can be seen as nothing more than rows of empty sheds, a few feet off the ground and probably leaning over with decrepitude. Not a soul is in sight and the few dogs nosing around for the remaining bits of litter merely accent the desolation of the scene. On bazaar days however, you pass the carts and the pedestrians with their small loads continuously bound for the centre long before you come to it. From eight o'clock onwards there is the hum and movement and push of quick sale and purchase, the food counters are packed with the hill people sitting on their haunches in a queue, waiting to be served. If New Year or the end of Lent is near, they will also buy some homespun of natural brown or dyed black material and have a suit of clothes stitched at the booths which have treadle machines whirring. They will buy an expensive towel of imported Chinese or Indian origin to double as a turban or sweat wiper on their long walks home. All this can be done with the proceeds of the crops they bring to sell wholesale if their village is more distant. By 2 p.m. the bazaar has 'broken'. The professional sellers like Ma Khin Su have their unsold supplies into baskets and loaded them and gone, in the rattling ancient buses which await them for the duration of the bazaar. The farmers' carts have gone, the food sellers have sold out and departed.

The empty sheds resume their leaning look and only one lone figure goes around bowed and bending at Taung-ni, 7 miles from the railhead of Shwenyaung. It is the wife of the richest man here, a Chinese who buys up farm produce wholesale, to retail profitably on the days in between. She is busy picking up the manure left by the tethered cart bullocks. She adds it to her store in a lean-to in their house and shop and works to make it drier and more easily handled to be bought back at top prices by the farmers for whom she is also chief money-lender.

Within the last year or two, Ma Khin Su has added a new line to her stock. Altar flowers. Most Burmese housewives regularly buy fresh flowers for the family shrine. The aim is to have something that will last reasonably long and not have to be constantly changed. For this, even in earlier years Ma Khin Su bought and sold asters and chrysanthemums. The asters would be plucked by uprooting the whole plant and laid in baskets lined with banana leaf. With the roots thus still part of them the flowers lasted better than the alternative gladioli which grow wild in the fields and are small by now for lack of proper planting.

More recently, she discovered in Thaton a foliage that she calls *Mya-sein-pan* – Green emerald or *hnit-taya-pan* – the hundred-years-duration flower. Naturally it is cheaper than real flowers and it sells in vast quantities. This green foliage which Ma Khin Su started selling serves excellently as the background for perhaps one or two smaller vases of roses or other fragrant flowers. There was hardly a stop to her sales of this foliage. It is a wonderful find – if you take one stem and plant it, it will root, as it roots even in the water and is self perpetuating if handled properly. However, it survives best in moist regions. Here, where she sold it, the rainfall is only about 60 inches; in Thaton from where her sister sent up the plants it is over 200 inches a year.

Sometime after she began working, Ma Khin Su acquired a house. All land in this part of Burma has to be leased from the state and if you get in early enough, or, like her, find some suitably connected friends to help you, you can get a grant of a still unleased plot free, and pay just nominal taxes on it yearly.

Ma Khin Su found a plot just one row of houses away from the high road and within ten minutes' walk of the railway station. She collected enough money and material to build with. Of the two main rooms in the house, she sleeps in, or rents out one. The other main room holds a high shelf for the shrine and it (the room) is where all the baskets are repacked or house sales are made from. She has a well from which water is carried to a side room for her bath and laundry. A narrow room connects this with the front entrance and in that space she washes her dishes, cooks, and eats.

Ma Khin Su's bazaar circuit is a busy one. One day in the week she stays home airing and selecting her goods and produce. She chooses Taunggyi Bazaar Day for this as Taunggyi is a small bazaar some 11 miles away and she does not like to go to it because there is too much competition from the big sellers.

The next day she goes to Taungnis, about 7 miles from where she lives. On the following day she stays in her own village – Shwenyaung. She hires male carriers to take her baskets to the bazaar and walks, returning early to prepare for the following day, which is spent in Yawnghwe, the capital city of this area. Being a fairly rich city, Ma Khin Su does her best business here. It is no use asking her how much profit she makes. Her main point is that she is also 'living' and eating out of this money, so even a small margin is worth working for as she is living the life she likes in doing it. On one of the days she also goes to Heho, a different centre 11 miles away, but across a range in the next valley. The drive there and back is longer and she gets homw late so she generally cooks the main part of a dinner on a little charcoal brazier, at the same time as she sells. Because she does reasonably well, Ma Khin Su gives more generously than her relatives ever expect. She is now 64. We have many conversations about the strenuous life she leads and the smallness of her profits. 'Isn't it time you stopped? Why not come and stay home quietly', I have often asked her. But she says she feels ill with many vague pains when she doesn't go on the round and keeps well when she does. Not only are her journeys strenuous, they are also disappointing. Occasionally, she is tempted to smuggle in some contraband merchandise. If she is ever caught, she runs the risk of losing her whole consignment. But she maintains, as many bazaar women do, that it is not forbidden in the Five Precepts to carry such goods as the government has labelled contraband today, and so she continues to do so. 'The next trip will make up for this loss', she argues. It is a gambler's addiction almost, and though Ying is now married and setting up house, Ma Khin Su is still postponing the day she will go and stay there. 'Call me when I'm too tired to go any more', she says and one of us surely will. She will be welcome anywhere. She knows this and so does not calculate her profits precisely nor worry about saving for the future.

Women and Small-Scale Home Industries

This chapter has shown us today's Burmese women working at their traditional occupations in so far as the work is family-sized and leaves the women comparatively free to rest on the days that they are not driven to work by necessity. One aspect of this tradition is that the women are largely self-employed in the way common to Southeast Asia as the figures below will show.

Women in their own account trade –

Country	Percentage of self-employed out of all women in trade
Burma	85
Thailand	40
Malaysia	74
Singapore	53
Philippines	61

In such works as we have seen, there is hardly a dividing line between a woman's domestic and professional worlds. In the next chapter we will see other women who work in factories. But, other than in the factories, there are women who work at home at traditional crafts. Such work includes making food, clothes, cheroots.

U Ba Khin and his large extended family made a comfortable living from their several shops, a knitting factory and a coffee production unit. When all such ventures were moved into the state's sector of the economy, U Ba Khin became manager of a state-owned People's Shop on a salary barely sufficient for their needs. In order to supplement the family income his wife, Daw Mya Yee, decided to start processing sunflower seeds to sell all over the country. She chose sunflower seeds because the family's home base is really the best sunflower growing area. The seeds were bought by U Ba Khin from the bazaar day meets around Taungni where Ma Khin Su goes. For the rest, Daw Mya Yee put into practice some ideas she had, in order to be able to sell her product more widely than other brands already on sale. She firmly discarded all small or imperfect seeds and chose only the best. She boiled them in large iron pans with a bit of water, salt and saccharine. She had her yard paved with cement and there, on reed mats, she spread the boiled seeds to dry in the strong sun, employing two male workers to help her. Despite many competitors she was successful in making rapid sales.

Three friends working together in the cheroot factory

The association of women with textiles is old as the hills. Old *Dhammathats* laid down the law that, in a separation of man from wife, she must have the loom. This consideration of the loom as a domestic utility and the use of it as a feminine accomplishments has long ago disappeared from the plains of Burma but it still lingers among highland peoples.

When we lived in Loimwe, the Hill of Mists, above Kengtung, we would see the short-kilted *Kaw* women walking back towards their hill-top villages. They used the time spent on such walking by spinning cotton as they went. With adroit pulling from one hand into the other they got the thread which now and again, they would, (pausing a second with one leg raised) spin tighter by twirling on the raised thigh. Lower down in the valley the ladies of the ruling family of Shans presented me with beautiful silk pieces which they had woven themselves.

It is interesting to note that Burmese women, usually the preservers of tradition, have largely turned, for their *longyis*, to a variety of imported fabrics, whereas the men use mainly Burmese handloom silks and cottons.

We now turn to the one big remaining industry associated with women – cheroot-making. The 'whacking great cheroot' of Kipling's day is rarely seen these days though it was part of my childhood background as our closest, favourite maiden aunt used to smoke one, usually one that she had rolled. Nowadays, it can be found in some delta towns. It was a 10-inch long cylinder with a diameter of about one inch and packed so loosely that its common accompaniment is a full sized enamel plate held under it by the smoking lady. Malcolm, the American Baptist missionary traveller whom I have quoted in Chapter I, gives a sketch of a Burmese lady walking out and in the illustration he includes the inevitable cheroot in her hand.

The Burmese distinction between a cheroot and a cigar is quite different from the English dictionary meaning which gives a cheroot as a cigar with an end (the smoking one) open and a cigar as having both ends pointed (and sealed). The Burmese 'cigars', a welcome present to connoisseur friends abroad, are in Burmese distinguished from cheroots simply by their *hsay-pyin* and *hsay-paw*, strong and weak. The strong are smoked by men, and the weak, the manufacture of which vastly predominates over the manufacture of the strong, this 'weak tobacco' is the pervading article in the female world's culture, and smoked by men and women alike.

In Rangoon and Pegu, there is a Chinese family that owns the 'duck' brand cheroot industry which is the biggest cheroot unit in that it employs 2,500 women rollers and a few hundred men helpers. The business, being Chinese and large-scale is controlled by the men of the family and the workplace is like a factory. All over Burma, however, especially in the town of Taunggyi with a population of 80,000 plus, the cheroot business is purely a woman's business, almost always in her house. The cheroots from here are considered the best in Burma for flavour, for good packing and rolling in that they hold well and spark less than the Rangoon or Pegu cheroots. The wrapper leaf used here is always *thanat* which is in fact very often called just 'leaf', so well known is it. In some parts of Burma, the dried outer leaves of corn (maize) are used for wrapping cheroots but cannot compare in the quality of the end product with 'leaf' cheroots. How much of it is women's business will be seen in the short sketch below.

During the sixties when my husband was absent from home for some years, I turned to livestock breeding. This was because, with the loss of our joint endeavours in the educational field, I had to move house to the home we had built in large grounds in the loneliest part on the edge of town. Breeding livestock also enabled me to employ labourers and their families who lived with us and provided us good company. This decision brought down a stream of disapproval on my head. Buddhists do not breed livestock (as it involves selling for slaughter), particularly if they have the means to work at something else.

Not far from where we lived was Hopong where there was a rice mill owned and managed by an elderly Burmese woman from lower Burma. The mill owner took a great fancy to me, calling me daughter and supplying me even when, for lack of stocks, she had to turn away the male farmers who came in carts for the bran.

As the years went on and rice milling became more controlled by government rules she lost interest in the mill and sent for her younger brother from Central Burma to come and help run it while she planted the *thanat* leaf which had become so profitable a product.

Since I was not in the cheroot business, I did not need to buy 'leaf' from her

Working in the cheroot factory

but I did come in contact with leaf buyers. I had family concerns in Rangoon for which I needed to send money now and again. Few transactions are done with cheques as to remit a sum we would have to go to a bank and buy a bank-draft which is a long-winded procedure. Waiting for it to be cashed at the other end is equally fatiguing. I had, however, heard of other ways of sending money and I went to see my friend Ma Kon who runs freight trucks between Taunggyi and Rangoon. A good part of her freight is 'leaf', packed tight in baskets which fill the 6-ton truck. Ma Kon's great capacity for friendship is well-known. She heard my wish to send money to Rangoon and she said 'Just the thing! The *thanat* leaf brokers need their Rangoon customers to pay for the loads I send down. You can pay them here and their man there will pay cash on seeing the note you get here.' She took me on a short walk from her house. Like all business women, her new house was built near to the bazaar and in the proximity of big brokers' houses. The house was a beautiful result in functionality. The whole of the downstairs hall was a huge room at one end of which a broad raised platform in polished wood ran along its breadth. When the farmers arrived with their baskets of leaf they could all lay out their bedding and sleep in comfort on this platform. The rest of the hall was swept clear and clean and round tables could be rolled out and their meals served. The yard outside was fully paved to admit buses and trucks easily.

Daw Nyo was the wife of U Than Tun, driver of our school bus. Soon after the school job stopped, U Than Tun suffered a seizure which developed into Parkinson's disease. At this point Daw Nyo took over and started a cheroot-rolling business. They had been lucky enough to get a grant of a site and had put up a wooden building before things went wrong for them. She employed three girls and both she and her 12-year old daughter worked alongside them. Thus cheroots with the new brand name of Thabye Nyo, 'the dark Eugenia', started.

A middling business is the Golden Pheasant business of Daw Nyo Sein who employs 15 girls, each of whom rolls 700 to 1000 cheroots every day and is paid at the rate of K.10 per 1000 cheroots rolled. If you go to the houses of any such middle-sized proprietors you will see the downstairs is all an open area, and sitting on mats on the cement floor are the girls. In front of each girl is a cane or bamboo tray resting on a stool. It holds tobacco mixture, scissors, glue pot, a pile of leaf, a wad of labels, a rolling aid in the form of wooden rod, and a pile of base stoppers. Each girl works very quickly and in silence. She takes up a leaf, rolls it round the rod and then, with skilled movements, tucks mixture between the rod and leaf. Very soon she is able to extract the rolling aid and leave mixture only in the roll. She stops the base with a stopper, glues the side end of leaf on to the roll, incorporating a label as she does so; then with the heavy scissors she cuts off the protruding end of the base stopper till it is level with the end of the leaf roll. When U Ba Kin, our driver, was unable to make ends meet his wife, Daw Mya, took to cheroot rolling. Being a superb worker, she would easily do as many as 1000 cheroots a day and make a good sum of money.

I have mentioned the base stoppers for cheroots. They are tightly rolled cylinders with a core of dried corn leaves and a final coating of paper to stick it firmly down. Women often make these stoppers in their own homes and then sell in quantity to a nearby cheroot house.

The wife of Ko Tin Hla, our goldsmith in Rangoon, in between tending her husband's business in the weighing and putting away of costly gold and gems, made such cheroot stoppers. The great attraction of this industry for women is the ease with which they can work without leaving their hearth and home. This struck me most vividly during a visit to Inle Lake. There, at the mid-lake bungalow we were quite a distance even from the watchman's cottage. We often had to call across for a pot of tea. The keeper's wife would come paddling with the tea-pot and cups and she would wait till our lunch was eaten to take them back. She brought over a cheroot-rolling tray with the mixture, labels, etc., from a cheroot house on the mainland and while she waited, rolled over 100.

I would like to end this chapter with an interesting story about women workers. During the days of economic recession in our country we took to saving everything we could as even small things which we would ordinarily consider junk acquired a resale value. Any kind of rubbish, including old newspapers, were bought by dealers. Such 'goods' were considered contraband by the government and if you were suspected of having them you could be liable to having your house searched. I had with me, at that time, a packet of letters written to me by a friend who had since died of cancer. These I put in a paper carton in an old cupboard. Not very long after this some friends of mine wanted to buy furniture in a hurry and I sold them the cupboard. It was emptied out in a hurry

Selling fans and iced drinks for hot passengers at bus stop

and all the junk came out. Not wanting to have it around, I called out to the junk collectors to come and take it away. The two sisters who came into my shed seized upon everything that they could find and asked if I had any more paper as that was what sold best. 'Here,' said one of them suddenly, coming upon my box of letters, 'here's some paper. We told you there must be some more!' I said the box contained personal letters which were not for sale. 'Haven't you read them yet?' said one of them. 'You have? Then what is the difficulty?'. I said I did not want other people reading my letters. Hoots of derisive laughter greeted this remark. '*Read* these papers? What an idea! That will take too much time to do. No, no, we assure you no one will read these. Nobody has the time. It's straight into the rolling they'll go!' These words have long since remained in my ears as so very apt for the Burmese women of this chapter who surely deserve to be called the salt of the earth.

9. Women at Work: Factory Workers

This Chapter could be written in two ways. One is to build up, with statistics at the national level, the picture of women at work in factories; how large a force they number, the percentage of female to male workers in different industries, wage levels, benefits allowed, the productivity of women, relative to that of men, conditions in factories etc. This method is possible only with the availability of the relevant statistics. Earlier on, in efforts to obtain statistics in another field of inquiry, the education of women, I was informed that government offices may supply such information only to other departments. Private citizens among whom I belong, have no source to which they can go freely to hunt up such information themselves.

Burma is not alone in this shortage of statistical data. Here is a paragraph I found in *Women, Society and Change* by Evelyn Suillerot. The book from which I quote is full of details, statistically tabulated diagrams and columns of women at work in countries of Europe and North America. Regarding countries such as of Southeast Asia, she says:

> In dealing with developing countries, one is struck by the inadequacy of statistical data on a problem as complex as that of female employment. The year books compiled by the main international organisations quote very low rates of employment, but do not indicate the sociological implications. . . . Africa, Asia and South America elude attempts to provide a measure of women's contribution to the production and the life of their country. But although their share cannot be calculated, they are certainly far from being unproductive.

In the face of this lack of numerical information, I have chosen to make this chapter much more descriptive of Burmese women who work in factories and whom I have been able to meet. Such an account will not be without its point for it will inform the reader about Burmese industrial women workers in comparison with other South-east Asian working women presently employed in the mammoth multi-national factories of Singapore, Malaysia and Thailand.

Radical Social Changes of Other Asian Countries

Linda Lim, assistant professor of Economics in Swartmore College, USA, has given us a masterly, and most vivid account of girls working in multi-national companies. She begins by assessing the value of female workers in recently established electronic factories in the above-named countries as offshore appendages to the big companies of electronic equipment in USA. On the one hand the deft fingers of Asian girl workers and the low wage level and operating costs of their environment make products cheap to the American consumer and profit-seeking capitalist alike. On the other hand, the workplace, with its piped pop music and cosmetic appeal based on American concepts of fashion and beauty, have had a long-lasting Westernizing and in a sense, 'modernizing' them, thus almost making them outsiders. At the same time, the push for production in this successfully industrialized set-up sets a 3 shift system throughout the whole 24 hours. Enterprising landlords put up dormitories of small sleeping cells within easy reach of the barbed wire factory enclosures, through which two thousand women workers may emerge at one time. To increase the numbers accommodated, the same bed may be rented out to 3 girls working on different shifts. The result is to produce in these cities, a corps of female industrial labour who, living in cramped conditions and maybe working on the midnight shift at a time when they may expect spirits to be abroad, are thought to be nerve ridden, anxious and often near hysteria.

I have gleaned much of the above from Linda's account of her researches in Southeast Asia.

Some Burmese Factory Women

Burmese factory women in general can be said to resemble Burmese non-industrial workers rather than industrial workers of other countries. Before beginning accounts of the women I met, I give a short note on general conditions regarding women in industries before 1962. The constitution in the revised version of 1950 in section 2, states that all citizens are to receive equal treatment in their livelihood. Paragraph 15 states that women workers must receive the same pay for the same work as male workers. Yet, in the days of private industry, employers practice discrimination in choosing male employees in preference to female whenever they had a choice, and in paying different rates such as are indicated by the following.

In the years immediately following 1962, factories except for those classified as cottage industries, came under the state sector and these factories now pay equal wages to both men and women employees. The government ensures that every working establishment numbering more than five workers must be registered, and this ensures that employees receive social security benefits. Women workers are thus entitled to maternity leave, sickness leave, medical treatment and compensation for injuries sustained in the course of work as male workers are.

Factory	Pay per month	
	Men	Women
	Kyats Pyas	Kyats Pyas
Rice Mills	93.87	67.76
Wheat Mills	115.03	57.03
Cheroots	119.00	58.07
Oil presses	107.18	58.60
Ginning and spinning	106.67	54.00
Hosiery	127.29	79.32
Timber Mills	92.51	46.41
Soap	50.13	64.30
Aluminium pots	160.42	75.00
Cinemas etc.	85.43	50.00

In general women tend to gravitate away from certain types of industry towards others in which they are found in roughly the same numbers as men and those where they predominate and sometimes even make up the whole workforce. Enquiries at the labour office yielded no figures, but such assumptions as I had made were confirmed; women do not join in saw-milling and logging industries, nor in tanning and leather works, nor in mining and related industries, foundries and automobile assembly works. They are found alongside men in agriculture-related industries, works producing consumer goods such as slippers, match, soap, hosiery; in factories producing food products such as biscuits, canned fish, sweet cordials. In certain industries such as cigarette and cheroot, spinning and weaving, they predominate sometimes to the virtual exclusion of male workers.

The women I first interviewed, belonged to factories not included in this short list. My first meeting was with A-Myaing. She had come to Rangoon from the Moulmein area as a child when her family moved. About two years previous to this, she had tried domestic service but was found to be incompetent by her employers and left shortly after. When I met her, the girls whom she came to visit remarked on her changed personality. She had been working in the intervening two years in a glass and bottle factory. She earned over 150 kyats a month as compared to 100 which is regulation wage for an average domestic servant, who, however, would get free food in addition to this wage. A-Myaing did not set too much store by this free food supply. She said they were a family of eight, and grew a large part of their rice though they lived in this capital city of Rangoon. When asked about her conditions of work, she said she was only a temporary hand unlike her elder sister who, as an established worker, enjoyed full benefits and would in any case be able to tell me better than she could, whatever I needed to know. She lived in *Ngamoyeik* on the outskirts of Rangoon where she said there were several factories in the vicinity.

Intrigued by the mention of paddy fields so near to us in town, I went to

Ngamoyeik. We drove till we reached a section where bamboo and thatch houses alternated with small wooden houses all continuously adjacent to each other. My companions pointed out the railway running alongside the road and beyond it, the paddy fields. On the other side behind the row of small dwellings, they told me was the big enclosure with office building for dealing with motor driving licenses and other controls regarding motor vehicles. All motorists in town had to come out here to get their papers passed. We walked about twenty yards down a path two to three feet wide. It was hard dry earth now but would be a quagmire during the monsoon months. We passed women bathing from a cement tank into which a faucet opened. I learnt that the faucet and pipe line had been provided by town supply, but residents in the area contributed to building the open tank where water during the hours of supply could be collected for common use during other hours of day or night. A-Myaing's house was of timber. We were greeted by her sister and mother. A-Myaing's elder sister came with a pot of tea and small cups. Her mother also came and sat by us. Ma Nyunt Khin, this elder sister, is 23 years old and unmarried. Third among eight children and eldest among the six to remain unmarried and at home. She takes a ten-pya ride to her glass and bottle factory where there are 32 women and 18 men workers. Her hours of work are 7 a.m. to 3.30 p.m. Her lunch has to be ready at this early hour and thus has to be cooked the evening before. Many women workers do some cooking at work and this is seen as normål. Neither she nor A-Myaing took on over-time work because they could depend on extra earning from the paddy fields.

My next visit was to this factory which, like the Mya Kalut factory in Ngamoveik had not been incorporated into the state sector but remained in the hands of private employers as still a cottage industry. The *Hman-myay Hpan-myay* factory was even less of an industrialized environment than Ngamoyeik, with its string of worker's houses and nearby small establishments producing soap, yarn, synthetic fabric, glasses and bottles. To reach this factory we left the main road and drove along a lane till we entered shady grounds in which there were nestled several low buildings. In one of these nearest the entrance, Ma Aye Than worked at packing the finished products for customers who came to buy attractive glassware in the form of coloured drinking glasses as well as vases, ashtrays and paper weights, well designed as owls, birds, fish and such like. Ma Aye Than is unmarried and she works here together with her sister. Their earnings support parents who stay home to look after young school going siblings.

Further along was the shed where the glassware was produced. Ma Mya Thaung who works here, is an older woman whose husband has a job as a radio operator in a government department. She has her mother living with her to look after a young child. Like Ma Aye Than she was dressed no differently and no more smartly than the bazaar women or other women working in the traditional roles I have described in the previous chapter.

Both Ma Aye Than and Ma Mya Thaung looked so much like bazaar women I referred to, in the previous chapter that I asked them whether they were happier at this work than selling food supplies in traditional Burmese women's occupation. Ma Aye Than replied that only those with a remarkably sociable nature enjoyed bazaar selling. She herself had no gift for backchat, and so preferred this job where she did not lose by her silence. Ma Mya Thaung said she preferred working here with an assured salary of a basic 200 kyats per month, whereas bazaar selling might leave her with a loss from perishable goods left unsold. I had before this thought about the differences between traditional occupations and modern industrial labour. This new environment, fully urbanized and deserving of the term 'industrialized', would, unlike traditional female earning, take a woman right away from domestic and home attachment to a different world of impersonal employers unremittingly regular hours, a complete break with domestic ties, and with far less control over earnings. The traditionally occupied bazaar seller, for example, desisted from selling on days when she did not need the sales or when she had work to do at home. The cheroot rolling girls also, in an enterprise like the one described in the previous chapter, worked in Daw Nyo Sein's house, where visitors came and went as their employer reclined on her raised platform with betel box and teapot to hand. If their own friends came to the open doors to talk briefly to them, they could rest to talk as they were paid on a piecework basis.

As it turned out, the atmosphere at this particular glassworks was more domestic and family oriented than any I saw up country. The proprietors, when they started in 1952, went to the Tennasserim area from which the wife had come, and recruited workers. To the other side of the shady grounds, she built wooden quarters to house workers whom they encouraged to come in families. Now they had a total of eighty workers, two thirds women and one third men. They could house only a quota of these, and the rest came by bus from a good distance away like Ma Aye Than and Ma Mya Thaung.

Turning away from works of such rural and family associations, I decided to find women who worked in the Burma Pharmaceutical Industry. This BPI which is a household word in Burma, occupies 79 acres in which have been built in slow stages. Starting from the use of imported raw materials in its early days, the industry now uses indigenous raw materials for about 50 per cent of its needs. It was set up to fill the whole country's pharmaceutical needs and its production for 1977-78 for example, amounted to 1,187,066 thousand tablets valued at 49.06 million kyats or ointment and similar preparations amounting to 183533 kilos valued at 11.30 million kyats (Burma Pharmaceutical Industry pamphlet).

I thought the surest way to meet women working in this big plant was to drive to its vicinity with someone resident in that area. We drove out to *Kyo Gone*, a suburb of the town of Insein, ten miles north of Rangoon. We saw no giant structure as might have been expected. The various plants are housed in separate and fairly low buildings. We went down a lane which showed low factory buildings on one side and on the other, small gardens with houses just as in a village. We stopped outside one and crossed the water ditch by a small bridge. Narrow stairs led us to the top storey of a timber house with a zinc roof and no ceiling. We were received by Ma Mya Win Kyi aged 31 and her husband Ko Tin aged 30. Ma Mya Win Kyi looked less like a bazaar seller than any of the women I had met hitherto. She told us she 'drove' a machine, set in a glass cubicle like 9 other cubicles in the factory room where she worked each day from 6 a.m. to 2 p.m. filling injection ampoules. Before entering this room, she and the other 9 women workers had to wash the *thanaka* bark cosmetic off their faces and remove the flowers from their hair. 'If you have to do this everyday, do you still put *thanaka* and set flowers in your hair?' 'I don't, because I live so close by, but others who have to come by bus, naturally must come with *thanaka* on their faces and flowers in their hair.' She took it for granted that despite the unfamiliar surroundings of their work place, Burmese women must still dress in the familiar conventional way and not forsake their native cosmetics although their plant produces lipsticks and nail varnishes also. She herself was a thin and spare looking woman with an intelligent face and said she appreciated the value of having to change into the uniform provided, (trousers and jacket) which made work more efficient because there would be no need to readjust her longyi to make it more firm. She earned over 200 kyats a month in addition to bonuses given to workers from time to time when production targets were exceeded. She had been ten years at the plant. She came originally from Moulmeingyun in the delta. Her husband Ko Tin has always been resident in Rangoon and started work in the plant's packing and delivery section at the same time. They met soon after joining, got married and now have four children. They bought the piece of land on which their house stands, but had to save and collect materials to build it for about three years. They moved in before it was completely finished, but are now quite comfortable. Ma Mya Win Kyi is pregnant again and we asked her if after this fifth child is born, she will seek contraceptive treatment at the hospital, but she smiled and shook her head decidedly. 'I have to keep fit to work. The treatment is unnatural and may not agree with my system in which case I will be ailing most of the time. A child will be no problem because our factory has a child care centre.' We asked if their combined wages sufficed for their needs and what they did if it was necessary to supplement their income. She told us that many women workers traded in order to make extra money. They did this by bringing goods and leaving them in small shops bordering the plant yard. Negotiations for sales took place among other women workers and the goods were then collected from the outside shops while money changed hands within the factory. She herself, in her job of filling ampoules, worked alone and in silence, but others who packed pills and tablets into bottles sat close together at tables and could talk provided they did not slip behind in the daily target that was set. Time off was given for women who wished to go outside to smoke, but as this entailed clocking out and clocking in again, smoking gradually lost its appeal and now she no longer smokes. She returns home for a quick lunch as she lives so close by. We asked to meet some of her neighbours and as word was sent across, Ma Khin Hta Yee came over. She was powdered and combed and altogether more ornate than Ma Mya Win Kyi. She also had met her husband after joining the plant. Her husband worked on the livestock farm which provides the factory with material for small pox vaccines and antisnake venom etc. She has three children but she did not use the child care centre provided by the plant. Instead, she deposited the younger child at the house of her parents nearby. We asked how they all acquired plots of land so close to each other, and were told that all the land here used to be *Bo Ba* meaning ancestral, that is privately owned land and could be bought cheaply till up to five years ago.

Roadside flower-seller

Some industries, such as paint and polish factories at Thaketa, a suburb to the south of Rangoon, do not attract many women. Out of 367 workers at the Burma Paints Factory, only 40-50 are women. I visited one of them, Ma Hla Khin, and was surprised that I had to go north in the opposite direction from her place of work. Her address contained the words 'guava orchard' and I was struck by the abundance of trees as we went down a dust lane flanked by houses. Ma Hla Khin's house was, unexpectedly, double storeyed. We went up a narrow side staircase to the upper floor where she lived. We faced a large alcove which held her altar. She told us that she got up at 4.30 a.m. every day so as to have time to make offerings of food at the altar. After these offerings, she put the rest of the cooked food into her tiered carrier and set out for work at 6.30 a.m. Changing buses twice, she arrived in time to start work at eight, paused for half an hour to eat lunch at twelve in the room provided for all who brought carriers like hers and worked until 3.30 p.m. They generally took half an hour or longer to clean up and change out of the blue overalls in which they worked. She came home late, hut her husband Ko Than usually had the evening meal cooked ready for her.

Bazaar vendor Daw Khiu Su in later years with the house she built

Despite the long bus journeys to and from work, they did not consider changing their place of residence. The whole area had been garden lands belonging to 'rich men'. People like her who came from Kyaiklat in the delta 30 years ago when insurrections made their home there unsafe, built small houses in these gardens and as more like them came and joined forces, the land became theirs as of right. Still the garden names persisted, the ward neighbouring them to one side was Jasmine Garden, to the other it was Acacia Garden. The abundance of trees and hedges made the whole area safer from fires than the normal squatter areas of Rangoon. The couple were better off financially than the average factory worker's family. Ko Than had been a driver in an army transport corps and had obtained an invalid pension though he looked barely forty. He was now free to make his wife's working conditions easier. He had used great resource and energy in collecting timber for their house, the lower portion of which they now rented out at 120 kyats a month. In addition, he often went to his wife's place of origin which is Burma's best source for pressed prawn and fish products. These were retailed at profit to neighbours or sold in the bazaar. He might himself sit down and sell there except on holidays when the wife was free to make the sales herself. They were also solvent because they had only one child to feed. This boy, now eleven, will have his novitiation ceremony during his school vacation in the coming summer. Ma Hla Khin's fingers showed traces of her work in the factory. She was employed in the section that made cans to hold paint. She explained that the rough metal sheets are unloaded by men who then cut them into required sizes, but forming them into cans with machines is a skilled task in which accidents can happen if one is not careful or skilled enough. She had hurt herself long ago before the factory became a state enterprise and had received compensation but not as much as would now be given. When the factory was a private one, there had been no child care centre and they had to depend first on an aged parent and after his death, on the government's social welfare centre to look after their child. Now there was a good child care centre at the factory itself. Ma Hla Khin had imbibed the lessons taught about Socialist goals for all people. When asked why she preferred this job to self-employed enterprises, she replied that this one helped production to serve the whole nation instead of just oneself. She said she always joined marches to exhibitions and rallies organized by

At building site 1

government out of a wish to do so.

I had been given the introduction to Ma Hla Khin by Daw Win Win who works as an assistant manager in the laboratory of this paint factory. The managerial staff contains two other women graduates who are engineers and work on the production side. Daw Win Win told me that as a rule, women work more overtime to earn incentive money offered for exceeding the target of 3500 cans daily.

At the glass factory

Ma Hla Khin's great regret was her failure to make the grade as a model worker. In order to encourage production, the state has, since 1964, instituted the system of choosing model workers for such points as lowest record of absences, highest production, good relations with fellow workers, co-operation, respect for rules, good character and initiative. Model workers are chosen from among both

men and women in factories employing over one hundred workers. They are
honoured at special dinners, sent on sight seeing tours and educative as well as
holiday sessions at special camps set up for the purpose. Any model worker
gaining this distinction for three years running is accorded the title of socialist
heroine. The years 1964 till 1972 saw a total of 408 women chosen as model
workers for one year only and 91 chosen for two years running and 25 as socialist
heroines. These figures are low compared to the total number of women working
in such factories. This is regarded as due to their dual role of housewife and
worker, and their absences for childbirth and child care.

Comparative Activity of Men and Women in Industry

Friends of friends at the central statistics office informed me that they had no
figure showing the breakdown of workers into male or female. I had obtained the
following figures earlier from Daw Kyu Kyu of the Economics Institute who had
worked them out from figures of the 1953-54 census. In the absence of more
satisfactory statistical information on the involvement of women in industry, I
give the following two sets of tables to indicate their activity in manufacture,
comparing this with the activity of men in manufacture on the one hand and with
female work in other fields, on the other hand.

Table 1953-54 Census Year
(Percentage participation rates of economically active population)

Occupation	All Burma		Rural		Urban	
	Male	Female	Male	Female	Male	Female
Agriculture, Forestry, Hunting and Fishing	64.67	58.45	74.59	66.75	13.10	10.36
Mining and Quarrying	00.73	00.36	00.77	00.41	00.49	00.11
Manufacturing	6.99	10.59	5.14	8.41	16.61	23.28
Construction	1.60	00.12	1.40	00.09	3.98	00.29
Commerce and Finance	7.31	17.75	3.73	12.06	25.92	50.65
Transport, Storage and Communication	3.55	00.16	2.16	00.08	10.75	00.62
Services	5.30	2.87	2.65	2.02	19.11	7.78
Activities inadequately described	9.75	9.68	9.80	10.18	9.51	6.83
Electricity, Gas, Water	00.10	00.02	00.02		00.53	00.68

Occupation	Union		Rural		Urban	
	Male	*Female*	*Male*	*Female*	*Male*	*Female*
Total %	100.00	100.00	100.00	100.00	100.00	100.00
Total No.	1,485,921	703,122	712,081	400,788	773,840	302,334

Based on these 1953-54 figures, Saw Kyu Kyu has worked out figures for 1975.

Table (in thousands)

Occupation	Total	Male	Female
Total	12,337	8,006	4,231
Agriculture	7,650	6,117	2,478
Mining, Quarrying	73	58	15
Manufacture	1,008	560	448
Construction	133	128	5
Electricity etc.	9	8	1
Commerce, Finance	1,336	585	751
Transport, Storage	291	284	7
Services	546	425	141
Activities not adequately described	1,191	781	410

Both sets of figures, though limited, show an undoubted involvement of women in manufacture which may be in small scale home industries or in factories of industrial value in the largest towns.

This chapter which is, in a sense, more fragmentary than the others does serve to reveal one point. Industrialization has hardly begun effectively enough in Burma to influence the life of urban women. Even if it increases, the rate of growth will not be quick enough to outstrip the adaptation of the Burmese housewife's life to new forms of employment. She retains her family commitments, her convention of dress and deportment, the traditional reliance on petty salesmanship to supplement the family budget and the traditional complementing of efforts by man and wife to make up family income.

10. Women at Work: Political and Professional Participation

Low Participation in State Organs of Power

We now come to a very different picture, from the last two chapters where women are often busier than men in making money for the family. Here the figures of their activity, in politics and national decision show far lower percentages than those of men. This is nothing extraordinary in a human world where in nearly every nation, seats of power are held as the last bastions of male predominance. Compare, for example, Burma's figures with USA, Britain and France.

For Burma, the precentage of women in the Pyithu Hluttaw (People's National Assembly) is less than 3% while there are no women in the Secretariat of officials in general administration. When the present Constitution was to be adopted, a Constitution Drafting Commission was formed with 97 people, including 3 women (3.1%). In the United States, before 1970, there were two women senators as against one hundred men, and eleven women out of a total of 435 in the House of Representatives. In France in 1967 there were 2.3% women among the deputies. In Great Britain, for 1967, women provided 5.5% of MPs in the governing party and 2.8% in the opposition (Suillerot).

What is extraordinary here are two points of difference. Women in Burma have been going about freely in the public places of trade and manufacture for centuries. Yet they have made hardly any inroads into the posts of government, politics or some professions. The second extraordinary point is that the reasons given for their inactivity in these spheres, which, elsewhere are rejected as discrimination disguised as protectiveness, neither needed nor desired by the women themselves – these reasons are here accepted by women in Burma in general as being sound ones.

Government

There is a marked difference in degree of participation between the professions, on the one hand and politics or government on the other. Some professions, prestigious, lucrative and academically high have been satisfactorily filled by women. I will deal with this professional participation later.

It is in government and politics that women are so remarkably inactive. I will discuss this failure of participation first. This examination begins with the distant British days as issues stand out more clearly in that static atmosphere of surface order before flux, national dynamism and untidy exuberance set in, with women appearing everywhere after independence.

Relaxing ·on campus

In tracing historical trends towards female inclusion in government, I will not stress queens or rulers. The odd woman like Empress Tzu Hsi, our own Queen Shinsawbu or Queen Elizabeth I of England, can be found in nearly every nation's history. We can see the woman Premiers of today in contrast to their subjected sisters under male authority. I will instead extract from my Burmese historical background an aspect more frequent and relevant to most women of today. I refer to the dues paid to the Chief Consort of reigning King – how she was held partly responsible for good or ill in her husband's domain, how she received separate offerings when the King got his, and how, in fact, she shared enjoyment of prestige and homage given to the male holder of a joint high estate. This old tradition has come through the British era down to present times.

With regard to this, let me refer back to Chapter II the term *kadaw* for wife if her husband is important (e.g. *Saya-kadaw*). So in the colonial administration, the Burmese word for ruler, *min* or King was not only added to the government *asoya*, but to the administrators, e.g. *Min gyi* or Big *Min*. The combination of the

British need for prestige with Burmese egalitarianism which existed side by side with complimentary aggrandisement in address, led to proliferation of *Mins* and *kadaws*. The lowest level called Township Officers got petitions addressed to *Myo-ok-Min*. These and the level just above (subdivisonal officers) were Burmese for the most part unlike their seniors who at first were largely British.

The share of wives in this prestige of even junior officials has been noted in descriptions of *Min-kadaw* in my book, *Burmese Family*. However, it is not right to stamp such prestige as British-inspired. It belongs to our traditions too, and the deference given to Burmese political leaders after Independence was no less than previous *Asoyamins* had received. The difference was that it was now expressed in a completely Burmese form. Wives of junior officials visiting wives of seniors helped and gave esteem, at home, away from office, in domestic and social rather than official areas.

In earlier days, when certain posts were open to Burmese men, and Burmese women were conspicuously absent from such areas, one of the reasons advanced was that conditions of service then were thought unsuited to women. I describe these conditions here, as some of them still pertain. Administrative officials (the most important, found it part of their duty to tour an extensive area. Roads were not always safe. There was not, and there is still not, the custom of finding hotel accommodation which is respectable enough for a woman to use, as a hotel (*haw-te*) still means a place where the ground floor has men drinking hard liquor, and no rooms that families commonly use.

The pattern for touring is to lodge in 'dak-bungalows' ideally situated in lonely sites next to woods, outside the village or town at which the touring man arrives with a bed-roll and a male domestic servant of his own. No woman sought to rise to such a life. It was far better to enjoy a husband's status as a *minkadaw*, to tour with him when he toured to places which were more interesting, for her and children to visit, or with special local products she could either buy cheaply or receive as presents from her husband's juniors there.

The unsuitability of such a life for women was even greater during those days before motor roads and cars became common. My elder uncle, who did best in government service did most of his touring on horseback and found his food where he could. The combined effects of long hours in the saddle and consumption of concentrated venison unbalanced by vegetables caused serious illness later in life. There was, besides, in such service the possibility of becoming a Judge, a prospect which made even many a male Buddhist quail, as it might involve passing a death sentence. Surely no woman wanted to try towards such goals. I think of two paternal uncles being given training in law degrees after their Bachelor degrees, by their elder brother, my father. Knowing of his intention to make them compete for the Judicial Service, my younger Uncle Pyant slipped away to the village where Father himself grew up as a monastery boy. He confided to us children that this was to avoid the prospect of becoming a Judge later on, though I think it was also to escape the other of my parents' plans – marriage with good connections. The elder Uncle San Lin stayed on to enjoy both these dignified estates arranged by my parents.

Directing traffic

Both Father and this uncle, though raised in days of purely male office holders, planned great careers for us four sisters. I remember the tones of pride with which Father told us of the experiment of having the first woman, Daw May May Khin recruited to the judicial service. I remember too that some years later, he told us sadly of the experiment's failure. Daw May May Khin had not been able to travel enough. No more women would be recruited. Daw May May Khin herself had a satisfactory career. She suffered no taunts or belittlement by male colleagues and rose to be Registrar of the High Court.

The Bar was, of course, a good place for a woman. She could plead while living in her own home town. As time passed Burmese discovered that the British distinguished, even in their home country, between lower levels, of law training and that for barristers. In time, the few Burmese families which were quick enough in amassing money, sent bright sons to London to 'take silk' or, in Burmese *Wut-lon-daw-ya* (able to wear the high mantle). Among this select band of the truly elite was Daw Pwa Hmi. She went in 1923 to England, studied at the Inner Temple of the Inns of Court and in 1925 'took silk'. In 1927, there was an official reception at the High Court to honour her appointment to the Thamadhi Juvenile Court. After a brilliant start to her career, she was unfortunately stricken with polio.

Mention of her means dwelling on the rare and distinguished few. I will mention two more in this train. For academic success, Daw Mya Sein passed Matriculation with distinctions in every subject, got a First Class Honours degree in History, and went on to an M.A. (Honours), then finally to an Oxford degree. In medicine, Daw Saw Sa in 1911, got her licentiate of the Medical Service Diploma; in 1912, she became an F.R.C.S. and got her D.P.H. from the Dublin Royal College of Surgeons, the following year. After still another year, she got her L.M. from Coombes Maternity Hospital. She served in many important posts on return to Burma until well into old age, serving as Assistant General Surgeon at the Women's Dufferin Hospital, Social Welfare projects and attending International Conferences.

Later on, I shall give profiles of todays' women in many more professions. They are, to suit this age, unsung wives working to supplement budgets with little thoughts of glory or accolade.

Politics before 1930

Much of the foregoing deals with the colonial era. During this time, much of political participation was in nationalist efforts which concentrated on speeding up the political machinery to include Burmese men as well as women. The landmark of the Burmese Nationalist Movement is generally held to be the successful boycott of November 29, 1920, of University and schools, in protest against Government's plans to make the University for Burma a residential one. This would have excluded a great many Burmese, who, being too poor for residential fees, could otherwise board with relatives in town to attend courses at a non-residential University.

The boycott achieved its aims and the plans were modified in the desired direction. In another University strike 16 years later, girls were to join in actively. In this one however, they were not present, but significantly for its success, the striking students encamped on the Shwedagon Pagoda slopes were supplied with food stocks by Daw Win and Daw Thein, members of the Burmese Women's Association of the Soortee Bazaar.

The idea of formal associations of women began in the second decade of this century when the early Buddhist associations were formed by men with the idea of promoting the national traditions to withstand the tide of new social goals consequent on the start of British rule. Thus the first formal association was the Burmese Women's Movement formed on November 16, 1919 under the umbrella of GCBA (General Council of Burmese Associations). The GCBA stemmed from YMBA's (Young Men's Buddhist Associations) formed as counterpoise to YMCA. Women recognized this as nationalist endeavour and resolved to be ready to support husbands, fathers, brothers and sons should the need arise. Though this was the chief aim, they also recognized that their own efforts should concentrate on the welfare and status of Burmese women in particular and later they took up a good number of feminist causes. At its inception, the Burmese Women's Association was formed with 300 members and an Executive Committee of officials' wives and business women, chiefly bazaar traders. The movement stated its aims were to model themselves on the great wives and mothers of world history, citing *Maya Devi*, *Yasodhara* and so on, hardly the orientation one would expect from a feminist viewpoint.

Nevertheless, they espoused the cause of women's status as needed. They curbed the tendency of poor women marrying foreigners (chiefly Chinese and Indian) and helped to bring about the Special Marriage Acts (Chapter III) by which the rights of Burmese women living with foreign husbands were safeguarded to the same extent as they were in Burmese-Buddhist marriages. They also pressed for and got special sections in city trams to be marked 'For Women Only'. They pressed the government to rescue and repatriate at government expense a group of Burmese women cheroot rollers who had been taken by their foreign employer to Penang, and were successful. They tried to raise the standard of learning and of religious knowledge among the members with reading rooms and classes. There were over two hundred branches of this movement all over Burma. Called *Wunthanu* (patriotic) Associations they decided to wear a uniform of light brown homespun cotton jacket (called *pinni*), longyis of *yaw* design from the western hill tracts of Burma, instead of imported cotton, and a scarf woven with a peacock design, the peacock being the symbol of the last Burmese dynasty. They once did away with tortoise-shell combs, a high quality comb around which their hair was usually wound, because the word for tortoise shell contained *leik*, the same sound as in the word *inga-leik* (English) as they did not wish to put anything expressive of English high on their heads. They pressed for concessions to allow women to stand for election to the Legislative Council. However, they did not succeed in getting this till much later, as these rights were being fought for by men at that time. They also tried to get on to Municipal Councils.

Later, this Association split. The split was caused not by religious differences, but by the coming of dyarchy and the creation of ministerial posts which were not enough for all aspirants. (*Burma's Constitution* Maung Maung, The Hague, 1961, p.14). With the split, the Buddhist members reformed into the Kalyani Women's Association. The parent association despite having branches all over Burma eventually dwindled. It may be that this would have happened as the nationalist movement grew more successful and enthusiasm had already reached its full height.

In 1919, general resentment had grown against the British decision to grant reforms (known as Minto-Morley Reforms) to India but to withhold consideration of extending them to Burma. After GCBA efforts got an agreement to send a mission to London to press the Burmese case, the Women's movement succeeded in getting a woman representative in, to include women in whatever concessions were gained. She was Daw Mya Sein, Secretary of the Burmese Women's Association. Dr Maung Maung in his book, *Law and Custom in Burma and the Burmese Family*, quotes from minutes of proceedings there.

> The women of Burma occupy a position of freedom and independence not attained in other provinces. Socially there is practical equality between the sexes. Purdah is unknown; women take their full share with men in the economic life of their country and the percentage of literates among women is far higher than elsewhere.

A limited franchise and popular elections were two concessions made at that conference. This first franchise for elections in 1922, was based on tax payments and property holdings, which allowed in far more men than women, resulting in a voters' list of 1.95 million men and 124,000 women. Elections were held for a Legislative Council or Lower House and a Senate. Attempts made to allow women to stand for the Legislative Council were defeated by 45 votes to 31.

Politics after 1930 till Independence

The tempo of Burmese nationalism can be said to have accelerated noticeably after 1930. There was also a distinct change in the style of nationalist efforts. The nationalism of the twenties was dominated by Burmese leaders who strove for British symbols of achievement such as the barrister's silk gown. These worthy gentlemen made a valiant stand for their Buddhist values to the rustle of silk longyis and the dignified tread of shod feet. Indeed, the first meeting of the YMBA began with a rendering of 'God save the King'.

The thirties were marked by the emergence of new and young leaders who had a very different style. They wore thonged slippers instead of shoes, homespun cotton instead of silk, and called themselves *Thakins*, meaning masters in their own house, with reference to the word *thakin* used for Britons by their subordinates. These young leaders went straight to the masses and joined with young monks in inciting Burmese feeling against the peasants' dispossession of land and their agricultural debts to foreign moneylenders coming in the wake of the British. Emerging with the *Thakins* were *Thakinmas*, women who joined the political association of the *Thakins* known as *Dobama Asi-ayone*. The high point of their exploits was in the oil field strike of 1938. At Chauk, a hundred women were among the leading strikers and had a loud and noisy confrontation with the police while they were picketing. The police turned water hoses on them, poured boiling tar on the roads where they might lie down to picket, and beat them with bamboo sticks. The *Thakinmas* did not disperse. Instead, if one was arrested, ten others would cluster around to get arrested too. They suffered their jackets to get torn in the beating, and chanted slogans in the rhythm used in joyful chanting at festivals, taunting the police with shouts of, '*Thakinma's* blood flows red and strong. Magwe's jail means nothing nothing! (Kyi Mah, p.35)' Twenty women were given two month sentences. These women were from Chauk; others from Yenangyaung and Pagan, were similarly active and got similar sentences. These women were regarded as so active that their husbands were dismissed from employment in the oil company. In the 400 mile march which the striking oil workers made to Rangoon, women not only joined in, but other women along the route were ready with cheroots, food and money to help the marchers (ibid, p.37). In Rangoon where strikes occurred in sympathy with oil field workers, women of the Dobama Association arranged meetings for nationalist speeches, as well as collections of funds to support strikers. Among the spate of strikers in Rangoon in this year were over two hundred women cheroot rollers of Ma Sein Nyunt's cheroot factory in Ya Kyaw and women workers from Thamaing rope factory, as well as women from soap, hosiery and rubber works.

hundred women cheroot rollers of Ma Sein Nyunt's cheroot factory in Ye Kway and women workers from Thamaing rope factory, as well as women from soap, hoisery and rubber works.

An equally significant part played by other women in the politics of the 1930s is that of a small group of University women in the years following Aung San's arrival in 1934. The image of the new nationalist leader was accepted by the girls chosen by some of Aung San's associates in these years. The University strike of 1936 was joined by 36 young women who made not only political history but also social history by going into the strikers' protest-residence on the slopes of the Shwe-dagon Pagoda where they camped side by side with male strikers. This, interestingly, did not cast any 'stain' on their character.

Proceeding from a different direction again, a lone woman, Daw Hnin Mya stood for election to the Legislative Council in the first elections allowing women to stand, and won her seat in Burma's first Legislative Assembly in 1936. By 1940 nationalists were involved with the possibility which Aung San had brought about of receiving strict military training and getting arms for their opposition to British rule.

In early 1942, the British and Allied forces withdrew from Burma and the Japanese occupied the whole country. As almost all senior administration in the government had been British, this withdrawal meant a collapse of government, and all schools were closed down while the population sought shelter in those parts of the country which was off the route of Japanese advance or British retreat. A few Burmese leaders at this point called on all Burmese civil servants to rally and keep going even amidst a hail of bombs and a breakdown in communications. A sense of national emergency arose as this was done.

Women were affected by the sense of emergency. During the war a reluctant merger was tried between Dr. Ba Maw's *Sinyetha Party* and the *Dobama Asiayone*. The single party was called the *Dobama Sinyetha Asi-ayone* of which Dr. Ba Maw was leader. The Women's section of the *Dobama Sinyetha* (poor man's) Party, plunged in to help in rescuing air-raid victims, setting up schools in safe areas, teaching and giving courses in such practical skills as soap-making in view of the current shortages.

When the Asia Youth Associations were formed with the encouragement of the Japanese authorities, girls as well as boys joined eagerly. It was a time when the emergency and dangers of war, combined with the resurrection of the Burmese martial spirit which had been greatest in Southeast Asia, but which the British had broken, was proudly reborn. This rebirth began when the Thirty Comrades, young nationalist leaders of 1937 and 1938, slipped off to their rigorous military training in Hainan Island. When the Pacific War started, these young leaders, together with their Japanese trainer and friend, Colonel Suzuki – who himself believed the promises given to the young Burmese that they would be left in control of their country once the British were pushed out – were joined in the Burma Independence Army by their countrymen in thousands. It was felt that at last the Burmese could again have a national army to carry on the tradition of their conquering forefathers who thought nothing of marching from the Brahmaputra to the Mekong, with mobility and stockade tactics which were acknowledged by all they fought against, as almost invincible. It had rankled that their King was led away quietly, 'without a shot being fired,' and so the common villagers all over the plain put up a long, fierce resistance.

Now in 1941, they did not realize that their entry into Burma was only a tiny part of the plan by which Japan herself would smash the colonial order in the world. When they did realize this, there was no time to repine. Aung San, clear-eyed like most Burmans, decided they would organize a resistance force and be ready if their overtures to the Allies, which they made now, were accepted. Under cover of the Asia Youth Association, the boys and girls now joined the resistance movement. The girls were especially active in passing messages to the underground group which must sometimes have seemed of little avail. They enshrined in their hearts the image of the new Burmese Soldier who would fight in this twentieth century, risking the tortures of the *Kempatai*, helping to hide arms and supplies.

Under the *Sinyetha* Party's consolidation, women also took to nursing which Burmese women had been slower to join than other ethnic groups. The nurses not only did nursing, they sewed clothes for their patients at this time of textile and clothing shortage. Two of the outstanding leaders in the Patriotic movements at this time married nurses, two sisters in fact. And the young daughter of the Surgeon, Ma Khin May Than, who organized all their efforts and kept up people's spirits with music and song, decided to train as a nurse and not as a doctor.

This patriotic fervour of young women continued in the post-war period to infect the populace and carry Aung San forward in wresting concessions and winning Independence in a very different way from that of the old leaders'. Events moved at a swift pace leading to an agreement with the Labour Party in Britain and Independence was proclaimed on January 4, 1948. During these two or three momentous years, no associations of a politico-social character would be expected outside of the AFPFL's all-embracing programme of civil resistance.

The women's part in all this leads me to conclude that, in general, Burmese women have stayed away from political and administrative areas, but when times have been critical and the need has arisen, they will act, organize and associate – something which they do only with religious or national need as inspiration.

Politics – Post Independence

After Independence was won and all those who had been active with the movements could feel that their time had now come, it may astonish the outside world how few women decided to take active leadership.

Though the Constitution stated that all citizens could be eligible for all offices regardless of sex, the list of women who stood for election to either parliament or chamber of nationalities in the years 1948-1962, is woefully short – 18 women only. These were: for 1947-51, Daw Saw Shwe, Daw Khin Hla, Daw Hla Shin and Daw Khin Pu. In place of leaders assassinated in 1947, their wives were appointed as temporary members of Parliament. These were: Daw Khin Kyi (Bogyoke Aung San), Daw Khin Nyunt (Thakin Mya), Daw Khin Khin (U Razak). In 1952 were elected Daw E Nyunt and Daw Saw Shwe. During 1953 and 54, Mrs Ba Maung Chein (Irene Po) held a Portfolio as Minister for Karen Affairs in the Union Cabinet, being the first and only woman Minister. In the elections for 1956 to 59, seats were won by: Daw Mya Si and Sao Hurn Kham in the Chamber of Deputies, and Daw Sein Pu, Daw Mya Mya and Daw Saw Shwe in the Chamber of Nationalities. In elections for 1951-61, Daw E May was elected to the Chamber of Deputies and Daw Hnin Hla and Amay Chit to the Chamber of Nationalities. From 1960-67 Daw Khin Kyi (Madame Aung San) served as Burmese Ambassador to India.

This side of 1962 the percentage of women has not been markedly higher though some increases have been seen. The Burma Socialist Programme Party (B.S.P.P.) has only 1 woman in 100 in its central committee. Two women members of note are included in the list of professional women whose profiles appear in the following section. A third woman party member in this list of professional women, works in the party in the one section where women predominate, that is, in the publication section. The national assembly of 1978 saw an increase over that of 1974 in its inclusion of 13 women members over 9 of the earlier session. However this is out of a total of 449 members.

Professional Participation: Training

Burma's University education has, in the years since 1962, changed its aim from one of general education for an intelligentsia, to being a preparation for one profession or another needed in national development.

Towards this end, University administration reformed a number of vocational preparation institutes for Medicine, Agriculture, Veterinary Science, Dental

Surgery, Engineering, Education and Economics, leaving other courses in Arts and Science Universities (2) or Regional Colleges (6). Since 1976, the number of Regional Colleges have been significantly increased. Special emphasis is given to Science courses, either introduced too late during British rule or not given sufficient push in the years before independence in 1962.

Intake for these institutions in 1975 are given in the following table.

Higher Education: Enrolment for the 1975-76
Academic Year

Institute	Male	Female
Rangoon Arts and Science University	9832	9800
Mandalay Arts and Science University	3988	3012
Institute of Education	561	1829
Rangoon Institute of Technology	3224	636
Agricultural Institute	674	244
Institute of Economics	1736	2872
Animal Husbandry and Veterinary Institute	646	259
Institute of Medicine (1)	1330	1176
Institute of Medicine (2)	494	266
Institute of Medicine (Mandalay)	636	344
Institute of Dentistry	257	63
Worker's College	4547	2434
Bassein College	1377	1654
Moulmein College	1688	1901
Taunggyi College	594	659
Myitkyina College	525	397
Magwe College	1072	903
Akyab College	241	175
Mandalay Evening Classes	764	370

(Source: *author's personal correspondence*)

Entry was granted in order of priority based on marks obtained in the nation-wide Matriculation examination, the top students entering Medicine as this is considered the most prestigious and lucrative profession. It will be seen that in the premier institute (Medicine 1) of this profession, there is an almost equal intake of boys and girls. However, other institutes, especially Engineering, Agriculture and Veterinary Science still show a big male predominance.

Some Profiles of Burmese Professional Women

Daw Yin Yin Mya, Economist, University Lecturer and Political Leader. In this short gallery of ten professional profiles, I begin with Daw Yin Yin Mya because she chose to subordinate her professional career to one as a housewife and this is a pattern which Burmese women up till about twenty years ago, generally followed. Daw Yin Yin Mya's distinguished academic successes are more remarkable because they were postponed till their pursuit could fit happily into her marital circumstances. Born in 1925, Daw Yin Yin Mya, after winning first prizes in High School and University, suspended study for the duration of the war. When universities reopened in 1945, Daw Yin Yin Mya's return to College was forgotten as she received a highly desirable proposal of marriage which she accepted. She married U Ba Aye of the Police Service. He was posted away from Rangoon where the University was situated and she accompanied him to Bassein. Although he was posted back after this to Rangoon, she confined her stay there to activities of a voluntary nature in the sphere of social welfare work and maternity and child care. In 1952, he was posted as Police Chief in the Military Administration that was temporarily set up in the Shan State to meet the emergency of Chinese nationalist troops entering Burma.

During this time, she visited the frontline. This took her far and wide through the Shan States to distribute gifts to the soldiers. In 1954, U Ba Aye returned to a senior Police post in Rangoon (Deputy Inspector General of the Union Military Police). She decided to re-enter the University and did so in 1956. She earned entry into 3 Honours courses and chose Economics. As the honours degree take three years, she sat for the ordinary Bachelor's degree examination after two years and obtained this B.A. degree in a number of other subjects. She was then appointed as tutor, that is the most junior level of University staff, in Economics. In 1959, she obtained her Economics Honours degree and was promoted to Assistant Lecturer in Economics.

She began work towards her Masters degree in Economics which she won in 1968. Her thesis was on 'Taxation in Burma.' During the years 1960-61, she took up the study of law so as to be qualified to practise if transferred again out of Rangoon. The Law course is in two annual parts and over the two years examinations, she gained a total of nine distinctions which is still the record in these law examinations. She was awarded the University Gold medal and the first prize by the Law Association of which she became the treasurer in 1961-62. She continued her work as assistant lecturer in the Economics Department until 1970 when she was promoted and appointed at the higher level of Lecturer and Head of the Economics Department in the Institute of Education. She continues in this post till today.

Her voluntary activities outside of work hours are as Vice President of the University Women's Association and also as the Treasurer of the Buddhist Association of the Institute of Education. There is also her voluntary work of a political nature which is highly important. She is a full-fledged member of the Burma Socialist Programme Party which is the only political party of the Union of Burma. The duties she carries out for the Party are done out of working hours and are purely voluntary. The posts she holds in connection with these are by appointment from Party leaders only, as they deal with the Co-operative movement and workers councils which are key instruments in the implementation of the Socialist Programme of Burma. I list these below.

Tin Tin Wint (third from left), volunteer literacy campaigner
with sisters and friends

Daw Yin Yin Mya after joining the B.S.P.P. in 1965, gave active leadership in the Party activities of the Institute of Economics from 1965-70. She served on the Council of the Central Co-operative Society from 1974-77. She was President of the Co-operative Saving Society of the Institute of Education from 1972, the day of its inception to the present day. She is also a Councillor of the Kamayut Township Co-operative Council, and Member of the Executive Committee of the Workers' Council No. 24 of Kamayut Township, also serving on various sub-committees in that capacity.

Daw Kyi Kyi Hla, University Professor. In using the term Professor, it must be explained that Burma still follows the British system in which only one position, the one and only chair in an academic department, is given the term of Professor.

This corresponds to the position of the Chair of a Department in an American University. The appointment, unlike that of the American academic chair, does not rotate between several professors. It is given after much more deliberation and accordingly, it is held until the professor retires. In such a context, a woman professor has been a rarity in Burmese academic life. Sometimes, a woman heads a department, but when the department is held to be a minor one, such as Anthropology, she is termed Head and not professor. The notable exception was the department of Geography where Dr Daw Thin Kyi who received her American doctorate as early as 1948 was Professor of Geography for many years. She is now retired and there remains only Daw Eleanor Kan Gyi as Professor of English, and Daw Than Swe and Daw Khin Saw as Professors of Burmese and Daw Kyi Kyi Hla, Professor of Philosophy.

Born in 1932, Daw Kyi Kyi Hla graduated with honours B.A. in 1964 and became an Assistant Lecturer teaching both Occidental and Oriental systems of Philosophy to first, second and third year students. In 1957, she got her M.A. degree, and her thesis was entitled *Developments in Symbolic Logic since Publication of the Principia Mathematica*. She was promoted to the position of Lecturer in the same department, but was posted out of Rangoon to Mandalay University where she taught for 15 years. Her writing over this period includes text-books in Burmese. *A Text-book of Elementary Logic* and *A History of Political Thought* in 2 volumes were published by the Rangoon University Press. A paper on logical foundations of the Burmese Language was read at the Research Congress in 1970. In 1972, she was posted back from Mandalay to Rangoon University where she became Head of the Philosophy Department till 1974. By now, her work included the study of the philosophy of the Burmese Way to Socialism in addition to previously taught systems. An external candidate was brought in as Professor for 4 years, until in September 1978, Daw Kyi Kyi Hla was appointed as Professor. Daw Kyi Kyi Hla's main interest outside of her academic work is her commitment to the Burma Socialist Programme Party which she joined in 1965 after the formation of the Party in 1963. She is secretary to a party group defined as a Party *Seit*. Her work is mainly organizational. She teaches ideology courses in the Kamayut Area bordering the University but she is also currently busy on compiling a glossary of political terms for use by the Party.

Tall, and beautiful, she is a compelling speaker and is eloquent both in Burmese and English. In February 1976, she attended the Union Day Conference as delegate from Rangoon division. Her speech there on an 'Evaluation of the first 5 year Economic Plan' made a great impression, as the economic situation of the country following its socialist programme is a burning and controversial issue.

Daw Kyi Kyi Hla became a full-fledged Party member in 1972. Confirmation as such a 'fully minted' member is an honour conferred only with good reason. She is married to a retired Army major. She has 2 children, a daughter who is a doctor and a son who is a budding engineer. Her other son Lieutenant Myint Ohn, was killed in action in 1977 in the great push made by the army against Communist and other border intrusions in the Northeastern areas adjacent to

China.

Dr Yin Yin Nwe. The Geology Department of the University where Daw Yin Yin Nwe teaches has one of the smallest proportions of women to men out of all Arts and Science Departments. Strenuous field trips, either up and down steep hills or under the burning sun feature largely in the course. It was found also that women students could not often complete the 20-mile walk that was a requirement for entrance to the department. Unlike other departments therefore, women are not readily admitted to the geological studies department.

Daw Yin Yin Nwe was born in 1949. She entered the Rangoon University of Arts and Sciences in November 1964 and obtained a B.Sc. degree in Geology in 1968 with distinctions in all six subjects. During this same year she had obtained a Fellowship of the Gemmological Association of Great Britain (F.G.A.), the training for which was conducted by Mr E.A. Jobbins, who came to Rangoon as a UNDP expert to set up a gemmological laboratory in Rangoon University with UNDP aid.

In January 1969, Daw Yin Yin Nwe became a demonstrator in the Geology Department of the University. She taught some undergraduate courses and was responsible for the gemmological training which Jobbins had set up. From 1969 to 1971 she took teams of students on field trips. These were to (a) remote areas lying between the Shan States and the Burmese plain, (b) the Mogok Stone Tract – a beautiful series of valleys and mountains, where almost every precious and semi-precious stone can be found, (c) Lead-zinc producing area near Bawzaing, Southern Shan States, (d) the hilly regions near and around the Pindaya Range. All these field trips involve extensive walks, as there is no other means of transport, and usually living in remote villages for at least a month or so. They were primarily to train undergraduate students in geological mapping.

In September 1971, Daw Yin Yin Nwe obtained a Colombo Plan Fellowship for post-graduate studies in England. She was sent by the government to Britain and admitted to Newnham College, Cambridge University, and commenced research for a Ph.D. in the Department of Mineralogy and Petrology under the supervision of the eminent petrologist, Dr S.O. Agrell. The title of her thesis was the *Aspects of the Mineralogy of the Skaergaard Intrusion, East Greenland*, and research for it was intensive laboratory studies using the electron microprobe, the electron microscope and other techniques. The thesis was submitted in April 1975, and a Ph.D. degree was conferred in August 1975. The months after finishing the thesis were spent in producing scientific papers related to the research done for the thesis. Three such papers were published in the journal *Contributions to Mineralogy and Petrology*.

She came back to Burma in October 1975 and since then, has been teaching several courses – both undergraduate and post-graduate. Post-graduate teaching is for the M.Sc. students and D.A.G. (Diploma in Applied Geology) students, and involved initiation of several new courses, field work and thesis supervision. She is also now in charge of the Gemmological Laboratory, and the Department's gemstone collection and is at the same time engaged in some research work on the marbles north of Mandalay. So far, she is the only woman to hold a doctorate in the geological sciences in Burma and was the first woman geologist in Burma to go abroad for post-graduate training. She was promoted in September 1978 to assistant lecturer.

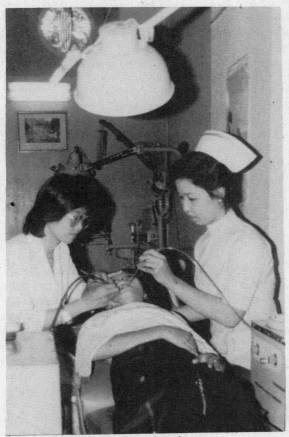

Dental surgeon and nurse at work

Dr Sao Mya Mae. Burma's closest link for the medical profession as well as specialized treatment for patients is Britain. The highest qualification Burmese doctors aim at is to be admitted either as a Member of the Royal College of Physicians or Member of the Royal College of Surgeons. There are more than a dozen women doctors at present who have obtained Membership of the Royal College of Physicians. Of these the one to be most recently admitted as Fellow of this august medical body was Dr Myat Kyi Than. This is being written a month after the death of the most eminent woman surgeon in the field of Obstetrics and Gynaecology, namely, Dr Daw Yin Mae, who was aged 81 when she died. Others and younger women Members of the Royal College of Obstetrics and Gynaecology remain active still.

Although Dr Sao Mya Mae has not sought the eminence belonging to the above members, she is my choice as the senior woman doctor in this list of professional women, because her career has been more wide in range and diverse in activity than her colleagues who have won greater eminence clinically. Dr Sao Mya Mae was born in 1921 as the daughter of a Chief of the small Shan state of Pwehla. She qualified as a doctor in Rangoon in 1950. She served as Assistant Surgeon in the Rangoon General Hospital till the end of 1951, and in the Rangoon Women's Hospital till the end of 1952. She was then sent by the Government to Calcutta where she gained her diploma in Child and Maternity Welfare. She returned to take up what she considers to have been a most important part of her life-work. As Assistant Maternity and Child Welfare Officer for the Shan states from 1954-60, she toured the whole of the state (approximately 57,816 sq.m.). In those years, women drivers were rare. Sao Mya Mae, short in stature looked remarkable as she drove her big touring van up and down the hill roads of her Shan environment. Most of the places she visited were what others would term villages, set in remote upland valleys. In the earlier section of this chapter I spoke of the exclusion of women from touring jobs because of their having to travel on lonely roads and live in isolated dak bungalows. Sao Mya Mae, as one of a Shan state family would have been welcomed in any of the Staff houses where doctors, nurses or midwives lived. She chose however, to stay alone in order to feel freer to report correctly without having to consider hospitality given her. To make her unmarried position 'respectable' in view of this, she befriended an efficient nurse whom she took everywhere as a younger sister, assistant and friend. This is the accepted pattern for unmarried women who need company in certain situations.

Dr Mary Krasu. Of the many women specialists with topmost foreign degrees in medicine and surgery, I give here the resumé of the career of Dr Mary Krasu, because she is among the youngest specialist to hold a senior consultant rank as well as Chief Surgeon in her hospital. Born in 1939, Dr Mary Krasu, a Karen Christian woman, qualified as doctor with an M.B.B.S. degree in Rangoon in the Institute of Medicine No. 1 in 1963. She was posted to the small settlement of Loilem in the Southern Shan States where, as Assistant Surgeon, she held responsibility for the general female ward with special charge of Obstetrics and Gynaecology.

In 1965 she was posted to the far larger town of Taunggyi where in the civil hospital, she rotated between the general female ward, the out-patient department and Obstetrics and Gynaecology, which had by now become her selected field for specialization. After three years of service in this hospital, she was posted to Rangoon, where in the Central Women's Hospital she worked for two years as Assistant Surgeon, O.G., obtaining her prerequisite training for taking a British degree in Obstetrics and Gynaecology. For this, she followed her two years in this Central Women's Hospital with six months surgery work in the General Hospital, Rangoon.

In 1971, Dr Mary Krasu was sent to England by the government of the Union of Burma as a post-graduate medical state scholar. She worked as Honorary Registrar in the Freedom Free Hospital, Plymouth, University College Hospital, London. She followed this with training in the Chelsea Hospital, and Queen Charlotte Hospital for Women in the course for her desired degree.

In February 1973, she obtained this degree becoming a Member of the Royal College of Obstetricians and Gynaecologists at her first attempt.

On return to Burma, she served as first Assistant to the Clinical Professor, herself a woman, Dr Daw Hla Kyi, in the Central Women's Hospital in Rangoon from 1973 to 1976. Then she moved up-country to Magwe where she had independent charge as a Consultant, O.G. During this period she made closer contact with the common folk in the heart of Burma and was selected as the workers' representative of Section 12 of the Magwe Basic Council of Workers.

Her next posting was to the Women's and Children's Hospital in Taunggyi, capital of the Shan states, where she is consultant in a 200-bed hospital. Though her present duties are far more onerous and responsibility heavier than her previous post in Magwe, she does less now of the administrative work, which was· her main strength in her previous posts. The administrative work in this large hospital for women and children is mostly the responsibility of an older woman, Dr Daw Tin E who is the Medical Superintendent as well as consultant for Pediatrics.

This hospital, run chiefly by two women is kept going and maintains what most observers and patients agree is a higher standard than the large General Hospital staffed largely by male doctors in the same town.

Lt. Commander Daw Mi Mi Khin, Burma Navy. Women's participation in the armed forces began with the formation of a small women's corps at the time of the Japanese occupation when the forces of Burma were called the Burma National Army. Before this corps could be fully formed, the resistance movement against the Japanese occupation started, the army went underground and the small band of girls followed into the jungle.

After Independence, attempts were made to recruit women into the Defence Services, after a resolution to do so was passed in Parliament in 1953. Recruitment, however, could begin only in 1959. Headed by Daw Kyin Si, eleven women were recruited to be trained as officers. After sixteen weeks basic training, they were offered training in their choice of courses as follows: Secretarial, Radio repair, Telephone switchboard, Nursing or Administration. Later, a batch was sent to U.S.A. for six weeks training at women's service training centres, followed by further training in England and Israel. After 1960, lack of funds stopped further recruitment. The plan to have a separate women's corps has never been realized, as other plans were made. Among these was the training given to all government servants (male or female, civilian or military) in batches, at

Phaunggyi. This training includes small arms and basic defence skill.

Lt. Commander Mi Mi Khin first became a Mathematics Tutor in Rangoon University after her Bachelor's degree in Mathematics. In 1960, she joined the Burma Navy as a sub-lieutenant. She received 7½ months training in navigation, seamanship and administration. Promoted to lieutenant's rank, she served for a term in the War Office at Administrative duties. She was then posted to the Naval Base called *Ratanabon* and during her years of duty there, chiefly at Accounts and Administration, she was promoted to Lt. Commander. She has 1200 men serving under her, ratings as well as male officers junior to her.

In her later years, she married Commander Aung Gyi, who is now retired. She has one child and keeps house in the Naval house prvided for her.

Daw Yin Yin (pen name Saw Mo-Nyin): (Journalist, editor, staff member of Burma Socialist Programme Party's Literature Section). Burma has eminent novelists, poets, journalists, editors and publishers among its women. I chose to include here the profile of Saw Mo Nyin, who is not necessarily the most famous in the writer's world. I choose her because the range, quality and subject matter of her prolific writing appears to me to be in tune with present day Burma as well as with the spirit of this volume on Burmese women's activities.

Daw Yin Yin was born in 1921 in Falam in the Chin Hills special division. She went to Primary School in that remote little town in the foothills of Burma's Western wall. After this, her father moved far east to the Shan states capital of Momeik, as Chief Minister to the *Sawbwa* or ruler of that state. Though Momeik has more status as the Ruler's seat, the neighbouring town of Mogok, higher in the hills, has greater prosperity and activity. Mogok is the site of the famed Ruby mines district of Burma which is rich in gems. It lies in a slight hollow, with blue hills on every horizon. Here, Daw Yin Yin had her Middle School education (Junior High). From there she went to the American Baptist High School in Mandalay to complete her schooling. The combination of ethnic minorities highland culture and the majority Burmese court traditions which were still strong in Mandalay have shaped Daw Yin Yin's interest in the cultural activities of widely divergent groups in Burma.

After High School, Daw Yin Yin attended Judson College in the University of Rangoon. On graduating she went as school teacher in Namtu and Lashio in the Northern Shan States. She had already begun writing under the pen name of Mogok Yin Yin since 1933 when she was 12, in such publications as *Thibaw Yadana Thiha* Journal and Judson magazine.

During the Japanese occupation of Burma in World War II, Daw Yin Yin was active in the Asia Youth Movement which was a front for keeping the resistance spirit strong. She worked chiefly at organizing the literacy section of the movement.

She married U Thein, a customs official who rose to become the Deputy Commissioner of Customs before he died in 1973. As the wife of U Thein, Daw Yin Yin accompanied him to such remote places at Kyukok on the Burma-China border, as well as to bigger towns like Bassein and Rangoon. Along with her keen interest in thoroughly indigenous activities, Daw Yin Yin also took a keen interest in the girl guide movement which many might have regarded as a foreign import. As guide leader she later went on a tour of England, Holland, Switzerland, and France to observe girl guide activities there. Her interest in sociological research and writings led her to attend social services conferences in the Republic of China, North Vietnam and Japan in the years 1957-58. During her husband's term of duty in Rangoon in the years 1957-58, she worked as a part-time lecturer in Burmese at the Worker's College. She also served as the women member of the Film Censor Board. She helped in constructing domestic science courses. She visited army units in the Central Division to talk on topics of educative value and of general cultural interest to Officers and men alike. She served on the committee for jail reforms. She was responsible for broadcasts from the official Burma Broadcasting Service on the topics of women's affairs and girl guide movements. With the formation of the Burma Socialist Programme Party in 1963, she applied for membership and became a party member in 1968. She joined the full time staff of Party Headquarters in the publication secton as publications officer, a post that she holds till today.

She wrote a series of Traditional Games for women to play, choosing games where the chant of question and answer gave scope for recapitulating old cultural verses. Her most recent effort is the production of anthropological studies on ethnic minority cultures which I have referred to in the bibliography suggested for Chapter XII, Saw Mo-Nyin has lost a soldier son, as well as her husband. She lives with a daughter, nieces and grandchildren continuing to be the cheerful citizen reflected in writings throughout her life. To commemorate Women's Year set internationally 1976, she brought out a volume containing the biographies of notable Burmese in all fields of life, generously including every segment.

Dagon Khin Khin Lay: Author. Dagon Khin Khin Lay, grande dame of Burmese letters, is often referred to as 'Mother of Burmese Literature'.

Born in 1904 she won a prize for a short story in 1917 at the age of 13. Belonging to a family connected with the court tradition, she was put to bed each night, not with stories of 'Golden Rabbit, Golden Tiger' as other children, but with tales of the Palace where a King had reigned till 1885. Such associations led to her writing her major work *Sarsodaw* which was first serialised in *Dagon* Magazine in 1920, whence she got her name of Dagon Khin Khin Lay. She did not succeed in keeping up her serial despite letters from the public urging her to do so. She determined to develop it into a major book, and completed the 3 volume work only in 1950. Meanwhile her output of stories and articles numbering over 500 during 4 or 5 decades continued. She entered the publishing business with the 1st Women's Magazine *Kyidawset* in 1922. Long ahead of today's whispers of women's liberation in the West, she fostered women writers purely from the wish to promote Burmese Literature which in her early days had fallen into Colonial neglect and a subsidiary place in official consciousness. In 1945 she published *Yuwadi* a magazine for which writers, typesetters and Bookbinders were all women while training was given to aspiring girl writers.

After she turned 60, she published her autobiography *60 years* in which she wrote of her marriage and subsequent quarrels with a well-known publisher *Bamakhit* U Ohn Khin.

At a library desk

I will deal here chiefly with *Sarsodaw* because of the particular Burmese women it portrays. The story concerns King Thibaw and Queen Supayalat though the title refers to another man. This title *Sarsodaw* has the literal meaning of Speaker of Literature and is the classical way of defining a scholar dating from the old oral traditions. In this tradition, a scholar must not only be able to write but must be able to declaim his work with eloquent and poetic effect, especially in the royal presence. This particular *Sarsodaw* was the scholar attendant of King Thibaw since his days as a bachelor princeling. The story tells of his love for the young girl Khin Khin Gyi whose parents adopted him as an elder brother to the girl whom he grew to love intensely when she was on the verge of becoming a young woman. Her charm caught the eye of both King and Queen and at their wish she was attached to the court. The King hoped that she would become a second Queen, and also wished to give his royal patron extra happiness, the *Sarsodaw* attendant helped to bring the girl close to Thibaw. Their love affair was discovered. Queen Supayalat got her way and the whole family was put to death after much suffering.

Dagon Khin Khin Lay was a Burmese nationalist when she wrote this book. Why reveal your dirty linen she asks. The answer is that so much had been written about the cruelty and bloody massacres attributed to Supayalat and her mother by British writers who dismissed the bloody trials and violence in European history as belonging to centuries long past, and expressed great revulsion at the liquidation of potential rivals in the 19th century, never thinking that the 20th century would see more slaughtering in Europe than in all the cruel Asian centuries put together. Dagon Khin Khin Lay does not omit the tortures of killing in her story. She even adds various details. Yet the reader is made to feel that all is logical and to be expected. The language throughout is in the fullest court tradition. The wealth of detail is immense. A royalist reading the book will be entranced by the refinements of expressions, utensils, ornaments, watergardens, flowering trees, and close-woven silks. He will be deeply moved by the unquestioning devotion and obedience given to royalty's desires. A socialist reading the same will be amply confirmed in his view that the institution of royalty deserved extermination. A Burmese uncommitted to either royalist or socialist views, will be swept away by the richness of imagery: the ready pens which versified so effectively and beautifully on the leaves of the *Pay* palm; the delicacy in portrayal of young female charm especially in the youthful Supayalat before she became Queen, and her need to maintain her position. 'It is time this Burmese woman was rehabilitated' a friend once said to me in referring to the early British depiction of her cruel ambitious nature. Dagon Khin Khin Lay did not set out to rehabilitate Supayalat, but in the course of her story, she has given us a Burmese woman as able as most Burmese women are believed to be. She was a character who decided to reverse the unbroken tradition that a King to be kingly must own so many wives. When in her first meeting with Prince Thibaw, she declared her love, she declared also her dream of lovers who could remain true to each other and for whom this would be enough.

Her father King Mindon had had 49 wives, 45 sons and 64 daughters. The struggles, manoeuvres, fears and hope for favor and for succession amongst such a company was understandable, and harrowing. Supayalat decided to have none of it. When her mother together with Ministers decided to install young Prince Thibaw as heir and King, the mother adhered to tradition and arranged for the elder sister of Supayalat to be crowned chief queen. Supayalat was stricken with hurt and anguish. You have stolen my sweetheart she burst out in uncourtly language. She could not move her mother. The ceremony had to take its course. The older sister, clad in full regalia was seated in her place with the King on her right. Coronation was about to begin. Suddenly Supayalat clad in identical

Queen regalia appeared from behind. She slid into position between the waiting King and sister. She looked around the hall and broke into the stunned silence with steady voice 'Carry on with the Proclamations if you please!' The ceremony went on and for the first time in Burmese history two chief Queens were consecrated at one stroke.

Dagon Khin Khin Lay has made the story of the last Burmese King's reign primarily a love story. The massacres, the pandering to royal wishes and the rewards heaped on faithful servitors all fall into place as part of a story of the monarchic tradition which was doomed. What continues, in Dagon Khin Khin Lay's own view, is the determination and strength of the Burmese woman amply seen in Queen Supayalat's character.

Sao Myawadi, Lawyer. Mention has been made in the earlier part of this Chapter (Section 2) of Burmese women's entry into the legal profession since the earlier period of Burma's emergence in the modern world. We have seen Daw Pwa Hmi, Bar-at-Law, taking silk in the Inner temple of the Inns of Court in London since 1923, and the ceremony of honour in Rangoon when she was installed as Judge of the Thamadhi Juvenile Court. We have seen Daw May May Khin also entering the Burma Judicial Service and rising till she became Registrar of the High Court before her retirement. These eminent women of law belonged to the era when high prestige of judges shown against the pomp and solemnity of British justice, and barristers with high earnings formed the elite in the British Indian world of litigation. All that has gone with the wind. The former judges or magistrates are now the technical referees and it is People's Judges who give the verdict. People's Judges are chosen not for their training in the law, but are elected to serve in turn from the position as Township Council members who are selected in turn for their contact with the common people and their devotion to the socialist goal. This was the pre-colonial concept of suitable judges and we have gone back to the old Burmese tradition. I have therefore chosen the career of Sao Myawadi to represent woman in law here, as she is young, totally of the present system and moreover specializes in cases of a problem which is a major concern of this Government: the drug addiction problem among youth. It is good to note the involvement of a woman in such a major sociological problem of today.

Born in 1945, Sao Myawadi spent five years in law studies at the University of Rangoon. She followed this with a year of Chamber practice in the city of Rangoon and by then became qualified to practice as advocate. A boy almost next door in her home town of Taunggyi had also trained in the same way, and they returned to Taunggyi where they were shortly married and started to practice with the husband specialising in civil cases and Sao Myawadi in criminal cases.

I asked Sao Myawadi what made her decide to concentrate on the cases associated with heroin, which are classified as criminal cases, and what there was for a lawyer to do in a problem which appeared to me more personal and sociological then criminal. She said it began with her keen sympathy for the parents who appeared to suffer most in the association of their sons or daughters with drug abuse.

> The Burmese law takes strong measures against use, possession, or trafficking with narcotic drugs. The penalty for any of these three types of involvement may extend from a light prison sentence to the death sentence. A lawyer's part lies in helping to get as lenient a verdict as possible. Somehow, either by luck or by what other factor I don't know, I succeeded in getting a lighter sentence than either the parents or I had hoped for. One case led to another, and in no time I found myself getting these cases almost to the exclusion of others.

After marriage, Sao Myawadi and her husband decided to live in part of the large house of her father. There, they receive clients and hold their discussions. There are five different People's Courts in Taunggyi, starting at the Ward Council level and going up to the Divisional State level as this town is the capital of the Shan states, a major unit of the Union of Burma. Before the first clients are due at 8 a.m., Sao Myawadi goes to market driven by her husband, and buys the fresh bazaar foods for her family. She cooks in the intervals of seeing clients who may or may not come during this period till 10 a.m., when offices open. By adroit management, she gets times and days fixed by the different courts to enable her to appear at every case she can follow. Sometimes the cases come from nearby towns such as Kalaw, Pindaya, Aung Ban, Yawnghwe. She may go and return the same evening on dates fixed by the courts in those towns, or she may spend a couple of nights away from home. She has three sons, the eldest being only nine; and during her absence, other relatives of the compound family household take care of them. I asked her if she thought of returning to the University for a masters degree, but she is quite satisfied that her present qualifications are sufficient for the work which she does not want to lose.

Daw Thein Nyunt, Member of the Public Services Selection and Training Board, Retired University Professor of English. This Board is a body of 8 members which interview and select personnel for posts in all branches of government administration. It is the only channel through which anyone can obtain a post with the government which is by far the largest employer in Burma. The Board members are usually senior persons who have already retired from service in their respective fields. Appointment as a member of this Board is regarded as a plum job. It is made partly in recognition of good service during the appointee's working years, and partly to utilise the knowledge of personnel and departmental needs gained from experience during a full service in an important branch of government. As will be seen from the earlier section on Government in this chapter, government Administration has been associated in the post with the prestige carried by men. The Public Services Selection and Training Board, therefore, was composed of male members only, till Daw Thein Nyunt's appointment in 1977.

Born in 1917, Daw Thein Nyunt secured a Master of Arts degree in 1948 after delays due to the suspension of academic education during World War II and the chaos of post-war reorganization. After taking her master's degree, she went on a British Council Scholarship to England for further studies in English literature. On return, she was appointed as a lecturer in English Language and Literature in the Department of English in the University of Rangoon.

During her ten years in this lecturing post, she was further appointed Warden of the women's hostel in the Teachers' Training College, a postgraduate Institution of the University of Rangoon.

In 1954, financed by a U.S.-Burma Cultural Exchange Programme, she spent a year at several major universities in the U.S. following courses in the teaching of English literature, as well as in the Dean of Womenship.

By this time, she had been serving as Warden of Inya Hall, the leading women's hostel of the Rangoon University of Arts and Sciences. Wardens of hostels are quite different from house mothers in American university dormitories. They carry a full measure of authority and must ensure that the strict care of unmarried girls which Burmese society expects is given. The Warden has spacious rooms in one of the hostel wings. These comprise a complete apartment with cooking and entertaining facilities. The job requires much efficiency and tact in providing food to the satisfaction of the women students on a spare budget, and in maintaining standards of cleanliness and orderliness in the years when expansion in student enrollment far outstrip extension of dormitories space. In accordance with the Burmese way of showing respect, tinged with affection, the students address this Warden as Ma Ma Nyunt, meaning Elder Sister Nyunt. Daw Thein Nyunt remains unmarried. Two or three female cousins lived with her, managing the apartment, being entirely supported by her.

In 1966, Daw Thein Nyunt was promoted to the Headship of the English Department, and in 1967, she was confirmed as Professor. With the reorganization of university administration, English became more relevant to the Teachers' Training courses in preparation for teaching it as the second language in schools. It was no longer desired to give English the important place in university curricula where formerly it had been the only foreign language to receive a special place. Daw Thein Nyunt's appointment as Professor of English placed her in the Institute of Education where she served until retirement in 1977. Following a short term as Special Education Officer attached to this Institution, she was appointed to the Public Services Selection and Training Board where, till now she carries out the much coveted duties which have been described earlier.

11. Conclusions

In the introduction to her book; *Women, Change and Society*, Evelyn Suilleroi states that only by comparison can you get the true picture of the condition you describe – it is only by comparing with the position of men that the truth of women's position can be realized. I use this chapter therefore to compare Burmese women (and men) with women and men from societies familiar to the reader. To do this will involve me in too many generalizations, to avoid some of which I will tackle the subject by recounting remarks made to me over the years on the two social systems regarding men and women, in situations which actually occurred.

I will begin by going right back to 1952-53 when I first visited the United States. At a small gathering in New York, a young man made some remarks consequent on learning something of my background during the course of the evening. I was at the time Principal of a co-educational high school within the system known then as that of private schools. By this is meant a school whose head is responsible to a Board of Founders or Governors and who engages staff to be paid out of the fees which pupils pay. Such schools are registered with the state and receive recognition as they must conform to requirements laid down by the state. The State schools in the main system have teachers who are fully state employees, the fees being either not charged or very nominal. My husband at the time was Principal Education Officer for the Shan and the Kayah state, two of the states within the Union of Burma; he headed an inspectorate of state education administrators whose brief covered both state and private schools within these two States.

'A difficult position,' said the young man. 'There must be a lot of conflict.' 'No,' I told him, 'there is very little conflict. Parents are free to choose the system they prefer.' 'I mean conflict between husband and wife being in the same field of work', he said. 'If you are as bright as you appear to be, you might get quick promotions and then won't your husband be jealous?' 'Oh no, you are wrong. In the first place I would not get such promotions. And even if I did, nobody in the community would give me the respect and regard they give him. We agreed early on, to settle in that community where, by his natural endowments and his attainments he was already a well-known and prestigious person.'

'Don't you mind that?' 'I would if someone else's husband got more regard than he did. As it is, I much enjoy what I get from being his wife, and I don't forget that I have got my present opportunities for work largely through his setting them up for me.'

The generosity of Burmese men towards their women's achievements is something that has struck me often during my long life. They are always proud of something successfully done by a *Burmese* rather than that it is a Burmese *woman* or man. In 1937, in the days of the British government, state scholars were chosen to study in England. Thirteen men and two girls were selected, one girl being an Anglo-Burmese, and I was the other. A grand dinner of celebration was held, mainly through the efforts of Ava Hall, a popular male dormitory. At the stage show held after dinner, the professional actors were given, to sing, the song these male students had composed for the occasion. Though the song celebrated everyone's awards, the refrain concentrated on the female part of it. 'Oh, Mi Mi! Oh, Kathleen! How much to be admired, how much to be happy about!'

All through the long ocean voyage and the years of study abroad, I continued to receive this generous kindness and encouragement from any Burmese male I came across. When my sister Mya came to do graduate study at Syracuse University in 1953, she was always 'with it' sartorially that the undergraduate girls identified themselves with her. When I visited her at their dormitory, I learned that the American girls often remarked at the way she could phone and ask any male of the small Burmese community there to visit or to come and escort her somewhere. Hearing that I would be going to visit friends in Niles, Michigan, one of these American girls suggested I visit Ann Arbor. My sister urged me to do this saying that there were four Burmese youths studying there and she would call one of them to see that I was looked after. I went to Toronto to visit friends and picked up a slight illness as a result of which I had to cancel a planned visit to Niagara. I caught a train for Ann Arbor. It was raining all that day. It was a slow train and when I changed trains at Detroit, a man chased me so that, in a panic, I ran with my case in my hand. As it was getting on for 11 p.m., my morale as we approached Ann Arbor was very low. To my dismay, the train stopped not beside any lighted platform but with my carriage facing a black void. I went slowly towards the door, not quite knowing what I would do. As I stood at the door, I heard suppressed laughter and some whispering. My ears caught the blessed words spoken in Burmese. 'I tell you it *is* her.' 'Yes it is,' I replied quickly and at once felt several pairs of hands reaching out to find my elbows. They lifted me down and I remarked that it was nearly midnight but they said everything was all right. One of their professors had offered to give me a night's lodging. On the morrow, they would come and fetch me, take me round, give me lunch and cook me a Burmese dinner at the apartment they shared. When next day I remarked on how good it was of them and their professor and Mrs Boyce to put themselves out to do so much for me, Ko Maung Maung Than said, 'Don't worry about that. But if you want to do something for us, please don't tell the professors to whom we are taking you, that you stopped only incidentally. Let them think you came to see us. Talk to them and be nice. We have told them about Burmese women but I don't think they quite believe all we say, so we told them you were coming here just for us to show them.'

On Ta Ta's arrival here in 1977 I was briefing her on various people and the kind of situations she might come across. I told her of what a friend had said about a young wife we both knew. 'She has had two babies within four years. No wonder she doesn't smile as much as one might expect her to do,' the friend remarked. I commented on my friend's remark 'they do make so much of what is natural or even enjoyable.' 'No', said Ta Ta, 'it's because their men have to give an image of masculinity. So they are busy projecting that image and feel they have to live up to it, and the wives are driven to show their own independence. Very few young men here, I am told, like to give help with small babies even if they are their own babies.'

Bearing this in mind, I was not surprised when Bill Gedney remarked to Pete Gosling at dinner a few weeks later, 'Have you noticed how gentle Asian young men are with small children?' This was said as he watched Khai, aged 23, sitting on the sofa with his three year old niece Mawn, feeding her spoonful by spoonful. It is quite true that Burmese males do not have to prove their masculinity nor be tough to give a male image. They enjoy the regard given to their *pon* from childhood and show regard for women as a consequence.

'Why,' I asked my friend Judy, 'Why do you so often comment on the favourable position enjoyed by Burmese women?' Judy is Pete Becker's wife, has spent three years in Burma and is now Director of ethnic music at the University of Michigan. 'Because Burmese women don't have to prove themselves' she replied, 'they get paid the same as a man if they get appointed to do the same job.' It is true that professional and all non-manual jobs in Burma bring the same wage for men and women in the same grade of appointment. The system of appointment is quite different. In the West it is a competitive society, and staff and workers are hired for whatever the prospective employer thinks he can get them for, resulting in terms fixed differently for each individual. Yes, it is a competitive society and in the restricted association of husband and wife more or less with each other, and without the extended family network, it is not surprising to find the spirit of competitiveness arising between spouses. Or, so I rationalized the surprising expectation of conjugal jealousy which that first young man in New York expressed to me.

'Isn't it all a terrible fuss about very little,' I asked Lola Nash who said how hard the first years of marriage are on wives. 'No, it is a genuinely bad situation', she said. 'The husband wants to improve his qualifications or at any rate get on with earning at a job. The wife has to stay at home with the children and it's an exhausting day every day for her. She has no desire or spirit left to make herself look attractive. The husband, meeting attractive women at his work place feels put off when he comes home to a wife who probably can't afford to buy expensive or smart clothes either but in any case she finds it too tiring to cope with two young children all day long. I did this for eight years so I know what I'm saying.'

Yes, Western society always takes the individual so seriously, in all the yearning and unexpressed longings of every sort which must be fulfilled if that individual has her due. And in no case does this belief take such strong root as it does with children. As much as the American woman's kitchen load is so easy compared to a Burmese woman's, the care of children is equally disproportionate in the opposite direction. It takes a heavy toll on the American mother. Children in Burma are a help or at least they give hardly any trouble to the mother who does not feel she must give them her attention to keep them amused or informed when she has other tasks to be done. When she goes visiting, the child can go along, but won't be tolerated if it becomes a nuisance there.

Our lives have been an almost continuous series of emergencies or hardship during the past thirty years. The family pulls together to survive or flourish. Grumblings and complaints are heard but they are against life in general, probably against the authorities, male or female. And if the wish is not to grumble against authorities in general, life itself according to the Buddhist sentiments heard since childhood, is trouble and suffering anyway. In the West, where the good material things of life are abundant and nature has been controlled to a great extent, the house feels safe enough to be divided, and it is possible to have spurs honed against spouse or parent.

Because America is a land of plenty, Burmese visitors to it often express surprise at how badly people fare as far as food is concerned. Meals may be just snatched in what seems a bare or poor fashion, when with so little trouble a delicious hot dish can be served. The Burmese meal takes time to prepare, but the Burman is used, since childhood, to expect two meals, properly cooked and composed every day and to sit down to them without haste or interruption. No one will disturb people sitting to a meal and the diners in turn will not let any visiting guests go by without offering them the meal or at least part of it. If they like to insist they will take an extra plate for the protesting visitor and fill it from the rice pot, all will push closer together and thus make room at the low round table. With the entry of an extra diner, everyone scales down their helpings from the central dishes and the visitor can be sure of at least having enough taste from the center to make the meal palatable. The appreciation of the two full meals daily certainly establishes the thanks due to the wife and mother who has, after years of cooking from scratch, acquired a specialist's dexterity at the job. If the family are on an outing, the man would not feel lacking in masculinity if the wife took out the money to pay for their meal then.

It is the natural thing to have the wife pay the bill if she has the money on her. In fact, when dealings are in cash they are more often done by women. Perhaps this is the same principle in operation in Burmese society as a whole. In Burma, the official trade, involving entry upon entry and check after check through papers, is mostly the job-work of salaried men. The quick direct trade of the bazaar is all the work of women who subscribe to the old saying which epitomises swift, satisfying trade as exemplified in this saying.

Here, here's a gryphon
So here, here's a cabuchon.

The swift thrust of exchange between two valuable commodities or between goods and money, is the complete opposite of entering in quadruplicate and cross-referring ledgers etc. This latter must belong to a state system as a check against cheating by salaried sellers and buyers. There is something about dealing in straight cash payments that seems to accord better with a woman's liking for direct, swift, practical systems. At home where everything necessitates the paying in cash, I keep the money and guide the pattern of spending.

A lot of uncertainty about sex roles does in fact stem from the developed nature of Western affluent society's economy. The equivalent to the Burmese concept of the wife being financially responsible cannot hold, for that concept is based on the premise that if the money does not stretch enough from the man's regular earning, the wife-cashier must do something to mend the hole. This is not tenable where mass production already provides enough of everything for everybody in its most convenient form.

Our idea of the woman being responsible for the solvency of the family and having the added responsibility of making up the money required by some, belongs with a non-industrial economy. Take a Burmese family setting out on a holiday, or pilgrimage as they call it. Pagodas can usually be found in scenic spots near to towns which are worth a visit and through the ages have become popular resorts. The wife and mother, before setting out, will buy a supply of whatever product her home region is known to make in good quality and quantity. It might be pickled meats of *lepet* from a Shan region, or handloom stout blankets of cotton from Mudon or slippers from Mandalay. When they get to their destination, they will lodge with friends, or friends of relatives, and the hostess will take her round to the houses of her friends who will gladly make a purchase. Though not much cheaper than the retail price in the local bazaar, this consignment is genuine, comes directly from *pin-yin*, root source, and it will be of good quality because the visitor obviously chose each article with care, wishing her hostess's friends to have the best. Since my childhood, as my parents were posted to one small country place another another, I got used to such ladies turning up with silk longyis from the Yaw region bordering the Chin Hills or lacy and tucked bodices from Moulmein always tied up in a square of cotton and only enough to form a handy bundle easily carried as my mother took them around. The stock was usually sold out before the visit ended and my mother was known to be a careful and knowledgeable buyer herself. The small profit accruing might pay for the expenses of the trip for the whole family and, with luck, may leave something with which to buy the speciality of this region to take home to the neighbours who look forward to some such souvenir of the holiday visit. Trade was never despised by the Burmese. Its low place in the lives of professional people was a British importation.

Postscript

'Unchanging Burma'

David Steinberg's comment was the one I heard most recently on the oft-repeated theme of an unchanging Burma. So many foreign friends who revisit Burma after long years of absence observe that nothing seems changed since 1951, or some such year. Presumably what they refer to is the lack of 'development' in modern economic terms, especially in contrast to high rise vistas seen in Bangkok, Kuala Lumpur or Singapore. 'It always seems to me', said David who is Director for Southeast Asia in the Agency for International Development in Washington, D.C., 'that Burma has been set in aspic since about thirty years ago.'

It was a kind of metaphor. Aspic is yielding, and it is pleasant to savour. Its mention evokes the green and gold of vegetables set in it, and reminds us sensitive Burmese that we eat well, even if we have not quadrupled our commerce, nor multiplied the stories of our buildings.

It is only to be expected that the view of Burmese who remain at home year after year may not coincide with that of the returning foreign visitor. True enough, some Burmese do see such changes as to make them deplore the eroding of Burmese cultural traditions.

These compatriots will think that in foregoing chapters I have depicted religio-social celebrations and family or social relationships as more intact than they are at present. This is possible. My age makes for such a tendency, while a sanguine temperament added to fortunate experience in family and social contacts makes me view the Burmese prospect as enjoyable, even in adverse personal circumstances. In this chapter, therefore, I make a closer scrutiny of some main topics dealt with earlier. I do this keeping in mind that the scene now observed is one from which I have been absent for three years. All over the world, we see the erosion of traditional cultural practices, and of family ties under the demands of modern life. Why should this not be the case with Burma as well?

If after this rescrutiny I still find Burmese traditions persisting amidst population shifts and other changes, I must hold to that as the keynote of this book, and I must be prepared then to have my stand pronounced wrong by other observers.

Urbanization: Incidence and Causes in Burma

A common feature of life today in many parts of the world is the shift of population from rural to urban centres. We see this tendency in Burma also. Dr L. Sundrum, writing a paper *Urbanization: The Burmese Experience* in the journal of the Burma Research Society in (1957), finds such a marked increase in town populations that he calls on government to provide facilities which cities need for these rapidly growing settlements. My reading of population papers published by the census department in 1954 confirms his findings.

For example:	*Name of town*	*1931*	*1953*
	Meiktila	9195	25180
	Moulmein	65506	102777
	Bassein	45562	77905

These are figures from earlier years. When, in the next section I make a more detailed case study of one town we will see the growth in more recent decades. Here, I note a point which may be of interest regarding this incidence of urbanization in a slowly developing country like Burma. Why, in the absence of industrialization in towns, have rural people still moved to them in such large numbers.

A major cause was the attainment of independence and the change in national consciousness which came with it. In the colonial era the Burmese had been mainly an agricultural and rural people. The capital city, especially, was the stronghold of British, Indian and Chinese. With independence the Burmese moved into the centres of governmental power, commerce, fashion and high living. They now felt the cities to be their own.

The scale of movement into towns was increased also by the insurrections of immediate post-Independence years as Burma struggled to form and stabilize a cohesive Union. The insecurity of villages with such insurrections made people flock into towns. This major cause of urbanization is still operative in a few areas of stubborn lawlessness, as will be seen in the case study which follows.

A minor cause of such population shift is the social shake-up following the revolution of 1962. Changes in the national economy as well as in personal fortunes have led people to seek new ventures in new environments.

It is to be expected that the change to urban life will bring changes in life style for rural people. Such changes may lead to altered family relationships. An extreme case in point may be seen in the study of Thai family life made by H.M. Graham. 143 families in Bangkok and its vicinity were interviewed by Graham's team of researchers. Bangkok, nearest neighbour to the capital of Burma, is well known for its provision of modern sybaritic pleasures, opulent hotels and places of fashion, so I need not describe it. The researchers found that once in town, Thai husbands became more pronounced in their tendency to take on extra wives. This meant that they had less and less money to spend on their 'first' families. This caused disruption in family life.

These schemes and diversions in Thai conjugal relationships stem from the nature of Bangkok's urbanization. They are perhaps to be expected wherever urbanization has brought amenities modelled on city life of the Western nations today.

It will be of interest now to examine the style of living found in Burmese town life, to see whether such changes in family relationships as noted above for Bangkok will also emerge. For this purpose I give a detailed description of one town, its structure and the life within it, in 1979.

Nature of Burmese Urbanization

To make a detailed case study of a Burmese town, I select Taunggyi for two reasons. One, its growth during the past two decades has been one of the most rapid in Burma. Two, I am able to make a satisfactory study of the town's structure and life, being a resident of it. Figures show growth in recent years as follows.

Taunggyi.	Population				
	1921	1931	1965	1967	1979
	6016	8652	45526	55606	80000

(Figures for 1921 and 1931 are from papers published in 1954 by the census department. Later figures are from records of the municipal office, Taunggyi).

The rapid growth of this town is due partly to its importance as the administrative capital of the Shan state. This state has border areas of hill ranges with poor communication and deep forests, which made it good ground for insurgents, and other forces fighting for its opium trade as well as for levies on isolated helpless villagers. In such an environment, maintaining security is a difficult job. This has led to an influx of refugees from many directions. They settle where they can in town, following their village skills to earn their keep. Loi Yang, coming from Nam Hsan to the north, left his tea and other plantations behind. He was lucky enough to find lodgings fairly near the edge of town, and he now grows vegetables and keeps pigs. He has eleven children and feeds them by a number of ventures based on rural pursuits.

Travelling 30 miles to the south west, he buys medicinal herbs which, after arrival in town and some processing, he can resell at five or six times the cost price. One son works at cutting down pine trees (and earns a good wage) in a project for sawing and making of crates.

One daughter makes *tofu*, which is sold wholesale to retail food sellers in the bazaar. Another daughter has taken up a completely urban profession. She has learnt tailoring and now goes to work daily in a tailor's shop in town where she makes shirts, trousers and other garments. There are other migrants of quite different origin. Due to economic changes in the central parts of Burma and the closure of private industrial plants, a great number of families like Ko Aung Nyein and Ma Khin Nyunt's have migrated here because their readiness to work as hired hands (in contrast to the independent-minded hill residents of this and nearby towns) ensures them a better livelihood than they can find back home. Such migrants live in a special quarter called Shwe-Daung, perched on the other edge of town where the dip of the ridge does not allow rural pursuits, but proximity to bazaar and congested streets facilitate other employment such as construction work, loading and unloading goods, road repair and, it is alleged, thieving. These form an influx of people in search of security or a better livelihood.

There is also an influx of people plying the new contraband trade which is a feature of life in Burma today. In the establishment of socialist economy, the present years are to be regarded as transition years. As such, a gap has occurred between the abolition of old capitalism and the success of new socialist production. To fill this gap a remarkable flow of goods have come in illicitly across borders to three or four main centres of such trade. Shorter and easier routes lead to centres other than Taunggyi, but a big volume of colourful eye-catching goods still pile up in this town after a three hundred mile hazardous trip from the Thai border.

The men and women doing lucrative trade may be transient, thus lending truth to the opinion many hold that the real population of Taunggyi is nearer 100,000 than the official figure of 80,000.

Despite this population which is of city strength, life in this town is structured on institutions derived from the village systems of centuries ago. These institutions are common to all towns of Burma today, extending to the capital city itself. I will therefore note them in some detail from the point of view of their impact on the life of residents.

The town is composed of twenty 'wards'. The formal term for the old Burmese idea of a neighbourhood. Although there is no physical division between one ward and another, each is conscious of it's entity as a community by the life that goes on within it. Residents join in to celebrate certain festivals of the year, such as the *Mahadoke*, drawing of lots described in Chapter XI of the Forest Ward. On the major occasions of the year, they take the combined offerings to specified points on the main road of the town joining with other wards in such a major all-town event. On other occasions their contributions as a ward compete with those of other wards. In all town emergencies, such as a burst dam in the valley below, or a need to patrol the forest path, the ward makes its contribution in terms of people who work, just as other wards do.

Residents holding large functions such as the feasts attendant on novitiations, birthdays, weddings and deaths get help from the ward most readily. Equipment is loaned from the pool kept for the purpose, and helping hands flock in, in greater numbers than some frugal housewives can use. The ward also recruits residents to form patrols in times of increased crime. These recruits keep an all night post to which residents can go for help in emergencies.

183

Most of the ward activities are carried on as voluntary service by elders who are elected, one for each area of a ward. Sometimes the functions of these elders recall the responsibilities which village elders had in the past, of ensuring that only 'good' and 'desirable' citizens dwelt among them. Here is an example of such a reminder.

In the capital city, Rangoon, government is ever watchful to nip in the bud any signs of a counter-culture intrusion from abroad. It sometimes raids houses holding card parties, or late evening dinners. In making such raids the police go first to the ward elders to get their consent, and take them along, thus stamping the raid as an act of community disapproval of a style of life.

The basis of each household's contact with the ward is another historical post which has been reactivated now. The ward leader is called the *Hse-aim-hmu* or 'ten house leader', though he or she has far more than ten houses in his charge in these populous times. Their main duties are to keep track of arrivals and departures in each household, to keep it informed of ward activities, to call for representatives, one from each house, to greet arrivals, such as top students or model workers, and to collect small donations for distressed residents, or for ward festivities. The leader, like all ward elders, is selected for his or her close contact and identification with the community. Thus, many residents in the capital, Rangoon, regarding the leader and all ward elders as interfering nuisances, will tell you they are normally someone's cook, gardener or watchman – quite ignorant. Here in Payapyu area, one of fifteen areas of *Ye-aye-kwin* ward of Taunggyi, however, our 'ten house' elder is a young Karen, previously a rural school master, and now on the education office staff. In addition to his routine duties he now collects weekly, from each house, either uncooked rice or a sum of five kyats. Some ten or fifteen residents of one area of this ward will, every Saturday, buy fresh foods and cook all night at the house of the Chief Ward Elder to put a meal into the alms bowls of nearly 1,000 monks who will walk by the house at dawn. This activity will go on during Buddhist Lent.

The suggestion of such rural and village associations in this account of community life must be balanced by a mention of the town's pleasant, if modest, development as an urban settlement. More than any other town in Burma, outside of the capital, handsome villas of international design have risen in Taunggyi in recent years, and stand in good gardens. For the main part they are served by good roads, and a satisfactory number of light Japanese cars ply for hire. The main road of the town, in contrast, wears a mean look. Improvement of its shanty-town look and prevalence of low shed-like buildings of colonial times, had just begun with two new cinema halls as well as with the cramming of the low built shops with textiles, foreign foods and such imported luxuries, when the change came which abolished private capitalism and private overseas trade. Now the five cinema halls stand shabbily and the people's shops are almost bare of stocks. The bazaar however teems with a cosmopolitan crowd and bursts with good foods of meats, fishes, fruits and numerous kinds of vegetables. There is, in addition, the blackmarket bazaar piled with bright wares from Thailand, ranging from medicines and cosmetics to fabrics and household linens. In its vicinity, as in the teashops, gather young men, dressed in clothes copied from foreign catalogues by the town's enterprising tailors. There is a great amount of illicit trade in drugs and pornographic magazines.

These last-mentioned features are submerged aspects hardly known to the average resident whose consciousness of urban life here is centered on the large number of houses, the wealth of goldsmith shops and proliferation of monasteries.

Effects of Urbanization on Religious Practices

A change that has been noticed in the neighbouring country of Thailand, and is no doubt a reflection of conditions in the West, is the falling away from religious observance. Such a change would be of great importance in a country like Burma where religion and socio-religious activities and relations are the very stuff of life. The important place of women in such Burmese activities is evident from chapters VI and XI especially. With the pressure of economic hardships and the diversion of funds to the new and often contraband, products available, one might expect a reduction in the scale of hospitality and entertainment in such celebrations as novitiation (see Chapter V) and *dana* feasts (see Chapter XI). Contrary to this expectation and inexplicably in the light of present finances, these celebrations appear even more lavish than before. A trader celebrating his 74th birthday in Taunggyi recently, invited 74 monks. Each monk was offered a set of robes, a full sack of rice and a 10 gallon tin of cooking oil in addition to the usual array of miscellaneous articles of use in the monastery. Hundreds of people were given a full meal of rice noodles with the best fish gravy possible.

Recently in the capital town of Rangoon, a doctor's wife in holding the novitiation ceremony for her sons, took advantage of the kingly splendours offered in the town's newest restaurant structure. This, a government project to incorporate the work of Burmese woodcarvers, lacquer craftsmen, painters, glass mosaic setters and such has resulted in the *Karaweik* restaurant. The *karaweik* is a lengendary bird, the figure of which, fashioned beautifully and embellished with traditional decoration and gilding, stood on the prows of royal barges through the centuries whenever king or sacred images moved across lake or river waters. Today, wishing to give the public a taste of such splendours, the government ordered a restaurant to straddle two long barges resting on the Royal Lake, which are graced by leafy shores and wooded islets, with a view of the golden Shwedagon spire across the water. Although the public find the prices in this restaurant prohibitive, it is occasionally used for religious functions. The three boys of the doctor, clad in silk satins and sequined head-dresses not only went round town in a procession of decorated cars but made a circuit of the decks and isles of this resplendent structure with white silk umbrellas held over them. Guests filled both long sections of the restaurant as well as the central connecting area where the boys sat on a dais. They were served a full meal of the richest fare –

butter rice and chicken curry with all accompaniments desired.

It is not only in such lavish expenditure that religious fervour is kept up. Meditation centres are crowded now to the point of proving a distraction for those in search of solitude. The University Congregation Hall recently held a series of evening sermons by the eminent Maha Si Sayadaw. The hall was crammed full with young men and women. The great scholar monk arrived, and I could not help thinking that the awed reverence paid him was comparable to the elaborate arrangements of deference made for the highest lay authorities, by a people who do enjoy showing such respect.

On the Shwedagon Pagoda Road leading down from the main entrance, a series of new *Dhamayones* or Congregation Halls have been constructed recently. by joint donations from such groups as the customs department or the railways department or the residents of Inlay Lake, up country. Such halls are open for use by groups of people wishing to invite *Sangha* of their own choosing, to give sermons or hold meditation sessions. Part of the hall has an upper storey away from the street front and this provides accommodation for monks who come from outside Rangoon, to perform these or similar services for their devotees.

Most recently, I visited the handsome *Dhamayone* of the Customs department. The hall is beautifully proportioned with a good wooden floor and doors leading out to side verandahs. At the head, a dais holds an elaborate *Buddha*-shrine. Below the dais is a chair on which the chosen monk Ashin Nanda-Wuntha to whom I wished to pay devotions, sat, instructing forty to fifty men and women over a ten day course of meditation which had been advertised in newspapers, thus bringing us together. The end of this course was marked by a gathering to which hundreds had been invited by the efforts of this small band of devotees. Ashin Nanda-Wuntha had been given donations towards his pilgrimages and his rural monastery in Amarapura, nearly five hundred miles up-country. He decided to divert part of these donations to the feasting of those who attended this closing ceremony. I had come to know well, Daw Yin Htay, the wife of U Po Si. Both husband and wife, residents of Rangoon, were active in the cause of religious celebrations.

The most remarkable phenomenon I witnessed in this field of observation however, occurred in April 1979, and takes us back to the direct transformation of a village into town precincts.

Part of the growth of Taunggyi municipality came from its spread northwards to include part of Payapyu village. This village, till about sixteen years ago, consisted in the main of bamboo and thatch houses with pear orchards between every two or three of them. The headman, Saya Nyo, called for volunteers from each house to clear lanes and ditches when needed. The village, though continuous with the edge of town, had no light or water supply laid on for residents to tap. Its small monastery served as the festive venue for perhaps a dozen villages further out in different directions. Residents were almost all of the Pa-O ethnic group. The monastery, set beside a small white-washed spire on the edge of the forest, was a simple shed with bamboo mat walls and a rough cement floor. We attended it in preference to the crowded and rich monasteries in town, and when we did so, sat on mats muddied by the feet of farmers before us. The monk was a simple Pa-O country man, not very learned, we felt. He was old, feeble, and had only one or two novices at any given time to serve him.

During the years following 1975, the pressure of population in the heart of town led residents to seek cheap sites in this village. They built solid houses of timber and stone. They pressed for lights and water. By 1978 a primary school had been provided by the government, and over 100 pupils attended it. The orchards had almost all gone. A young woman doctor who lived nearby in the town had set up a clinic which gave treatment for a small fee.

Before 1975 the old monk had made many attempts to collect donations for a monastery more like the others in town. His plans were considered grandiose. Unfortunately, he died before he was able to complete the structure.

At *Thingyan*, our New Year period in 1979 and our first *Thingyan* after resettling in our house near this place, we went across with our offerings. Everything was transformed. Roads had been laid, windows shone in the monastery, which was laid with smooth clean mats, and a new monk sat to receive devotees.

He was younger of course, of Pa-O origin also, but trained and educated in a nearby bigger town. Cars from the town brought city folk whose presence added festivity to the occasion. The greatest surprise was that the number of novices was now 40. The greater educational qualification of the monk attracted them and the arrival of urban fashionable attendance had greatly enhanced the activity at this monastery. Novitiations held here during this summer brought the total of resident novices temporarily to 80, during the school vacation months. What a change from the desultory attendances of its village days! Under its row of great banyans, foundations were laid for new structures such as a dining hall, extra dormitories and an ordination hall.

Religious practices and celebrations in Burma have always been invested with social status, enjoyment of good food and a show of fine clothes. As town life raises the standard of living in these respects, and sets fashions which those seeking upward mobility are eager to share, the result for such religious occasions is an increase in scale and a continued lavishness despite hard times.

Observations in these two sections dealing with Burmese town life today tend to confirm the adherence of the Burmese to their traditional life, especially in socio-religious activities in which women feature so largely. Still, there have been so many changes of residence and of personal social positions since World War II, that the pressures of family and social opinion on the individual have surely decreased. In this regard I add some notes in the section following, on the present position of women regarding some aspects treated in Chapter V.

Changes in Female Self Perception

In looking for changes regarding the situation of women in Burma, I think it will be evident from the rest of the book that no changes regarding legal status for

Burmese women need be expected, as the customary laws defined in Chapter III are acceptable to both sexes. What might yield more results is a scrutiny of the attitude of Burmese women regarding their own lives and plans. The greatest change in this respect observed over the past two or three decades is the attitude of young Buddhist Burmese women towards marriage with foreigners or non-Buddhists. Before World War II, the value placed by all Buddhist Burmese girls on the approval of, and full integration with, the family was (as described in Chapter V) important and accepted with hardly any qualifications or exceptions. The family system regarded as aberrant marrriages not only with foreigners from abroad, but with persons of mixed blood within a country, or of a different religion. Such mixed marriages were contracted only by Burmese Christians, by girls of good families amongst the hill people, or girls of little or no means and family background among the majority of Burmese. Apart from these, girls of what were known as 'respectable' Buddhist families with official, financial and educational backgrounds considered that they must give up the idea of marriage with anyone of divergent religious or racial background, even if they happened to be in love with him.

After World War II, girls of ruling families amongst hill peoples, especially the Shans, began to marry foreigners belonging to what had been the ruling race, in an effort to get away from frustrations of post war unsettlement. These few girls, being the vanguard of such counter culture decisions in favour of individual wishes were given cool treatment even by younger relatives who had lived abroad. Unrelated Burmese men also expressed strongly the male resentment present in every culture against such marriages contracted by their girls. Gradually, however, girls among the majority, Christians only at first, but later non-Christians as well, in going abroad to study, decided to marry such Britons and others as they grew to love. This has been increasing in the last 15 years. Government, in an effort to deter such a brain drain of selected scholars whether male or female, has levied heavy compensation fees to be paid in such defaulting cases. It is worth noting that the decision to pay such heavy fines or to incur official disapproval is painless compared to earlier decisions to brave family disapproval and cause sadness and disappointments to mothers and aunts. By now, aunts and mothers of girls making such marriages talk freely in society about their sons-in-law, though their hearts still feel pangs of passing envy whenever they hear of marriages in the traditional manner by daughters of friends.

It is not only women who have moved out of old attitudes towards immersion in foreign cultures. For a long time, the Burmese were conspicuously slow to seek material enhancement and the pleasures of life in more developed countries abroad. They said, and they may be believed, that they preferred life in Burma with its cultural richness, its Burmese food, the leisurely tempo, warmth of friends and access to pagodas. However, changes in personal fortunes and prospects have meant that there has been an increasing migration of Burmese abroad in recent years. This migration has meant a change in family relations. Yet the decision to migrate is readily made, and now there are colonies of Burmese flourishing in Thailand, Malaysia, Singapore, U.K. and U.S.A. Within Burmese in Burma itself, women are becoming more modern – they will drink socially more readily than they did before, and many are becoming more independent. In following careers, there is a distinct difference between younger working women of the present day and professional women of an older generation. The difference may be due as much to current economic hardships as to a greater concern for her own career by the young wife. The fact remains that, whereas the older woman did not hesitate to resign from a career, when her husband was posted away from her town of employment, young couples nowadays struggle on living in different towns, so that both husband and wife may continue their jobs until the government sees its way to posting them in the same place again if professional conditions allow.

The Population Mix

This most marked feature of Burmese life in recent decades is treated here, because flux and new social contacts, especially for women, may be expected to work a change-oriented attitude, even if, up till this time, traditional attitudes have prevailed.

The mixing of people evident all over the country between small ethnic groups and the majority, between different income groups and between different geographical areas, will be seen in the movements I have already referred to in the earlier sections. In those, I have touched on the causes of such movements. I must now underscore the government's great part in this. It organizes, with a great deal of vigour, visits by ethnic representatives to the capital, conferences, exhibitions, sports meets, reward camps, reward tours and other such occasions. This is a driving factor in the mixing of people, and has had some effect.

In this mixing of people, the new presence is that of families of the army men who are stationed all over the country, especially extending to the borders which used to be so remote and unheard of to the common person in the heart of Burma. It is to salute the women who follow these Burmese men now to such untrammelled areas, that I end this chapter and this book with the portrait of one of them. I quote from a newspaper article I wrote in 1974. I apologise for the Burma style of English language journalism in which the article is written. The reason I do not attempt to rewrite this profile in more suitable language, is that the young woman portrayed there was completely alive to me when I wrote it. Time has passed and memories have faded, so, instead, I offer you the portrait of yet one more Burmese woman, the youngest and most contemporary of all in this book, born of the people whom present day Burma must honour above all others.

BEYAN

Can you conceive of a lotus rising naturally out of dust and a ragged beginning? Not a sumptuous white lotus such as rises from rich murky waters, but a slender dark-red budding one. This beauteous formation is the story of Beyan. What her name means her mother cannot say; she knows only that it is a common name with them.

With recent years have come small waves of people from Taungdwingyi area to our upland town. One family arrives and is soon joined by friends and relations coming after. They settle on the edge of the town in a new quarter that has a bad name among some old residents. The kind ones realize that, as Taungdwingyi area is well-farmed, with dam waters old and new, those who leave it must be the idlers among a worthy community of farmers.

Can you believe that in a family where male relatives are constantly chased or caught as thieves, where spouses are changed often, where everyone lives light-heartedly with such things as the norm, one young member, without cutting adrift can quickly acquire a taste for continued work, can respect possessions bought with well-earned wages, while retaining the happy liveliness common to her beloved and shiftless kin? This too is the story of Beyan and a true one.

Before Independence, the frontiers of Burma were remote areas to the average citizen from the main bosom of the country. How adventurous I felt on first journeying into these Shan fastnesses, to cross the unbridged Salween and then the serried mountains of Kengtung State into the water divide of the unknown Mekong, and even further to the magical creation of an English settlement out of a hill of mists in Loimwe.

Can you appreciate the jump from those times to this, when teams of administrators, botanists, climbers, welfare workers and many others have become familiar with such frontier regions? Among them are soldiers, and with them their wives. So to many humble families, names like Takaw, Loilem and Loimwe have become as tame as Kyaukpadaung or Chauk. This again, is the story of Beyan.

Soldiers are generally anonymous to citizens like us. They live, move and fight unpublicized and necessarily apart. But when one young girl whom one knows closely becomes a soldier's wife and goes off to one distant new place after another, snippets of her life are retailed back to keep hearts warm. This, then, is the story of Beyan up to its sunny present.

Beyan first came here in a family of construction workers. Tall for thirteen, she was passed off as an adult. When a few days' work revealed her intelligent quickness at every task, no one grudged her adult wages.

Having just arrived, the family had no warm clothes against this cold, so wore all the clothing they possessed in layers. Beyan collected the most. Over threadbare jackets she wore one cloth as a cape from her shoulders, another from her head, with her skin having been burnt by the sun down there, then shrivelled by the cold here, with curly hair an uncombed tangle, with the brightness of her small eyes lost in a sharply lean face, and a stutter when she spoke, you could only think 'Poor child', and pity her.

During pauses in work, however, her high spirits and antics with uncles and cousins soon revealed a coltish grace. Orchid hunting and walks in woods on holidays next revealed her eye for all aspects of Nature. She came from bare plains, and here she was enthralled by all new forms of growing things, the profusion of flowers, above all by the beauty of the tiniest wildflowers. We became friends on this basis alone. It was her role to discover the first hidden florescences in these wild acres and to come with excited bounding run to tell of them.

She started domestic work when construction was over. She learnt to cook, to wash and iron the clothes she bought from her wages. She got a room of her own, a tin trunk, a mirror. She learnt to read just by inference from labels and signs around her. Now she was 14, her face softer, her stutter almost gone.

She offered to take on livestock for extra wages and did more than feed them well. When thefts occurred, she tracked them downhill, intrepidly exposed an uncle and sent him fleeing right back to Tawngdwingyi. She plucked and sold flowers, bunching them attractively enough to sell well. Fifteen now, she had acquired gold earrings and ring, with a red stone, a watch, and an ability to run in high-heeled sandals.

Her elder sister, always pretty and pleasant, eloped afresh and often. But Beyan declared she would marry, and for a lifetime, only when she turned eighteen.

We heard her sing as she carried poultry feed about in pouring rain. Even for her this was unusual buoyancy. When her sister eloped again, with the worst prospect up to date, there was speculation as to how she must be finding things. Beyan's answer was different from earlier occasions.

'Happy of course. She is with the one she desires.'

A group of soldiers were given sentry duty at our village post. What obstacle are green hedges to a youth of 22? Beyan did not wait till she reached eighteen. At 16 she was ready to wed. She was 17 when she brought her baby from Loilem to show us.

We read of army wives getting trained in small arms use. We could picture Beyan putting first foot forward, cocking an accurate eye. Her mother complains that soldiers' wives are under discipline. They must get leave to visit parents back home, must even wield hoes to clear grounds. We can picture Beyan laughing and wielding her hoe. But not too thoroughly if it is just to scrape the earth bare.

This is the story of Beyan who must have turned 21 now in another distant place.

Bibliography

Abbreviations:

JBRS: *Journal of Burma Research Society*
BSPP: *Burma Socialist Programme Party*
BRSFAP: *Burma Research Society Fiftieth Anniversary Publications*

Ba Than; *The Roots of Revolution* (Rangoon, 1962).
Bennet, Paul, *Conference Under the Tamarind Tree* (New Haven, Connecticut, 1961).
Boserup, Ester, *Women's Role in Economic Development* (London, 1970).
BSPP, *Myanma-amyothamimya i Nainganye Hlokeshahmu,* "Women in Political Upheaval", (in Burmese, Rangoon 1975).
        Taingyintha Yinkyehmu Yoya Dalayhtonezanmya – Chin, "The Culture of Indigenous Peoples – Chin" (in Burmese, Rangoon, 1968).
        Taingyintha Yinkyehmu Yoya Dalayhtonezanmya – Rakhaing, "The Culture of Indigenous Peoples – Arakanese" (in Burmese, Rangoon, 1976).
        Taingyintha Yinkyehmu Yoya Dalayhtonezanmya – Kachin, "The Culture of Indigenous Peoples – Kachin" (in Burmese, Rangoon, 1977).
        Taingyintha Yinkyehmu Yoya Dalayhtonezanmya – Mon, "The Culture of Indigenous Peoples – Mon" (in Burmese, Rangoon, 1978).
Christian, J. Leroy, *Modern Burma: A Survey of Political and Economic Developments* (Berkeley, 1942).
Cochrane, H.P., *Amongst the Burmans* (London and Edinburgh, 1904).
Coomaraswamy, Ananda K., *Buddha and the Gospel of Buddhism* (Bombay, 1956).
Dagon Khin Khin Lay, *Sa-sodaw* (Rangoon, 1937).
Dharmasakti, Honorable Suriya and Wimonsiri Jamnanwej, *Status of Women in Thailand* (Bangkok).
Djamour, Judith, *Kinship and Marriage in Singapore* (London, 1959).
Donnison, F. S. V., *Burma* (London, 1970).
Enriquez, *A Burmese Loneliness* (Calcutta, 1918).
Fielding-Hall, H., *The Soul of a People* (London, 1898).
Forbes, J. F. S., *British Burma and its Peoples* (London, 1878).
Foucar, E. C. V., *They Reigned in Mandalay* (   )
Furnival, J. S., *Paganmyo Sittan* (JBRS, vol XXXIII, pt. 1).
Geertz, Clifford, *The Religion of Java* (Glencoe, Illinois, 1960).
Geertz, Hildred, *The Javanese Family* (New York, 1961).
Graham, Henry M., *Some Changes in Thai Family Life: A Preliminary Study* (Bangkok, 1961).

Hall, D. G. E., *A History of Southeast Asia* (London and New York, 1955).

Harvey, G. E., *History of Burma* (London, 1967).

Hickey, G.C., *Village in Vietnam* (New Haven, 1964).

Hundley, H. G. and U Chit Ko Ko: *List of Trees, Shrubs and Principal Climbers, etc.* (Rangoon, 1961).

Interviewer's Reports: (i) Patricia Kingham; (ii) Sao Hseng Sanda; (iii) Thi Thi Ta; (iv) Toe Aung Kyaw.

Jardine, Sir John, *Notes on Buddhist Law* (Rangoon, 1882).

Kaung, U., *A Survey of the History of Education in Burma before the British Conquest and After* (JBRS, vol XLVI, pt. 2).

Kinwunmingyi, *Digest of Dhammathats: 2 vols.* (Rangoon, 1909).

Kyi Mah, Tetkatho, *Myanma-Amyothami Lawka*, "World of Burmese Women," (in Burmese, Rangoon, 1975).

Lahiri, S. C., *Principles of Modern Burmese Buddhist Law*, 5th ed. (Calcutta, 1951).

Lu Gale, U., *Paddy Planting Songs* (JBRS, vol XXXI, Pt. 1).

Luce, G. H., *The Ancient Pyu*: (JBRS, vol XXVII, pt. 3, reproduced in BRSFAP, no. 2, from which pages are quoted).

　　　　Economic Life of the Early Burman (JBRS, vol XXX, pt. 1, reproduced in BRSFAP, no. 2, from which pages are quoed).

　　　　Old Kyaukse and the Coming of the Burmans (JBRS, vol XLII, Pt. 1).

Malcom, Howard, *Travels in South-East Asia* (Philadelphia, 1853).

Maurice, David, *The Lion's Rora* (New York, 1967).

Maung Maung, *Women in Law and Custom in Burma and the Burmese Family* (The Hague, 1963).

Mya Than Tint, *Myanma Kyetawne doh i Kabyamya* "Folk Songs of Villagers," (in Burmese, Rangoon, 1975).

Mya Sein, Daw, *Administration of Burma* (Rangoon, 1938).

Nai Pan Hla, *Mon Literature and Culture over Thailand and Burma* (JBRS, vol XLI, pt. 1 and 2).

Nash, Manning, *The Golden Road to Modernity* (London 1965).

Nisbet, John, *Burma under British Rule and Before*, vols I and II (London, 1901).

Pe Maung Tin, *Women in the Inscriptions of Pagan* (JBRS, vol. XXV, pt. 1, reproduced in BRSFAP, from which pages are quoted).

Personal Correspondence (from researcher in the Ministry of Information, Rangoon).

Personal Correspondence (from Shan State Education Office, Taunggyi).

Rhys-Davids, C. A. F., *Outlines of Buddhism: A Historical Sketch (London, 1934)*.

Saw Mohnyin, Bama-amyothami mya, "Burmese Women," (in Burmese, Rangoon, 1976).

Scott, Sir James George, *Burma – A Handbook of Practical Information* (London, 1906).

Snodgrass, Major, *Narrative of the Burmese War* (London, 1827).

Sullerot, Evelyne, *Women, Society and Change* (New York, 1971).

Than Yun, *Social Life in Burma* (JBRS, vol. XLI, Pt. 1 and 2).

United Nations Statistical Year Book, 1973.

Warren, Henry Clarke, *Buddhism in Translations* (New York, 1976).

White, Sir Herbert Thirkell, *A Civil Servant in Burma* (London, 1913).

Yeway, Htun, *Thilashin Thamaing* (Rangoon, 1965).

Glossary

Abhidhamma: most advanced section of Buddhist Tripitaka Scriptures
Ahnade: 'the strength hurts', constraint felt at causing inconvenience
Aingyi: jacket
Ain-oo-nat: father, literally 'spirit head of the house'
Ainshin: house owner, lord
Ainshinma: lady house owner, housewife
Aintha: husband; 'man of the house'
Akyaw: bark, ground for cream applied to sores
Amay, mikhin: mother
Anatta: no soul
Anneiksa: impermanence
Aphay, ahpkhin: father
Apyos: young virgins
Arahatship: the state of being ready for deliverance (in Buddhism)
Ariyas: right living persons of highest virtues
Asoya: government
Atetpa: property from a previous marriage
Atthagahta: higher level of commentaries on Buddhist scriptures

Bamakhit: name of newspaper
Bazin-yinkhwe: cicada
Beindaw: herbal remedies
Bikkhunis: order of ordained nuns
Bikkhus: order of monks
Bo Bwa: ancestral, privately owned (of land)
Boddhabatha Amay-aphyay: Buddhist catechism

Chet-myok: 'burying of umbilical cord' — part of traditional ritual for birth
Chit-kyauk-yothay: love-fear-respect

Dak: Indian word used in colonial period for 'postal association'
Dama'u-kya: 'land belongs to the first axe' to clear it
Dana: giving, in accordance with Buddhist precepts
Dandalun: soup leaves or fruit from a tree (*Moringa oleifera*)
Dani: a kind of thatch
Danyin: fruit with strong aroma, for dip
Daw: name prefix for woman
Deva: celestial being
Dhamayones: congregation halls
Dhamma: Buddhist doctrine
Dhammacariya: 'Teacher of the *Dhamma*', title awarded to the winner of the
   annual scriptual examinations, open to monks and nuns
Dhammasetkya: Sermon on the Wheel of Law (the recurrent cycles of existence)
Dhammathats: law books
Dobama Asi-ayone: name of nationalist movement
Dokkha: suffering

Ekote: larva of a beetle

Gandakayaka: 'Treatise Writer', title won by writer of theological treatise of high standard
Gonyin: creeping plant, the seed of which is thought to prevent conception
Gyaung: vale or glen; today usually affixed to name of nunnery

Haw-te: hotel
Hnalone: heart
Hnama: boy's younger sister, 'cherished girl'
Hnapazon: property acquired jointly by couple after marriage
Hpon: Buddhist concept of potential spiritual glory, which may be possessed by individuals
Hsay-paw: mild (of cigars)
Hsay-pyin: strong (of cigars)
Hse-aim-hmu: 'ten-house leader', selected leader of a ward
Hsoon-ama: woman in charge of alms food, such as is supplied to a monastery
Htoke-sii-dow: game played by two teams trying to cross lines without being touched

Inga-leik: English
Ingee: jacket
Inn: (1) leaf used for roofing; (2) magic formula for good or evil purposes. (Distinguished by context.)

Jatakas: stories of Bhuddha's past existences

Ka-chin: red ants
Kadaw: prestigious term to mean wife
Kahtein: a robe-donating ceremony at the end of Lent
Kan-Karma: destiny or fortune in this life, dependent on good or evil done in past existences
Kanwin: legal term for presents given to a bride by the groom and by both sides for joint use in the marriage
Karaweik: legendary bird, traditionally carved on the prow of royal barges
Kauk-yu-mwe-sa, appatititha: adoption out of compassion, not with a view to inheritance
Kaung-tin: folded cloth worn on the head by *Thilashins*
Kaw: a small ethnic minority group
Kempatai: secret police in Japanese occupation of Burma in World War II
Khawut: light brown sarong worn by *Thilashins*
Khinpun: friend; or 'husband' if said by wife
Khon: the court of arbitrators
Kike: calf-length gown worn by *Thilashins*
Kilitha: child 'begotten in pleasure', that is without the parents contracting marriage
Kin: guards appointed by neighbourhoods to keep law and order
Kinmun-tat: ceremonial hair washing and name-giving of one-month old infant
'Ko: name prefix for young man
Ko ko: elder brother
Ko-yon: length of cloth worn over the shoulder by *Thilashins*
Kyat (K.): unit of currency
Kyaung: monastery or school

Kyaw-paung-ta-taung: weed used for infusion or poultice to cure a variety of ills
Kyet-le-san: leaf boiled for infusion to reduce blood pressure
Kyidawset: name of a journal

Lanzin Lu-Nge: Youth Who Follow the Way (youth organization for 15 to 25 year olds)
Lepet: steamed tea leaf
Letetpwa: property accruing to one spouse during coverture
Letkyat: special jacket worn by *Thilashins*
Let-the: 'hand-operator' or untrained midwife
Lin ka htan tet, maya ka hten chet: Proverb: 'Husband climbs the toddy tree, wife cooks it into jagaree'
Lin-maya: married couple, literally 'husband-wife'
Lin-nhin-mya, sha-nhin-thwa: Proverb: 'As the tongue and the teeth, so the husband and wife'
Longyi: skirt
Lupyos: young bachelors
Luyechun: top student awardees

Ma: name prefix for girl
Mahadevi: chief wife of *sawbwa*
Mahadoke: festival with drawing of lots to decide offerings to be donated
Mahasi: name of most important meditation centre in Rangoon
Ma ma: elder sister
Maung: (1) name prefix for boy; (2) a girl's young brother
Maya devi: name for mother of Buddha
Mezali: soup leaves from tree (*Cassia siamea*)
Mibaya Khaung: Chief Queen
Mi-hpa: parents; literally 'mother father'
Min: ruler, king
Mi-nay-khan: birth chamber; literally fire-application room
Min gyi: form of address formerly used to senior administrators
Mi-tha-su: family; literally 'mother offspring group'
Mway-the-mikhin mway-the-hpakhin: 'The mother who gave [me] birth, father who gave me birth'
Mwe-gan-mwe-sa, kittima: adoption with a view to giving inheritance
Mwe-sa: adoption
Mya-sein-pan/Hnit-taya-pan: green foliage known as 'green emerald' the 'hundred-years'-duration' flower
Myo: kin, 'the friendly people'
Myo-ok-min: form of address formerly used to low-level officials

Nat: spirit
Nat kadaws: spirit wives or mediums
Ngan-say: fever specific
Nibbana: Nirvarna; Buddhist idea of bliss in cessation of life and desire
Nissata: dependant
Nissaya: supporter
Nyarnasaryi: name of a renowned *Thilashin*
Nyaung-te: fatigue from strain

196

Nyi, nyima: boy's younger brother, girl's younger sister

Orasa: eldest child, literally 'child of the breast'

Palu: winged termites
Pakhet-tin: cradle placing; ceremony when a new-born baby is moved from a box in its mother's bed to its own cradle
Pa-o: an ethnic minority group
Pareit: chanting orisons against evils
Pareit-kyo: sanctified yarn
Paripatti: practice
Pariyatti: study
Patamabyan: scriptual examination
Patamagyi: senior/*Patamalat:* intermediate/*Patamange:* junior: doctrinal examination for monks
Pattala: musical instrument like xylophone
Pay: species of palm
Payin: property held by husband or wife personally, before marriage
Payit: cricket
Peon: office errand boy
Pinni: light brown homespun cotton jacket
Pin-yin: root source
Pya: cent
Pyissi pahtan: section of Abbhidhamma Buddhist scripture
Pyithu Hluttaw: People's National Assembly

Rahanmas: ordained nuns; no longer existent

Salamu: teacher
Samsara: cycle of existences
Sangha: order of monks
Sankri: elders
Sanlyan: assistant elders of villages in past centuries
Sarsodaw: 'speaker of literature', i.e. a scholar of the old oral tradition who had to be able to declaim as well as write
Sasana: religion, meaning the way to deliverance
Sawbwas: chiefs subject to a central authority; ruler of a state
Saya: master or teacher
Sayadaw: senior resident monk of monastery
Saya-lay: form of address used to *Thilashins*
Say-me-toe: 'quick fire remedies'
Sazingadaw: sergeant's wife
See-te-yay, hse-te-gazin: Proverb: 'the water which flows, the ridge which conserves it'
Seit: section of the Burma Socialist Programme Party
Sinyetha Party: Poor Man's Party
Shabutsay: pellets for sore throat or chest congestion
Shay-Saung Lu-Nge: Youth's Vanguards (organization for children aged 10 to 16)
Shinbyu: ceremony marking the beginning of adolescence for boys, when they spend a short time as novices in a monastery

Shraddh: part of Hindu funeral ceremony
Shwe-myo: 'the golden kind', meaning relatives
Shwe-phi-mo-lut: brand of tea
Sonma saga: admonitory epistles
Sukhri: headpersons of villages in the past
Survasti: spirit of learning
Suttas: parts of Buddhist scripture
Swemyo: relatives, literally 'the friendly breed'

Ta-tha-mway, ta-thway-hla: Proverb: 'One child born, one blood changed into more beauty
Taungtangyi, Meikthalin: species of fragrant woods ground to make cream
Taw-lay-wa: four exemplary wives from the *Jatakas*
Tazaungdine: festival of lights one month after the end of Lent
Teza Lu-Nge: Youth Power (organization for children aged 6 to 10)
Thadingyut: end of Lent
Thakin: 'master in one's own house', leaders of the nationalist movement in the 1930s
Thakinma: women members of nationalist movement
Thami: daughter
Tha-mi-tha-hpa: family; literally 'offspring mother offspring father'
Thanaka: bark cosmetic
Thanat: leaf, for wrapping cigars
Thathana wunhtan: 'servers of religion'
Thedansa: death bed testament
Theragatha: songs of revered teachers (male)
Therigatha: psalms of the Sisters
Theravada: Southern School of Buddhism as practised in Burma, Thailand and Sri Lanka
Theri: ordained nun, meaning revered female teacher
Thet-htar, thet-hsut, thet-nhin, thet-pan, thet-le: 'life entrusted'; 'life plucked'; 'life conferred'; 'life a flower worn on hair'; 'life exchanged'; terms men use to refer to their wives
Thingyan: New Year. Prelude to new year; a festival lasting for three to four days
Thugyigadaw: headman's wife
Thugyis: head persons of villages
Tofu: bean curd

Vinaya: monastic code
Vipassana: form of meditation with concentration on breath

Wunthanu: patriotic
Wut-lon-daw-ya: 'able to wear the high mantle', i.e. take silk (qualify as a barrister)
Yazaguru Egga Mahapandita: Buddhist title
Yetsa: a digestive powder
Yuwadi: name of womens magazine

Zani, amyothami, meinma: terms used for 'wife' by husband
Zani-maungnhan: married couple, literally 'wife-husband'
Zeyathiri: girls orphanage run by *Thilashins*